INFORMATION FOR INNOVATION

INFORMATION FOR INNOVATION

Managing Change from an Information Perspective

STUART MACDONALD

OXFORD UNIVERSITY PRESS

1998

Oxford University Press, Great Clarendon Street, Oxford OX2 6DP
Oxford New York
Athens Auckland Bangkok Bogota Bombay
Buenos Aires Calcutta Cape Town Dar es Salaam
Delhi Florence Hong Kong Istanbul Karachi
Kuala Lumpur Madras Madrid Melbourne
Mexico City Nairobi Paris Singapore
Taipei Tokyo Toronto Warsaw
and associated companies in
Berlin Ibadan

Oxford is a trade mark of Oxford University Press

Published in the United States by
Oxford University Press Inc., New York

British Library Cataloguing in Publication Data
Data available

Library of Congress Cataloging-in-Publication Data
Macdonald, Stuart, 1946–
Information for innovation : managing change from an information
perspective / Stuart Macdonald.
p. cm.
Includes bibliographical references.
1. Information technology—Management. 2. Technological
innovations. 3. Organizational change. I. Title.
HD30.2.M33 1998
658.4'038—dc21 97–18064
CIP

ISBN 0–19–828825–5

1 3 5 7 9 10 8 6 4 2

Typeset by Graphicraft Typesetters Ltd., Hong Kong
Printed in Great Britain by Bookcraft (Bath) Ltd., Midsomer Norton, Avon

For Sarah

*who has accomplished much more than she is
willing to admit*

PREFACE AND ACKNOWLEDGEMENTS

Each of us has a dominant perspective from which the world and its issues are seen. This book seeks to show how the view is altered when the perspective is changed. It justifies the adoption of what it calls an 'information perspective', but to complement prevailing perspectives, not to replace them. Perspectives, being enmeshed in values, experience, and identity, are entrenched and will be defended to the last. It would be disingenuous not to admit that an information perspective can also become entrenched, not to acknowledge that this book would have been more balanced had it been written from other perspectives as well. At least it will be read from other perspectives.

Hindsight reveals that what sometimes feels like an obsession with information had its origins in research conducted more than two decades ago. Fate decreed that research on the history of agricultural innovation was closely followed by a study of innovation in the semiconductor industry. Despite the polar separation of contexts, it was impossible not to be struck by what their innovation had in common. In both, innovation required, above all else it seemed, new information. So, how information was found, acquired, and used went a good way towards understanding the activity. A reckless disregard for disciplinary boundaries and career development led to the application of this approach to the study of change in other areas. The results were interesting —an inconvenience in an academic world which prefers conformity to controversy, and a serious impediment to acceptance in a real world which expects from empirical research confirmation of the wisdom of its ways.

Only very gradually did a general approach to the study of innovation firm into a specific information perspective. Don Lamberton, who has fought tirelessly for the elevation of Information Economics within the discipline of Economics, is largely to blame. His own fascination with information proved infectious, converting approach into perspective by adding theoretical structure to empirical observation of the role of information in innovation. The information perspective has now been applied in many situations, a few of which are reported here. It does seem to reveal much that is hidden from other perspectives.

I am grateful to those from whom I have learnt and whose ideas are too embedded in my own thinking for appropriate acknowledgement. I am also grateful to very many colleagues for their interest in an information perspective; their careful criticism has encouraged much thought. A more obvious debt is owed to Don Lamberton, Richard Joseph, and Robin Mansell for providing comments on drafts of the text, to David Reams for drawing some of the figures, and to my editor, David Musson, for his faith and optimism. I am also strangely indebted to those whose unrelenting opposition to both the book and its ideas confirmed the need for the latter and assured the completion of the former.

Stuart Macdonald
University of Sheffield
March 1997

CONTENTS

Contents

LIST OF FIGURES

LIST OF TABLES

LIST OF TABLES

Introduction

This book is about information. It is not just another book about how information is changing all our lives. There is already scribbling aplenty on the 'information revolution'. In particular, there is much discussion of information technology, of the wonders it can perform and of the social and economic consequences of performing them. What is not much considered, despite its apparent relevance to information workers toiling with information technology in an information society and information economy, is information itself.

The argument to be presented here is that what is done with information, be it ever so clever, and therefore what results from what is done, is influenced—sometimes even determined—by the nature of the good. It is necessary to step back from applications to consider just what is being applied. It is necessary because what is being applied is not like other goods, other resources. And while some of the strange characteristics of information allow wondrous things to be done, others constrain and prohibit. If the direction and success of our endeavours is so influenced by these characteristics, it would surely be wise at least to know what they are. Wiser still would be to understand how they affect what is done with information and how best to deal with this situation.

The argument heads into uncharted territory: whence it has come also has no clear map. Its provenance is to be sought in the efforts of many who have explored their own routes, most commonly those who have abandoned the safety of a disciplinary core to seek their fortune at the periphery and sometimes beyond. There are clear signs of the thinking of those who have journeyed from the heartland of Economics to explore elsewhere the peculiarities of information and the mystery of innovation. There is evidence of the investigations of those who once called the History and Philosophy of Science home and were drawn towards Science and Technology Policy. Many of these have continued their journey from policy towards the strategic concerns of Management, though they have not abandoned their empirical roots to swing from the treetops with the Management gurus. There are traces of those disciplines which claim the world as their preserve—History, inevitably, for everything is History; and Geography, though everything is certainly not Geography just because it has a spatial dimension. And there are signs of thinking mined from deep inside disciplinary strongholds, from Physics and Engineering, though to bracket the two suggests a misunderstanding of both; from Political Science, Law, and Sociology. And there is thought stolen from such subjects as telecommunications, agriculture, and patents, convoluted enough to consider themselves disciplines and to mark their territory with boundaries. Major contributions have also come from beyond the academic pale, from the vast and unruly world of empirical information where academic writ does not run. In short, the argument presented here has no conventional academic foundation. It is a creation of the very situation it explores—how information is found, acquired, and mixed with other information to create something new, in this case an argument about how this happens. The argument may not be correct or convincing, but its very existence as the product of information drawn from so many sources is itself indication that an information perspective is relevant to the understanding of innovation.

What, then, is an information perspective? The explanation is embarrassingly simple: an information perspective puts information first. It sees information as the primary concern in any issue. We all use information; we all have information and are surrounded by very much more of it—a familiarity which breeds not so much contempt as complacency. Just as most of us survive without knowing in any detail, or wanting to know, how our bodies work, so we feel we can manage well enough without bothering too much about how information works. And just as we abdicate responsibility for our bodies to doctors and medical technology, so we leave information problems to information specialists and information technology. This confidence that there are experts somewhere who do bother about information on our behalf, to whom an information perspective is second nature, is misplaced. True, there are information experts galore, but they are a diverse lot. The librarian is as much an information expert as the telecommunications engineer, the teacher as much as the advertising manager: they have little in common, and certainly not their approach to information. The econometrician who lets information equal I only mystifies and infuriates the sociologist worried about freedom of information. If the experts have little to convey to each other, they offer still less to those who are not information experts.

Whatever this book might offer, it is certainly not a crash course on how to become an information expert (of any sort). Its information perspective is based on nothing more sophisticated than the observation that information has some very odd characteristics, and that these seem to be fundamental to just about everything that is done with information. The more that is done, the more appropriate the perspective would seem to be, but as nothing is done without information, it could be argued that an information perspective is universally applicable. What the perspective reveals most starkly is how the awkward characteristics of information tend to be ignored in favour of its more convenient ones. It is exceedingly handy that information can be stored and processed in such vast quantities by computers; that it can be transferred so cheaply in similar quantities by telecommunications; that it can be owned through the intellectual property system; that it is sufficiently nebulous to satisfy the requirements of government policy and programmes; that it can be contained and administered by organizations, reinforcing their systems of structure and control in the process.

This is a convenient view of information as amorphous stuff, its characteristics endowed entirely by the systems in which it plays a part. Established economic and social systems have within them information systems; it is as important for the validity of these greater systems as it is for information systems themselves that information be seen as explicit and neatly codified, that existing channels are accepted as capable of its transfer without the inconvenience of transactions. The nearest this formal, institutional view of information comes to acknowledging any inadequacy in its systems is its concern that they are too capable, that they can handle too much information. It is fascinating how information overload, the rights of access of the many to so much information, and the accuracy and security of databases are perceived as problems of abundance, simply the result of too much of a good thing. Concern about the productivity paradox—the observation that investment in information technology does not always yield increases in productivity—is equally intriguing. To paraphrase Solow, the concern is evident everywhere except among IT specialists and those who invest in IT. Note that, when something does go wrong with an information system—not an infrequent occurrence—it is frequently argued that responsibility should lie with those who designed the system rather than the system itself, as if it is inconceivable that a proper system could ever be deficient. If systems fail, whether they be the dedicated systems of information technology, or the systems of the organization, or the systems of the market, it is because of imperfections in these systems, not because of any inherent weakness in the notion of system. Perfect systems would not fail.

It is change which challenges this assurance. Existing systems cope very well with information that is already in use, with what is already being done. They cope less well with anything different, with anything new. From an information perspective, change is seen to require the addition of new information to that already in use. This raises questions: how is such new information found? how is it acquired? how is it mixed with that already in use? Such questions present not the comfortable problems of information transfer, but the almost intractable problems inherent in information transactions. No longer is it possible to evade the awkward characteristics of information, for these are the very characteristics at the heart of information transactions.

Part II of the book applies an information perspective to a selection of issues. They have little in common (one chapter sets semiconductor electronics cheek by jowl with eighteenth-century threshing machines) except that each involves change, and for each there is an established perspective from which change is viewed. Here an information perspective has been brought to bear on each, throwing a different light on the issues and suggesting conclusions which would not otherwise seem appropriate. Much of the change is technological change, but that is just because the fortunes of funding have pushed much research in this direction. Examples of any other sort of change would have revealed much the same thing. Thus, what has long appeared to be an organizational rejection of the efforts of independent inventors seems from an information perspective more like organizational resistance to all new information, whatever its source (Chapter 6). Nations and firms alike are anxious to secure exclusive use of the information most crucial for innovation, and yet, from an information perspective, their attempts seem more likely to discourage than encourage innovation (Chapter 7). Common notions of how high-technology firms acquire the information they need for innovation are inspired by the ease of its transfer rather than the difficulty of transactions in such information. An information perspective finds that technology parks are unlikely to facilitate the complex information transactions underlying the rapid pace of innovation in high-technology industries (Chapter 8). Greenery and ducks are no substitute for information exchange networks. The attempts of policymakers to acquire information overseas for innovation in firms back home seem equally absurd from an information perspective: foreign information obtained at marginal cost does not find its way to firms quite so cheaply (Chapter 9). The belief that information for innovation in eighteenth-century agriculture was dispensed through an agricultural establishment, that labourers and farmers learnt from their betters, is upset by an information perspective suggesting that labourers and farmers are much more likely to have exchanged information with each other (Chapter 10). And the same perspective reveals the patent system, that bastion of innovation policy, as often ineffective in disseminating and protecting the information required for innovation (Chapter 11). Lastly, the information perspective is turned on organizations to examine their strategic change (Chapter 12), a topic normally examined from a strict organizational perspective. The requirements of information would seem to be in conflict with the requirements of organization.

It is not just the desire for fun, the love of contention, which yields conclusions that are so often so counter-intuitive. The conclusions emerge from the application of a perspective from which information cannot be taken for granted as a ubiquitous, undemanding, and infinitely flexible resource. Information is not like that at all; it is tricky stuff. Part I of the book explores the oddities of information, and is inevitably less fun. It tries to explain what is actually very simple, though what is very simple is often very hard to explain simply. What has emerged may be too naïve for some, too convoluted for others; it may be too strange for many, too obvious for a few. Despite its exhortations to look beyond the simplicity of information transfer to the complexity of information transactions, this book may not achieve even the transfer of information from author to reader. That will depend as much on the reader's existing perspective of the world, and on its ability to accommodate another, as on the information contained in these pages.

PART I

Information and Theory

1

The Nature of Information

Perspective is the view of the world and its contents gained from a particular vantage point. So determining is perspective that it is often confused with the view itself. How the world is seen may depend as much on which perspective is selected as on the reality. Indeed, as reality itself is hardly an undisputed absolute, perspective is crucial. There is, of course, no single, correct perspective. The information perspective which is offered in these pages is simply one of many. It is offered not as the best perspective for viewing reality, not even as a better perspective. It is offered not to supplant other ways of looking at situations, but to supplement them. An information perspective is simply another way of seeing things. Why, though, with so many perspectives already available, would there be any advantage in adopting yet another?

Most of us have several perspectives, but dedicate only one of these to any particular subject: we typically see the same thing in the same way. If we are accustomed to seeing gardening as a pleasure and do-it-yourself as a chore, it is difficult to exchange perspectives so that gardening is regarded as a chore and do-it-yourself as a pleasure, or to combine perspectives so that gardening and do-it-yourself are seen as both chore and pleasure. The more experienced we become in our activities, the more difficult the leap to an alternative vantage point becomes. [1] This has less to do with declining mental ability than with increasing intellectual capital. Expertise and attachment to perspective go hand in hand. Each expert acquires a particular approach to her subject, and a growing disinclination to alter an approach so integral to her expertise. Even were there incentive to change perspective, the expert's years of familiarity with but one view renders his subject almost unrecognizable from any other. More threatening is the potential damage to reputation of what can seem, to those practised in another perspective, a naïve approach to the subject. For example, only when eminent scientists are safely retired do they risk becoming historians of their own subject. Given what they often make of an historical perspective, it is generally as well their careers are not at stake.

[The] social effects [of the stirrup] over the years were enormous. It led to the development of a specialised corps of mounted soldiers who needed considerable support not only from foot-soldiers, but also from other men to feed and care for the horses. The mounted soldiers took to wearing armour and special methods had to be used to get them into the saddle. It was these mounted soldiers who became the squires and aristocrats and the medieval society was born—through the stirrup. [2]

So, an economist sees technological change from a perspective very different from that of a sociologist looking at precisely the same subject. An historian will have another perspective, a political scientist yet another, and within disciplines there is yet further variety, the perspective of the econometrician being quite distinct from that of the industrial economist. And subdivision within subdisciplines produces schools of thought, which are also—perhaps only—schools of perspective. Such profusion of perspectives should encourage the sharing of views. It does not; or at least not much. The more a group perceives its perspective to be exposed to distortion, the more protective of its perspective it becomes. Thus, doctors, assailed on all sides by those with other perspectives on the subject of health, defend to the death the peculiar validity, and therefore value, of their own set of perspectives. Their defence is that many years of training are a prerequisite for an 'informed view'. Thus, not only does perspective influence what is seen, but what is seen also influences perspective.

The entrenchment of perspective is reinforced by the confirmation of those who share it. The peer review of academic life depends on all the group seeing things at least roughly the same way. In any organization, there is an expectation that individuals will see things as their colleagues do. To share perspective is to be part of the team, one of us: conversely, those who do not share the common perspective tend to be regarded as unreliable, indolent at best, treacherous at worst. In such an environment, it is difficult and even dangerous to maintain a different perspective. Most do not: they either seek surroundings compatible with their existing perspective (in the Army, perhaps), or allow their own perspective to be moulded to a shape acceptable to the organization. They march to the same drumbeat and sing from the same hymnsheet. Even were there real incentive to try another perspective for a while, and even were ostracism not the penalty for the attempt, prolonged familiarity with a single perspective renders any other awkward and uncomfortable. Thus, readers of the liberal *Guardian* newspaper tend not to try the conservative *Telegraph*, nor the populist *Sun* for the change in perspective this would provide. They stick faithfully to the approach which allows them to relate most easily to the news.

This is not to say that the value of a fresh perspective is unappreciated, but—like a multi-disciplinary or interdisciplinary approach—it is more welcome in theory than in practice. To acquire expertise in more than one subject is not only rather hard work, it is also to risk the accusation of expertise in none. Much safer to develop expertise in a single subject with a single perspective and then to present this expertise not only to peers with the same perspective, but also in such a way that it can be recognized and valued by those with other perspectives. In the academic world, this might take the form of a scholarly paper for other academics, a separate report for funders, another for those who have been studied, and quite different stories for the *Guardian*, the *Telegraph*, and the *Sun*. Such a solution to the problem of disseminating research results neglects altogether the contribution that fresh perspectives can make to the research itself. Research is conducted from a single, fixed perspective and then the results are translated by adjustment to the focal length of other groups. Thus is expertise spared the distorting influence of other perspectives.

As the heading is the first thing that will be read, it is essential that it leaves the reader in no doubt about content of the briefing and its relevance to business. A report entitled 'A Postfordist analysis of labour relations in Bradford's clothing industry, 1963–1992', for example, might be an accurate description of the study, but it is too historical and specialised. Better titles would be, 'What lessons can the clothing industry learn from labour relations in Bradford?'; or 'The future of labour relations in the clothing industry'. [3]

AN INFORMATION PERSPECTIVE

From an information perspective, the dominant feature of the world appears to be information. No doubt this is a distorted view of reality, but then so is that from any other single perspective. The value of an information perspective is derived from the difference between information and other goods. Were information much like anything else, particularly were it capable of being found and acquired and used just like other goods, an information perspective would have no particular distinction, and consequently no particular value. The view it would give would differ little from that offered by other perspectives. Though many of these may seem to be radically different from each other, they are actually more remarkable for their commonality. An agricultural point of view is certainly not the same as a manufacturing point of view, and each depicts the world in a very different way, but they still share fundamental assumptions. Turnips have to be grown in fields and sold in markets; widgets made in factories and sold in not dissimilar markets operating under not dissimilar rules of engagement. Information is not like either turnips or widgets: it is neither grown nor manufactured as they are, nor can it be sold in markets quite as they can. Information transactions are very different from those by which turnips and widgets are bought and sold. In consequence, an information perspective is also very different. Therein lies a large part of whatever value it might have.

A larger part still is derived from the very ubiquity of information. Information being everywhere—even embodied in turnips and widgets—and required for everything—even the sale of turnips and widgets—a perspective which focuses on its characteristics and relationships is widely applicable. Indeed, it is argued that information is now more ubiquitous, more important, than it ever has been; we live in an Information Society, an Information Economy, we are going through an Information Revolution. [4] It is no more the purpose here, any more than it is usually the purpose of those who resort to these terms, to explain and justify them. [5] Some of the justification for the proclamation of a new information world is quite unfathomable.

[Information flow] is an essential ingredient in the recipe for survival in a world which is turning ever faster and becoming increasingly information-rich, but shrinking by the ability to transfer information globally and make use of the information. [6]

Acknowledgement of the dominant role that information has come to play in society and the economy has not really been accompanied by any fundamental change in the way we look at society and the economy. The perspective we enjoy of, say, the Quaternary Sector is not radically different from the perspective long enjoyed of any other sector; [7] we see the information society much as we have long looked at manufacturing or the service sector, information as just another good—an enormous turnip or a giant widget. Indeed, a major concern of many who resort to these grand information concepts is fitting them into existing social and economic models.

The fundamental difference between information and other goods both requires and provides another perspective from which to view the world. [8] Though the difference between information and other goods is rarely denied, it is commonly ignored. No act of faith is necessary to appreciate the difference, no appropriate set of values and beliefs. All that is really needed is observation, which may have something to do with why the difference is typically admitted, then disregarded. Everyone is accustomed to dealing with information; there is no one who does not, and it is precisely because dealing with information is second nature to everyone that the fundamental nature of information is overlooked. It is hard to see clearly—to put in perspective—what is all around. This chapter will rely on observation—and just a little interpretation—to illustrate some of the fundamental aspects of the nature of information. In demonstrating the difference between information and other goods, the potential value of an information perspective may begin to become apparent.

DEMAND AND SUPPLY

Consider the very basic problem of obtaining information. Not all information is equally desirable: only some is wanted. The problem lies in identifying what is wanted, and what is not. This is often hard enough to do even after information has been acquired, but the task is infinitely more challenging before. In as much as one cannot know what one does not know, the problem would seem to verge on the intractable. One can, of course, know *that* one does not know; for example, that one has little to contribute to a discussion on the life cycle of the tsetse fly, but this inadequacy in itself offers little guidance to what might be said on the subject. One does not know *what* one does not know.

Total ignorance, as opposed to relative ignorance, can be a great comfort in that one is oblivious not only of what one does not know, but also of that one does not know. The tsetse fly might not exist. From this emerges the paradoxical situation—and there is much paradox in the nature of information—in which those who know a lot about a subject are more aware of what they do not know than those who know much less. The scholar, knowing how much more there is to know, sees himself as student: the student, oblivious of what else might be known, sees herself as scholar. This is why the columnist is able to scribble easy opinions on every topical issue while the expert on any of these has trouble reaching any conclusion at all. Perhaps it is as well that those who have little information manage so well on their ration, for they have great difficulty acquiring more. Snippets of information are readily gathered—they are almost unavoidable—but further acquisition of information to complement the snippets, to tell the whole story, is very much harder. This is because the acquisition of further information demands the use of information already obtained. Those who have information are better placed to demand information than those who do not. The behaviour of the bookworm or the swot suggests that the demand for information increases with the consumption of information, but it should also suggest that such consumption increases the ability to demand information. The more an individual knows, the more aware he can be about the information he wants to acquire. This is not to suggest that the mere accumulation of information reduces the problem of expressing demand for the unknown. The urge to collect—information or anything else—may simply reduce the discrimination which is an essential component of demand. Information overload, then, may be not so much the burden of trying to use a mass of acquired information, but—again paradoxically—the inability to use this information to acquire yet more information.

In a world where attention is a major scarce resource, information may be an expensive luxury, for it may turn our attention from what is important to what is unimportant. [9]

All demand for information is expressed in some degree of ignorance. Were there no ignorance, there would be no need for information, and presumably no demand. This is a little different from the situation in other markets. In these, buyers are certainly not fully knowledgeable about what is for sale in that they cannot have perfect information about all goods, but ignorance is not actually a prerequisite of demand. Moreover, in most markets, buyers can reduce their ignorance, and hence their uncertainty, by discovering more about the goods for sale. The very structure of markets for other goods gives the buyer some assistance in that even the most ill-informed is likely to realize that a garage sells cars, a tailor's shop clothes, a florist flowers. There is no equivalent information shop, no informationist's. A visit to the florist allows the buyer to see and smell the good, a visit to the tailor's to try it on, a visit to the garage to try it out. With very little initial information, and no more initiative, the potential buyer can acquire more information about many goods simply by examining and comparing them. To be sure, not all potential buyers display the same information-gathering behaviour. Some will arrange for a thorough mechanical inspection of a car; some will kick its tyres. The point is that a buyer—even a tyre-kicker—can acquire information about a car, and about most other goods, in order to express demand. This is not the case with information itself. A library—or its electronic equivalent—will certainly provide information on a subject, but it is actually very poor at providing information about information. The system allows the identification—perhaps the very precise identification —of a subject on which information is required, and then seeks to fill the lacuna with whatever is available. Curiosity, mitigated by relevance, substitutes for demand.

Consider the predicament of someone trying to sell not a car, nor clothes, nor flowers, but information. The good is intangible and there is nothing for the potential buyer to smell, nothing to try on or out, nothing to kick. Not only is it difficult to gather further information about the information for sale, but the good itself must be kept under wraps. Only the seller really knows what he has for sale, and yet the seller may not disclose what this is. To do so would be to give it away, although, in that the acquisition of information always requires some time and energy, it is hard to acquire information without buying it through the expenditure of resources. The best the seller can do is to disclose only part of the information he has to sell in the hope that this will promote demand for the remainder. This taster strategy is fraught with uncertainty simply because the seller does not know what the potential buyer does not know. How could he? His sample may as easily satiate as stimulate the buyer's appetite. It may well prove completely uninteresting; knowing half a football score is no improvement on knowing no score at all.

The seller of information is further constrained by the nature of information, even if he does manage to effect a sale. Information is infinitely reproducible and what the buyer has bought, the buyer can resell. Buyers may pass on to others the information they have bought, and pass it on as new, undiminished by their own use. Other goods do not share this characteristic. There is a second-hand market for other goods, but the concept of second-hand information is meaningless. The seller of information, then, would seem to be in an unenviable position in that even a single sale creates an immediate potential competitor, and any competitor's sale creates the threat of yet further competition. Actually, another characteristic of information renders the seller's position even less comfortable. Information is typically expensive to produce and inexpensive to reproduce. Thus, the producer of information must sell dearly to the first buyer if he is to cover his costs and reduce the risk of being undersold by the resale of his own information. Mitigating this misfortune is yet another odd characteristic of information. While other goods are transferred, usually physically transferred, from seller to buyer so that the latter has what the former once had, this is not the case with information. Though information be transferred to countless buyers, it still remains with the seller—and with all subsequent sellers, of course. There are not many goods that can be disposed of and yet retained at the same time.

Let us assume for a moment that the difficulties inherent in matching a buyer of information with a seller of information are somehow overcome. What price is to be charged? If the seller is the producer of information, he will be anxious to relate the price he charges to the cost of production, but the calculation becomes increasingly irrelevant for subsequent sellers of the same information. Pricing by what the market will bear is hardly a feasible alternative when the market itself is so imperfect. The problem arises not just because buyers do not know what they are buying, but also because sellers, not knowing what buyers do not know—or much of what they do know, for that matter —have little idea what value their information might have for buyers. Only after he has bought, perhaps some time after he has bought, can even the buyer place a value on the information. Even then, it will be very much a personal value, dependent on a whole range of individual circumstances. To others, in different circumstances, the same information will be worth much more—or much less. It is not the case that information is always worth more if no one else knows it—the stock-market scenario; it is much more common for information to be valued precisely because everyone else has it and to be without is to be at a disadvantage. Those who acquire information have something in common with collectors. The value of the item which will complete a set is generally much greater than the value of the first item in the set, and much greater still than an item that is not part of a set at all. But collectors of other goods know whether what is being sold will satisfy their requirements, and sellers may well know too. Buyers and sellers of information do not.

The very uncertainty that surrounds the buying and selling of information and the associated difficulty of matching supply to demand through price sometimes lead to price itself being used to signify the value of information. Just as demand for some fashion goods is as much for their high price (or rather for their reputation for high price) as for the goods themselves, so demand for information can be encouraged by great expense. There may be heavy demand for a costly consultancy report when there is none at all for the equivalent academic paper, freely available. The difference, of course, is that the buyer of the fashion good values the price itself, while the buyer of information desperately looks to price as an indicator of the value of information. That buyers should do this with so little justification is itself an indication of the problems they face in information transactions.

MAKING INFORMATION ORDINARY

All markets are imperfect in as much as buyers and sellers can never have perfect information about what is bought and sold. Information markets are quite splendidly imperfect in that, ironically, there is an even greater shortage of information. There is no way that the information market can arrange its stalls so that all buyers and all sellers may gather together to examine the quality and price of goods. Though it is often assumed that the conjunction of computing and telecommunications technologies overcomes this problem by making massive quantities of information available cheaply and anywhere, the problem is scarcely addressed. Modern information technology deals—and very impressively—with the transfer of information: it does little to effect information transactions. It can supply masses of information, but it cannot easily identify just what information is wanted. The Prestel venture in the UK failed not because of the technical challenge of making an infinity of information available to the citizenry, but because individuals were unable to relate their demand for information to an endless supply. A similar problem may await those compiling something grandiloquently entitled the 'World's Innovation Database'.

The World's Innovation Database forms part of the MFP Australia's promotion of proactive interaction with industry, government and the community. MFP Australia is the organization responsible for the development of Australia's Multi Function Polis. It is committed to developing a unique community of advanced design; a smart city that will balance innovative economic and social development, be technologically advanced and environmentally sustainable. If you have any information which may be suitable for inclusion in the World's Innovation Database, please fax or send details to . . . [10]

So glaring are the imperfections of the information market that for centuries society has intervened in an attempt to rectify them. Society has met with limited success. The patent system is the classic example of response to the failure of the information market. Faced with a situation in which inventors could not disclose their inventions for fear of others copying them, it seemed sensible to give them exclusive rights to their own inventions, sufficient to allow them to recoup the costs of invention, and to provide them with an economic incentive to invent. This was not because society sought to be fair, but because economic benefits for inventors were reckoned to bring economic benefits for society as a whole. Eighteenth-century masters faced similar risk of competition from those to whom they taught their trade, and required that apprentices serve a period as employees before launching out on their own. The traditional patent term of fourteen years was derived from a simple doubling of the usual duration of an apprenticeship. The solution was found not in trying to deal with the peculiar characteristics of information, but in official declaration that information was an honorary ordinary good. This has been the approach to information of legislation and regulation ever since.

Thus it is that, because information is so difficult to measure, goods which are easier to count are often allowed to stand in its stead. For example, because the output from R&D is hard to assess, the input is measured instead, usually in terms of manpower or expenditure. Under any circumstances, indicators, precisely because they are so pre-eminently measurable, tend to create their own markets: there can be more incentive to produce the indicators than to produce whatever it is they are supposed to indicate. When this is information, thoroughly intangible and invisible, the incentive is especially great. Thus, academics may strive not to disseminate information through the publication of papers, but simply to publish papers. [11] It is the indicator itself which determines promotion prospects and institutional research ratings. With the same reluctance to deal with the distinctive nature of information, duty on information entering a country is levied not on the information itself, but on the medium which carries it. This logic persuades courier companies that they should charge more to carry computer discs than other material of similar weight. Or again, the price of telephone calls on switched networks, which might have been expected to bear some relation to the amount of information transferred, bears none at all. Because this would be difficult to calculate, prices are traditionally related to the time taken to convey the information and the distance it has been sent. The same ingredients still comprise the formula for charging for telephone lines used to transmit data from computers or fax machines, though here the amount of data transmitted is very easy to measure. Indeed, the distance ingredient is retained even though it has long since ceased to have any major influence on the cost of providing telecommunications.

Such examples suggest that there are considerable problems in getting to grips with information. Indeed, there is considerable reluctance to try. Given the nature of information, this is understandable. More intriguing are the implications this fudging of the issue might have. If reliance on indicators of information tends to create a market in indicators, a demand for indicators themselves, is it not also possible that other attempts to represent information in terms of ordinary goods may also distort demand for information?

INFORMAL INFORMATION TRANSACTIONS

The usual response to the difficulties of market transactions in information is to avoid them altogether, or at least as much as possible. Thus, organizations are far more comfortable dealing with their own information, information contained and controlled within the organizational boundary, than with external information. Certainly it is true that systems to handle such organizational information are shaped to replicate and fortify the power structure of the organization, but they also have the advantage of avoiding market transactions in information. Indeed, they may become so efficient and so geared to handling the highly codified information on which organizational efficiency depends that there is little need for any transactions in information. Where the organization simply cannot ignore external information, there is still a tendency to avoid acquiring it in the market. The preference is to be able to treat external information as if it were internal, basically to internalize the external. It may be a mistake to ascribe this preference entirely to a desire to avoid market transactions in information; such an assumption suggests that managers have more understanding of the nature of information than they make evident. [12] It is perhaps more realistic to attribute this urge to internalize information to the desire of managers to exert the same sort of control over an important external resource as they exert over internal resources. [13]

There are alternative means of arranging information transactions which avoid both the problems presented by the market and those associated with internalizing information. Broadly, these means can be regarded as informal information transactions, in contrast to the institutional arrangements of the organization and the formality of the marketplace. These are basically non-market, non-institutional transactions. The characteristics of information pose problems for market transactions, problems which are masked rather than solved by such devices as affording information the status of honorary ordinary good; and the characteristics of the organization tend to make demands on information that discourage information transactions. Informal information transactions seem to have advantages over the transactions that can be arranged by either the market or the organization. [14] The characteristics of information remain the same, of course, as do those of the organization, but it would seem that informal transactions can cope with some of the oddities of at least the former in ways that the market and the organization cannot.

Informal information transactions take many forms, most of which allow the exchange of information for other information, something which the market and the organization both find difficult. This barter is a common enough transaction in daily life: most obviously, it is the basis of conversation. It seems axiomatic that conversation entails not just information transfer, but information transaction. Information is exchanged for other information, and with only the crudest accounting of whether the transaction is balanced. The most rudimentary calculation leads to the conclusion that bores—those who provide only information that is unwanted—are to be avoided, as are the taciturn—those who provide almost no information at all.

This ease of transaction stands in sharp contrast to the difficulties experienced in formal information transactions. What explains the difference? Nothing too complicated. Individuals will generally go to some lengths to converse with those who both give and receive information. Receiving is just as important as giving. Only by listening can an individual select from his own store of information what is likely to be of use to the speaker. Listeners are valued not just because speakers love an audience. When participants in a conversation know each other well, they also know what information the other can use. A whole range of factors affects individual ability to use information—basic intelligence, preoccupations and prejudices, attitudes, convictions, values—but perhaps more important than any other is the information the individual already possesses. Information is required to use information and if information cannot be used, it cannot be valued. If information received is not valued, there is little incentive to give information that will be of use in return. End of conversation and end of information transaction.

Receipt of useful information encourages demand for yet more of the same on the grounds that further information is likely to prove equally useful. But even before any information has been received, it is possible for the individual to assess the chances of acquiring useful information. If the information an individual gives is well received, it indicates that the recipient has information of his own with which to use the information received. This compatible information is available if the recipient chooses to give it. Thus, the ability to use information that is given signals to the sender the availability of information that he might be able to use himself. He does not know what this information is; he does not need to know; he can express demand in ignorance.

A further advantage of simple conversation is that it allows both parties great variety in their means of conveying information. A shrug of the shoulders, a grunt, a sneer, a yawn can often convey more information than paragraphs of prose. Moreover, conversation provides the opportunity to question, to verify, to amplify where understanding has been inadequate. This is particularly essential for transactions involving uncodified information, irregular information for which there are no neat and obvious categories, and tacit information, the sort that is implied rather than expressed explicitly. In the real world, probably most information is tacit and uncodified. Certainly it is upon the transaction of just this sort of information, rather than the simple acquisition of information contained in a patent specification, that successful technology transfer is dependent. [15] This transaction seems to be accomplished best by face-to-face contact, by those who have experience of the new technology talking, on site, with those who do not. Much personal conversation takes place at a distance rather than face to face. The overwhelming preference for the latter when information transactions are crucial suggests that there are aspects of face-to-face communication which are generally more conducive to information transactions than communication from afar. It is also likely that the means of communicating at a distance are often associated with institutional communication, and are themselves an obstacle to information transactions between individuals.

This is not, of course, to say that personal communication is always the best means of effecting information transactions. Where order and completeness of information are essential, conversation is hopelessly inadequate. What is an appropriate means of effecting information transactions depends, to some extent, on the type of information involved. That conversation, despite its limitations, is so often used suggests that it has certain advantages over other means. Conversation avoids the need for the pricing of information, allows the transfer of tacit and uncodified information, and permits demand for information in ignorance. It stands in stark contrast to formal market mechanisms, which allow none of these.

INFORMATION NETWORKS

The argument is that informal mechanisms, as exemplified by conversation, are more appropriate to the basic characteristics of information than are formal information transactions. Informal information exchange, however, is constrained not only in that it does not cope well with highly structured information, but also in that information transactions would seem to be restricted to a single source. Of course, an individual may have many such sources, each independent of the others, or may gather sources together in meetings. Neither is an ideal solution to the problem of tapping two sources at once; the first because it is impractical to be constantly hopping from one source to another, the second because group meetings have their own dynamics which can easily interfere with information transactions.

The information network goes some way towards overcoming the limitations of bilateral information exchange. The network permits multilateral exchange, which clearly gives access to much more information than would be available from any single individual. This, then, is a powerful concept. Individuals may draw information from any part of the network, from any other member. In return, they must contribute information. They can do this through any other member and need not reciprocate at the time they receive information, but contribute they must. Not to contribute, and not to contribute information that other members will value, leads to excommunication from the network. Where individuals, and perhaps the organizations to which they belong, have come to rely on network transactions for the information they require, excommunication can be devastating. Classic models of the personal and informal information network—and of this dependence—are the invisible colleges of academics and the professional peer networks of the high-technology industries. Although the latter are particularly associated with the Silicon Valley environment, and particularly necessary in its information-intensive industries, information networks presumably exist in other industries. [16] Certainly there is much discussion of networking these days, though frequently with scant appreciation that an information network of this sort is rather different from a telecommunications network or a firm's distribution network or its ties to research collaborators. [17] An Australian government scheme exhorting small firms to join networks makes no distinction.

Sharing resources, information, production costs and storage facilities can reduce your running costs. The development of new markets or new products as a result of a network can increase your profitability. [18]

An essential characteristic of the informal information network is that its members make personal use of the information they receive. Indeed, they use this information very much for their own benefit; their employers benefit only indirectly through this personal use. This is important for two reasons. The first is that if the individual were not to use the information he received, he would be less able to express demand in ignorance. Information, having no intrinsic value, is valued in terms of the use to which it is put. Consequently, familiarity with how information might be used is essential for the expression of demand. Gatekeepers, those who pass on information from the outside world to others in their organizations for them to use, appear to have only primitive information networks. [19] Such people rely on contacts for their information rather more than on networks, on bilateral rather than multilateral exchange. The second reason is that information can rarely be used in isolation: it must be mixed with other information. This mixing is not easily achieved. The individual is keenly aware of what information he already has; he is much less aware of what information others in the organization have and therefore of what new information will mix with theirs. He is much less able to demand information on their behalf than on his own.

It seems, then, that personal and informal means of information transfer are more suited to the characteristics of information than institutional and market mechanisms. Yet, there are occasions, as when information is highly codified, when formal mechanisms are more appropriate to information transactions. There are many more occasions when institutional imperatives demand the formal. There is no way that a large corporation can handle all the information needed to conduct its business purely through its employees chatting to each other. Other considerations than efficient information transactions demand system and procedure. The report and the committee are the product of these considerations. Such mechanisms often struggle even to transfer information and can be grossly inadequate for information transactions. It would be wrong, though, to conclude that they are therefore necessarily inappropriate to the characteristics of the good. Information is power in a plethora of ways, not least in that it supports the structure of organization and all who cling to it. Information is essential for every activity, and power falls to those who can manipulate information. This skill is most commonly restricted to managing information transfer, and then to restricting the transfer of some information, or of some information in some directions. [20] In that this manipulation seldom extends to interference with information transactions, an appreciation of the characteristics of information is suggested that is more instinctive than intellectual. The manager who tells his subordinates only what they need to know, the politician who provides the electorate with only what it wants to hear, the lawyer who tells judge and jury only what will convince; all are taking advantage of the obstacles to information transactions that institutional systems present. All transfer information instead. In much the same way, public relations resists all involvement in information transactions: its function is simply to transfer information.

Thus, there are institutional and there are market mechanisms for effecting information transactions, and there are informal mechanisms; they do not operate in separate worlds, but together in the same environment. Just what may be the relationship between the formal and the informal is an intriguing question, but one that is rarely asked. Organizations would prefer to rely on information transfer alone, using their own systems to move about information they already contain. Where transactions are unavoidable, they prefer to use the same institutional systems because their use reinforces organizational structure. They are deeply suspicious of informal information transactions because these are thought to undermine this structure. Yet, there is *prima facie* evidence that it is the informal mechanisms which are damaged by the formal. Formal transaction mechanisms have a structure to support them: informal mechanisms do not. The information exchange network is a subtle and delicate creation existing quite independently of organizational support. Such a fabrication is easily damaged, perhaps deliberately, perhaps merely through an inability to appreciate how the mechanism operates and what its role in information transactions might be. [21] The US semiconductor industry has long provided classic evidence of the importance of informal information networks, [22] yet even here their importance can be obscured by the bulk of formal mechanisms. Sematech is a government-induced consortium of US semiconductor companies, a formal collaboration calculated to reverse decline in US competitiveness.

Prior to the establishment of Sematech, there was no mechanism for manufacturing personnel in any of the US semiconductor companies to meet, exchange information, and provide consensus technical direction on equipment and materials needs to the supplier community. Today, Sematech has over 200 such meetings per year . . . [23]

Thus do the trappings of formal systems overshadow even the most evident informal information exchange. Where this is less evident and where the importance of information is acknowledged in the absence of any understanding of the complexity of transactions in information, the crushing of informal mechanisms is even more likely. For example, reductions in organizational hierarchies to improve information flow may well damage existing networks and have just the opposite effect. [24] Similarly, universities seeking to protect information by means of the intellectual property system may well undermine the invisible colleges which provide the information. [25] An information perspective, in as much as it reveals that much of what is done because of the importance of information is inappropriate to the nature of information, may help prevent what is little less than the abuse of information.

GOLD AND INFORMATION

In a modern economy, gold has value for various reasons: it is pretty, it does not decay, it conducts electricity well, it is easily worked, it does not react to other materials. But beyond its aesthetic and material value, gold has the advantage of being in short supply. Certainly gold is mined, and dredged and panned, but only with some difficulty, and what is found each year is but a small proportion of all the gold that has ever been found. Had these arrangements not been made by nature, they might well have been made by man, for his economic system is much facilitated by the use of such a commodity. The properties of gold allow it to represent wealth, and it is this ability of gold to represent which overshadows all its other uses. [26]

However, it is not nature but man which allows gold to represent wealth: common agreement that this shall be so is essential. To be sure, there are other representations of wealth, but these demand rather more trust—also in short supply—among nations, between those who exchange goods for these representations, and particularly between a population and its government. There is always the temptation to increase representation beyond the value of that which is represented, and paper is much easier to print than gold is to mine. So, faith in the value of currency is much bolstered by the knowledge that it can always be converted to gold—the gold standard, which is intermittently defended as the best way to maintain probity and stability in financial affairs. Such a system, however, apart from bestowing enormous value on a tooth filling, would deny governments and institutions the flexibility they insist is required to manage, and manage in, a large and complex economy. So, whatever the medium of exchange in use these days, only a

proportion is backed by gold, an unknown and variable proportion at that. Fort Knox no longer holds gold to back every
dollar, and every other currency convertible to dollars, if it ever
did; and the promise on every pound note to pay the bearer
on demand has only nostalgic worth. These arrangements are
expedient rather than perfect; individuals and institutions still
scurry for gold, or for whatever else might retain its value as a
medium of exchange, whenever the world becomes unsettled and
faith falters.

Because gold has for so long had this very special role in the
representation of wealth, it is easy to forget that only common
agreement allows gold to represent wealth, that beyond a few
handy material properties, gold has no intrinsic value at all.
Limited supply makes this common agreement worth while, but
it is the agreement rather than the limited supply itself which
allows gold to represent wealth. Though there is too much variety of wealth for it all to be equally represented by gold, and
some wealth—health and happiness, for instance—cannot be
represented at all, it is easy to believe that those who have more
gold are richer than those who have less. As the supply of gold
is limited, it follows that those who procure gold from others, by
whatever means, become richer and the others poorer. Thus pirates
and privateers made themselves and their backers wealthier by
seizing the gold of others, who consequently became poorer. In
a sense, a very limited sense, this is exactly what did happen;
their exertions provided them with more to exchange for whatever was of value to them. But there are other ways to acquire
wealth—basically to create it. In a world populated entirely by
pirates, no wealth would be created and the only way to increase
wealth would be to seize that of others. But wealth is not finite,
and those who plough and scatter can make themselves richer
than the most rapacious pirate. And those who do not, though
they fill their galleons with New World gold, can become relatively poorer.

In essence, assuming that wealth is the goal, behaviour is
determined by judgement about whether it is best created or
acquired. For many, the latter offers a more tempting option
than the former, which is why societies and governments take
measures to restrict this option and to encourage the former.
Some, of course, would argue that these arrangements benefit

only those who are still permitted to acquire the wealth that others create.

INFORMATION MERCANTILISM

Mercantilism is the belief that the amount of wealth in the world is finite and therefore that wealth can be gained only by acquisition, by taking the wealth of others. The assumption that merchants, those who buy and sell, do not create wealth through their endeavours is quite erroneous of course; they simply do not create goods. Those who trade in goods certainly increase their value by placing them in the hands of those who value them most. The term 'mercantilism' is unimportant, but the disposition it describes is as relevant now as it has ever been. It is still hard to picture how wealth can be created, and very much easier to see how it can be acquired. If this is difficult even when wealth emerges from the factory gate as a physical product, composed of the tangible raw materials that entered the factory, it is much more difficult when the wealth created is intangible. The debate over the relative importance of the service and manufacturing sectors is less about value added than about whether the intangible is really wealth at all. It is yet more difficult to appreciate that there can be wealth in the intangible when the intangible is not of value in itself, but only in that it contributes to the creation of value elsewhere. What value is there in design, for example, or in research and development for that matter?

Information mercantilists display an attitude towards information akin to that of other mercantilists towards gold and the wealth it represents. Information can be created—of course it can—but this is a slow and uncertain process. It is much easier to acquire information from others. So far the stance, whether applied to information or to gold, is hard to fault, but the argument goes further, much further. Just as it is the having of gold that is imagined to bring wealth, so it is the having of information that is considered important. Those who have more information are considered richer than those who have less, and acquiring the information of another increases the wealth of the acquirer as much as it diminishes the wealth of the supplier. There are two obvious problems with this further step. The first is that

while possession of information may provide as much enjoy-
ment as the possession of a gold ornament, information is not
itself wealth. More information is not more wealth. Much like gold,
information has an important representational role—towering
hierarchies are built on the notion that only those at the top have
access to all the information the organization contains. Unlike
gold, though, information can be used to create wealth. Later
chapters will explore in some detail the contribution of information to the creation of whatever wealth innovation brings. The
second problem is that the accumulation of information is not
quite like the accumulation of gold. There is no limited supply
of information—quite the reverse—and the acquisition of information, unlike the acquisition of gold, does nothing to diminish the
stock of the supplier.

Notwithstanding these objections, the argument proceeds. Because the possession rather than the use of information is imagined to bestow wealth, it seems necessary to guard information
that has been acquired lest others seize it. Those who keep trade
secrets are guarding the information they possess, as are those
who maintain commercial confidentiality, or who look to intellectual property legislation to establish rights over information.
Because the having of information is seen as an essential precon-
dition to the using of information, security to retain information
is frequently judged appropriate. With security comes the hoarding of information, it being much easier to mount guard over
hoarded information than over information that is flowing or in
use. Thus does the value attached to information reinforce the
distinction between the having of information and the use of
information, so that information which can be properly secured
can be regarded more highly than that which cannot.

In its extreme form, this attitude presents very serious problems indeed. At first sight, it would seem to facilitate change in
that information is being sought to swell the hoard, but then
others are equally anxious to prevent the loss of the information they possess. Market transactions in information—always
problematic—are further impeded by a greater reluctance to
sell than to buy. Systems for the exchange of information are
much more efficient than market transactions, but such systems
require that information be given if it is to be received. This is
anathema to the mercantilist mentality. When the organization

becomes a storehouse of information because the mere possession of information is assumed to bestow wealth, leakage must
be prevented at all costs.

INFORMATION MERCANTILISM IN PRACTICE

This all sounds quite absurd; surely no one would expound and
defend such a philosophy. Well no, certainly not in its entirety.
Information mercantilism is an attitude rather than a logical
explanation of behaviour. Like racism and sexism, it tends to be
covert, and apparent in part rather than in whole. If the attitude
is defended at all, it is with emotion rather than with logic. But
prevalent it certainly is. Take the example of national security
export controls, the system employed by Western governments,
and especially that of the United States, to prevent the acquisition of Western dual-use technology—that with both military and
commercial application—by the Soviet bloc. With total justification,
it was argued that the hardware itself was much less valuable
than the information required to make the hardware, the know-
how. So, this information had to be prevented from leaving the
West; it had to be guarded. The extraordinary measures taken
to do this, the complications and implications arising from their
imposition, and their inevitable failure to achieve their declared
aim are the subject of Chapter 7. Of relevance now is the information mercantilism which supported such a preposterous system, a system which would not have been tolerated but for the
instinctive appeal of its justification. It was sheer information
mercantilism which reduced high-technology firms, accustomed
to creating wealth through rapid innovation dependent on the
ready exchange of information, to paranoid hoarders of this same
information.

Information mercantilism is all too evident in many organizations. The approach of firms to industrial espionage is redolent
with the attitude: information is to be retained within the firm
because management is convinced that the firm will lose wealth
if it goes elsewhere. This often regardless of experience that the
firm's information is of more value to it outside than in, that
each firm in an industry innovates and prospers more when the
whole industry advances together. Government programmes

which seek to stimulate the flow of information into a nation's firms, but which refuse to let information out—the subject of Chapter 9—are wonderfully mercantilistic. Similarly, a large part of the justification for governments providing firms with incentives to perform R&D is that the firms should be compensated for the loss of their research information to others. [27] The use of the patent system to protect information rather than to disseminate it—the nub of Chapter 11—displays the same mercantilistic approach. So, too, do attitudes which discourage employee mobility on the grounds that employees will take to new employment what they have learnt in the old. Restrictive covenants and non-disclosure agreements seek to prevent this, as do understandings among employers not to steal staff from each other, golden handcuffs on employees, and even the reluctance to train employees on the grounds that they will only leave and take their information elsewhere. Where firms also aim to encourage innovation, a more self-defeating policy would be difficult to imagine, and it is entirely mercantilistic.

THE RISE AND RISE OF INFORMATION MERCANTILISM

The mercantilist transforms common agreement that gold represents wealth into personal belief that gold actually is wealth. The information mercantilist makes a very similar transference with information. Just as the actual value of gold usually requires its combination with teeth or jewels or whatever, so the actual value of information generally demands its combination with other information. A lump of gold has little more than curiosity value, much like an isolated fact. Information has no intrinsic value; its value is derived almost entirely from its use and this demands its amalgamation with other information. Yet it is quite common, and becoming increasingly common, to refer to information in the abstract, as if it really does have an inherent value. Thus the information economy and the information society are less distinctive for the use they make of information than for the sheer prevalence of information. [28] Information technology, from the laptop to the Internet, is more remarkable for the amount of information it can handle, for the mass of information it can make available, than for its assistance in the use, and even the acquisition, of information. This is mercantilism in practice. Hence the importance attached to computer memory, the capacity of information technology to store information. Even the processing of information is seen less as the means by which information from the electronic store is used, and more as the system by which it is handled. It is akin to the sifting of gold through fingers. Thus it is that, despite the difficulties of finding much direct link between increased productivity and the adoption of information technology—the productivity paradox—adoption is still almost universally justified on the grounds that more information technology means greater productivity. Despite Solow's trenchant observation that 'You can see the computer age everywhere but in the productivity statistics', [29] a mercantilist view prevails that to have information technology is to have information, and to have information is to have wealth. If information technology reflects and reinforces many mercantilistic attitudes, so, too, do attitudes towards the removal of information, towards discarding and forgetting. The mercantilist treasures every scrap.

There is now no dispute, as once there was, that information is important. While this represents victory for those who have argued long and hard that information has been neglected, [30] it has also given an unintentional fillip to information mercantilism. If information really is important, then it would seem to follow that special care should be taken of it, that it must be guarded. Information is valued simply because it is information, because it exists, an attitude previously confined to the filing clerk, but which is now evident wherever there is information technology. With very few exceptions, information has no value except in use: in as much as hoarding of information restricts the use of information, hoarding also restricts its potential to contribute to value. The next few chapters consider why, although a store of information can certainly be used, it is unlikely to produce value indefinitely. There is mounting pressure for change; innovation becomes essential. The following chapters argue that neither is likely without fresh information, and that usually from external sources. So, whence the information comes is considered together with how it comes and how it is used. A basic observation is that information must be given if new information is to be received, which fits nicely with earlier observations on information networks and the nature of information, but which is totally at odds with information mercantilism.

REFERENCES

1. See Stuart Macdonald, 'Technological change and the expert', in W. Ward and M. Bryden (eds.), *Public Information: Your Right to Know* (Royal Society of Queensland, Brisbane, 1981), 53–9.
2. G. Badger, 'ASTEC: planning for science and technology in Australia', public lecture, Griffith University, Brisbane, 10 Sept. 1977.
3. Economic and Social Research Council, *Writing for Business* (Swindon, 1996), 5.
4. e.g. Marc Porat, *The Information Economy: Definition and Measurement* (USGPO, Washington, DC, 1977) and 'Global implications of the Information Society', *Journal of Communication*, 28:1 (1978), 70–80; Ian Miles *et al.*, *Mapping and Measuring the Information Economy* (British Library, Boston Spa, 1990).
5. For some assistance, see Ian Miles and Kevin Robins, 'Making sense of information', in Kevin Robins (ed.), *Understanding Information Business, Technology and Geography* (Belhaven, London, 1992), 1–26.
6. Irene Wormell, 'Gatekeeper as relayer of information', *International Information Communication and Education*, 10:2 (1991), 145–52 (146).
7. On the merits of delineating a Quaternary Sector, see Barry Jones, *Sleepers Wake! Technology and the Future of Work* (Oxford University Press, Melbourne, 1982).
8. A masterly review of the scholarship in this area is Don Lamberton, 'The information economy revisited', in Robert Babe (ed.), *Information and Communication in Economics* (Kluwer Academic, Dordrecht, 1993), 1–33. See also Don Lamberton (ed.), *The Economics of Communication and Information* (Edward Elgar, Cheltenham), 1996.
9. Herbert Simon, 'Rationality as process and product of thought', *American Economic Review*, 68:2, (1978), 13.
10. *Wollongong University Campus Review*, 26 Jan.–1 Feb. 1995, 24.
11. Ralph Adam, 'Laws for the lawless: ethics in information science', *Journal of Information Science*, 17 (1991), 357–72.
12. See O. E. Williamson, *The Economics Institutions of Capitalism* (Free Press, New York, 1985).
13. Stuart Macdonald, 'Learning to change: an information perspective on learning in the organization', *Organization Science*, 6:2 (1995), 1–12.
14. G. R. G. Benito, C. A. Solberg, and Lawrence Welch, 'An exploration of the information behaviour of Norwegian exporters', *International Journal of Information Management*, 13 (1993), 274–86; Hokey Min and William Galle, 'International purchasing strategies of multinational US firms', *International Journal of Purchasing and Materials Management*, 27:3 (1991), 9–18.

15. Lawrence Welch, 'The technology transfer process in foreign licensing arrangements', in S. Macdonald, D. Lamberton, and T. Mandeville (eds.), *The Trouble with Technology* (Frances Pinter, London, 1983), 155–68.

16. Stuart Macdonald and Christine Williams, 'The informal information network in an age of advanced telecommunications', *Human Systems Management*, 11:2 (1992), 77–87.

17. For an altogether different concept of network, see H. Thorelli, 'Networks: between markets and hierarchies', *Strategic Management Journal*, 7 (1986), 37–51. See also Benjamin Gomes-Casseres, 'Group versus group: How alliance networks compete', *Harvard Business Review*, July–Aug. 1994, 62–74.

18. AusIndustry, *Business Networks* (Canberra, 1995).

19. Stuart Macdonald and Christine Williams, 'Beyond the boundary: An information perspective on the role of the gatekeeper in the organization', *Journal of Product Innovation Management*, 10 (1993), 417–27.

20. Adam, 'Laws for the Lawless'.

21. Kristian Kreiner and Majken Schultz, 'Informal collaboration in R&D: the formation of networks across organizations', *Organization Studies*, 14:2 (1993), 189–209.

22. Ernest Braun and Stuart Macdonald, *Revolution in Miniature: The History and Impact of Semiconductor Electronics* (Cambridge University Press, Cambridge, 1982).

23. William Spencer and Peter Grindley, 'Sematech after five years: high-technology consortia and US competitiveness', *California Management Review*, 35:4 (1993), 9–32 (p.23).

24. Rebecca Marschan, Denice Welch, and Lawrence Welch, 'Control in less-hierarchical multinationals: the role of personal networks and informal communication', *International Business Review*, 5:2 (1996), 137–50.

25. Irwin Feller, 'Universities as engines of R&D-based economic growth: they think they can', *Research Policy*, 19 (1990), 335–48; Stephen Hill, 'Moving boundaries: transformations of the interface between academic institutions and their environments', in Irmline Veit-Brause (ed.), *Science Policy and the Case for Realignment between the University's own Values and the Society's Real Needs*, (Deakin University, Victoria, 1995).

26. Inevitably, J. M. Keynes, *The General Theory of Employment, Interest and Money* (Macmillan, London, 1936).

27. See Stuart Macdonald, 'Theoretically sound: practically useless? Government grants for industrial R&D in Australia', *Research Policy*, 15 (1986), 269–83.

28. See, for example, Nick Moore and Jane Steele, *Information-Intensive Britain* (Policy Studies Institute, London, 1991).
29. R. M. Solow, 'Review of Cohen and Zysman, *Manufacturing Matters: the Myth of the Post-Industrial Economy*', *New York Times Book Review*, 12 July 1987, 36. See also Don Lamberton, 'The information revolution in the Asian-Pacific Region', *Asian-Pacific Economic Literature*, 8:2 (1994), 31–57; Diane Wilson, 'Assessing the impact of information technology on organizational performance', in Rajiv Banker, Robert Kauffman, and Mo Mahmood (eds.), *Strategic Information Technology Management* (Idea Group, Harrisburg, Pa.,1993), 471–514.
30. Most notably, Don Lamberton. See in particular Lamberton, 'The information economy revisited'.

2

Change and Innovation

THE QUEST FOR INFORMATION

Most people are hard put to say what information is, perhaps because information itself is needed to attempt the explanation, but more likely because of the intangible ubiquity of the good. Because information is intangible, it is easier to picture its physical associations than the good itself. Because it is ubiquitous, information is more remarkable in its absence than in its presence: total ignorance is more exceptional than partial knowledge. Information is even commonly described in terms of what it is not—not data, for example—as if elimination of what need not be defined automatically defines what remains.

Here the concern is with information as that resource which allows change to occur. [1] To be sure, other resources are almost certain to be required as well, but it is hard to see how anything new, anything different, can be done without an addition of information to that already in use. Thus, understanding of change is likely to be increased by considering—as these next few chapters do—whence information comes, how it comes, and how it is used. Change, of course—the transition from one state to another—provides its own perspective on the way things are done; the lessons of history are learnt through understanding what is done now in the light of what has been done before. An information dimension augments this perspective, supplying the flesh of meaning to the bare bones of comparison.

Some would argue that all information already exists, that all the hand of man must do is find information and use it. [2] Yet, man does tend to distinguish between information that is available and information that is merely out there somewhere, between that which is known and that which is not. More particularly, he distinguishes between that which he knows himself and that which is known by others. While what is not known at all—whether the information is yet to be created or is out there somewhere—has value in its potential to become known, more value is commonly perceived to lie in the acquisition of information already known by others. Information may be sought for its own sake, to satisfy the thirst for knowledge: much more commonly it is sought to add to the resources already available to do things. Information is a means rather than an end.

This compulsion to know more can lead to the supposition that it is the quest for information, rather than information itself, which is fundamental to change. The searching, finding, and acquiring of information may overshadow the contribution of what is sought, found, and acquired. The consequences of this perspective are considerable. Innovation is seen entirely as a function of man's endeavours, his research in particular, or of those of his creations to facilitate these endeavours—his institutions, customs, and organizations. Change is seen as a process, something devised by the wit and will of man. This view is not necessarily wrong, but, like any dominant perception, it is intolerant of alternatives. An information perspective serves to put man in the background for a moment; it allows change and innovation to be seen were there other than man to see them.

CHANGE AND PROGRESS

The terms 'change' and 'innovation' are used synonymously, innovation most commonly in the context of technology, change more generally, though increasingly in the context of the organization. Both are associated with progress, though they are certainly not synonymous with progress. Change may indeed be required for progress, but change does not necessarily bring progress, except in the purely pedestrian sense of progression to a succeeding state. Progress in the sense of the betterment of something or someone is not an inevitable consequence of change. [3] Things sometimes have been better in the past and there is no justification for seeing change and innovation as inherently good. Why, then, is optimism so prevalent?

The view that change is progress may be clearest to those who are not directly involved in its practice and to those who benefit from change. Many gain little from change, some nothing at all, and some lose; most are averse to the uncertainty which even beneficial change entails. [4] Thus, many employees in the early Eighties, for example, were extremely apprehensive about the impact of technological change on their skills and working conditions. [5] This at the very time when public servants and their political masters were fired by the need for technological change and were extolling the benefits of innovation. The proponents of innovation are seldom those who undergo its traumas; the innovation they advocate is innovation elsewhere, innovation by someone else. Similarly, different perceptions of change are evident in those who direct change and in those who endure its consequences: to have some control over change—perhaps even the illusion of control—is at least to perceive a reduction in the uncertainty it entails.

This is straightforward enough, but there is another dominant perspective on change which is less obvious. Clearly any change that does not happen instantly involves some sort of process, progression from one state to another, perhaps through several intermediate stages. But is this the sort of process that can be repeated like a scientific experiment? Some change is unquestionably stochastic: some can be depended upon to occur precisely as planned. Most change—and perhaps all change wrought by man—falls somewhere in between. This poses problems for those who can accommodate no mystery in the means by which change is brought about. [6] Frustration is particularly evident in those who would guide policy or strategy for change, those who are intolerant of the uncertainty in the relationship between cause and effect. The guide who can lead only part of the way may want for patronage.

Consequently, there is a tendency among the proponents and leaders of change to disregard the unpredictable—the random element in change, serendipity in innovation—and to focus on what seems to be predictable. Past experience of change should warn us that transition is neither smooth nor predictable, yet it does not. The view of how present change came about is very much bounded by what elements eventually contributed most, and most directly, to the change. Hindsight tends to exclude what seemed relevant and promising at the time and proved to be anything but, and it inevitably excludes the uncertainty which pervades all efforts to change. The impression of smooth passage

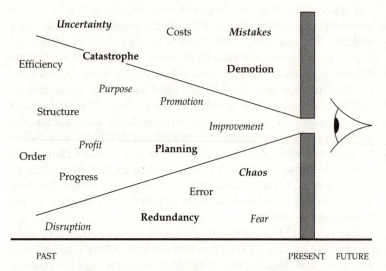

Efficiency
Uncertainty Costs *Mistakes*
Catastrophe
Demotion
Purpose
Promotion
Structure
Improvement
Profit **Planning**
Order
Chaos
Progress
Error
Disruption **Redundancy** *Fear*

PAST PRESENT FUTURE

FIG. 2.1 Change seen with hindsight

from initiation to innovation is all that remains, and only the most traumatic of interruptions to progress are indelibly impressed on the memory (see Fig. 2.1). [7]

Perceptions of past change as the outcome of a neat and ordered process, sanitized of all uncertainty, [8] lead inexorably to the notion that how to change can be learnt in much the same way as what to change. [9] Learning to change is taken to be the transfer of information from those who know to those who do not, a process which can be directed and controlled. Such learning, in its implication that there is nothing worth knowing that is not already known—usually elsewhere in the same organization—is really training. It reinforces both what is already done in the organization and those who decide what is done in the organization.

Learning should be linked to freedom from dominance and ownership. Learning is a voluntary activity intended to achieve improvement. If 'learning' occurs in a situation of dominance and control it should be termed training. [10]

Indeed; understanding how to change and innovate comes as much from appreciating what is not known as from absorbing

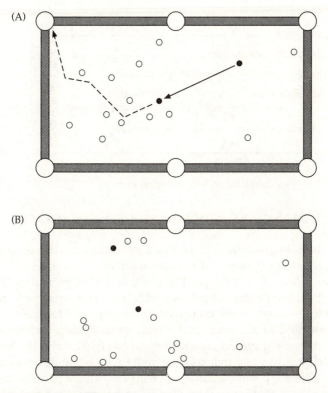

Fɪɢ. 2.2 The billiard-ball effect

what is. Yet the exigencies of order and control deny the importance of mystery and curiosity, of ignorance and forgetting. [11]
In their place there is often a sterile environment of best practice and benchmarking, of innovation which, having been created, then diffuses as ordained to produce adoption dots on maps
and to have impact and implications. Fig. 2.2 depicts in A change
as it tends to be perceived by those who implement and direct
it—as a process akin to potting a billiard ball. The designated
ball somehow finds the corner pocket, avoiding all other balls
on the table. In B, the ball never reaches a pocket, but does scatter all the other balls. It is hardly possible to change a part of
the whole without affecting the other parts, an effect which adds
to the uncertainty of the intended change.

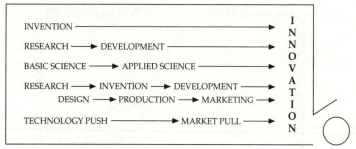

Boundary of organization

FIG. 2.3   Linear model of technological change

CHANGE AS PROCESS: THE LINEAR MODEL

The best example by far of the desperation to disregard the uncertainty in change and to claim mastery over a process is the linear model of technological innovation. This depicts new technology as the product of process, with innovation emerging from a series of steps in the industrial management of technology. It is presented as axiomatic that science must precede technology, invention must precede innovation. In its classic form, the linear model portrays research coming first, followed by development and ultimately innovation—a perception which permits those who believe that innovation is good to be convinced that R&D, as a prerequisite for innovation, is also intrinsically good.

Technological advances are possible only because of major investments in research and development [12]

Fig. 2.3 shows variations of the linear model with the associated dimension that, because a process is at work, it can be controlled and therefore contained within the boundaries of an organization. Even market pull is the organization's interpretation of demand rather than actual market response to prototypes, so that too is conceptually within the organization. Only once the linear process is quite complete does the organization open its doors to deliver its innovation to the outside world.

. There is also a sociological dimension to the model stemming from the perception that research initiates the process that culminates in technological innovation: those responsible for setting the process in motion are accorded greater status than those who follow in their footsteps. The scientist, who starts the ball rolling, is regarded as a professional; the engineer, who keeps the ball rolling and maintains its direction, regards himself as a professional; and the salesman, who simply passes on the ball to an eager market, neither regards himself, nor is regarded, as a professional. The scientist wears a white coat, the engineer a brown one, and the salesman something flashy and tasteless.

I remember vividly when I proposed switching from science to engineering at Cambridge being dissuaded by the disdainful assurance that I was 'clever enough' to do science. [13]

The linear model is a simplistic portrayal of technological change as an inevitable, unidirectional, and discrete process. It is this very simplicity which has long been the model's strength. The function of any model is to simplify in order to facilitate understanding. The more complex the phenomenon—and change is decidedly complex—the more needed the simplification. Precisely because it is so welcomed and because it presents such a tiny target, simplicity is actually very difficult to challenge. Even so, the reputation of the linear model of technological change has been thoroughly and convincingly destroyed by a barrage of research and practical observation. Most devastating has been the revelation that much contribution to change comes from outside the closed system of the model, from beyond the confines of any one organization or single system. [14] Almost as damaging has been the finding that links between science and industry, even within a single organization, are not especially close. But the *coup de grâce* has been recognition that the unidirectional flow of information fundamental to the model is in fact multidirectional, with innovation as likely to inspire research, and much else, as research innovation. It follows that innovation is not the culmination of a process, and consequently that there may be no particular process involved. Innovation would seem to be inherently incremental with change itself stimulating and contributing to further change. With doubt cast on the very existence of process, the linear model of technological change would seem to lie in ruins.

Although most innovations can be traced to some conquest in the realm of either theoretical or practical knowledge that has occurred in the immediate or remote past, there are many which cannot. Innovation is possible without anything we should identify as invention, and invention does not necessarily induce innovation, but produces of itself . . . no economically relevant effect at all. [15]

And yet the linear model survives, even thrives. In part this is because even a model which is wrong has a fundamental utility for those who would demonstrate its inadequacy; as a straw man, of course, but also as a convenient encapsulation. If even its opponents can find a use for the linear model, it should not be surprising that others for whom its acceptance brings specific advantages are supportive. Scientists are not opposed to the notion that their efforts are responsible for technological innovation, nor policymakers to the idea that innovation can be summoned up by the programmes they implement, nor managers to the control the linear model lets them feel they exercise over innovation. [16] Beyond these partisan interests, there is a vague and general feeling that if innovation happens—which it obviously does—then it must have started somewhere. For every omega there must have been an alpha. There is also a basic organizational requirement to deny the reality, and certainly the virtues, of disorganization. It is all very well to allow that disorder produces unfavourable outcomes, but the favourable must be claimed as the product of good management, good decisions, good organization.

This *mélange* of basic reasoning, basic self-interest, and basic emotion permits persistent resort to a model which is quite wrong. Most often its use is implicit—as when policymakers and politicians proclaim the importance of R&D in national competitiveness—and there is no obligation to defend the model explicitly. But often enough its use is quite explicit, as when senior management declares innovation to be a central plank in its strategic platform, and that resources have been allocated for its carpentry. In such cases, it is not uncommon to find fervent denial of the linear model cheek by jowl with thinking that is derived directly from nothing else. This triumph of the sense of process over common sense is intriguing. Obviously the linear model presents an obstacle to any other understanding of change and innovation, but—far more serious—the concept of linearity buttresses a much wider range of thinking and action that would collapse without this support.

Technology push and market pull

While apparently a concession to the reality that forces outside
the contained world of the organization influence innovation
within, the notion of market pull is really no more than a
mirror image of technology push, which is transparently the
linear model in another guise. The idea of the forces producing
innovation within the organization as a cohesive unit shoving
technology along a single track is fanciful enough, but that of
external influences all heaving together to haul technology from
the organization is even more unrealistic. [17] A major distinction of external forces is that there is no prospect of directing
and controlling them in the same way as forces within the organization, or perhaps at all. To portray them as a neat obverse of
linear forces pushing out innovation is to misrepresent both the
nature of these pressures and their impact on innovation. It
would be rather more helpful to picture the market pushing
innovation every bit as much as technology, but this would
convey the awkward impression of forces opposed, in conflict,
of disarray and uncertainty.

Technological determinism

It is understandable that scientists and engineers should be
inclined to assume that their own contribution is seminal in the
creation of innovation. It follows that, in as much as innovation
brings increased competitiveness and other benefits, scientists
and engineers see their efforts, and themselves of course, as directly responsible. From this vantage, it seems clear that technology
is the driving force in innovation, and that all which technology
produces is tributary to it. The linear model has been extended
from the idea of technology pushing to the idea of technology
forcing, and therefore causing. So, cause becomes the legitimate
concern of scientists and engineers, while effect is quite distinct,
the province of social scientists. This division of responsibility
obviates any need that either group might have felt to become
too entangled with the other. This is most evident in the scientist's
easy and eager assessment of the social benefits which will flow
from technology, but it is also apparent in the social scientist's
aversion to any detailed involvement with technology. [18]

Acceptance of cause and effect allows resort to various indicators of technological development to reveal what the world will
make of innovation. This is a large part of the purpose of comparing the R&D expenditures of firms, or of countries for that
matter. Interest is not in R&D itself, but entirely in what the
expenditure is assumed to reveal of future innovation and thus
competitiveness and thus prosperity. This is also a large part of
the purpose of comparing the patent applications of firms and
nations. [19] Patent statistics have no more inherent interest than
R&D statistics, and that is very little indeed. In much the same
way, some of the cruder notions of technology trajectory, of a
set course for technological development, are dependent upon
the acceptance of linearity.

Technology and industry policy

Innovation is considered to be essential for national prosperity and governments are seen to have a responsibility for its
encouragement. The linear model is a godsend: governments
may restrict their intervention to one of the most abstruse of
industry's activities, as distant as could be from the commercial
interests of industry in the market. [20] Additional support for
this approach is derived from the theory of market failure as
applied to technological change, the notion that individual firms
cannot reap all the benefits from their own R&D, that some will
escape into the economy at large. [21] Therefore, the economy,
represented by government, is to compensate firms for their
loss by subsidizing their R&D. Failure to do so, it is argued,
will result in firms underspending on R&D and consequently in
fewer benefits for the economy from innovation. [22]

The deficiencies of market failure theory are considered elsewhere. For the moment, it is relevant to note only how linear
are the assumptions surrounding this application. The theory
leaves no room for doubt that R&D results in innovation and
that the link is direct. It is the linear model which underlies the
justification by which governments seek to encourage maximum
innovation with minimum interference in the affairs of industry. This is despite ample evidence that government assistance
for industrial R&D has little impact on innovation from industry, [23] and every suggestion that assistance in the market would
be much more likely to have the impact that governments desire.

High technology

Even when governments are expected by their electorates to be more interventionist in their innovation programmes, it is hard to ignore the influence of the linear model on their efforts. Take high technology, a category once defined by the immense benefits presumed to emerge from the innovation it produced. Immense benefits naturally required immense innovation and this, in turn, immense expenditure on R&D. Indeed, high-technology industries were identified by their generous expenditure on R&D, if not by their capacity to spend yet more. High-technology firms found governments everywhere eager to encourage yet higher levels of spending on R&D. As their programmes were commonly evaluated not in terms of innovation output, which would have been difficult, but in terms of resources put into R&D, which was much easier, the success of high-technology programmes was assured. The stock market, industry itself, and society as a whole were less impressed by benefits which were easier to measure than to effect. Yet their reservations have been interpreted as an indictment of high-technology industry itself, and not of the linear justification for the means by which high technology was encouraged.

Science and technology parks

Most prominent among the alternative means of encouraging innovation in high technology has been the science or technology park. Significantly, the terms are used indiscriminately. These parks provide accommodation and an environment considered appropriate for high-technology firms, generally new and small firms. The firms are even to look like the benefits they are supposed to produce; they are to be clean and modern, the very opposite of 'smoke-stack' industry. In the same vein, their environment is to be green and grassy and as natural as artifice can contrive. In the technology park there are shades of the greenfield R&D of large corporations some thirty years ago, when R&D was regarded as such a precious activity that complete separation from anything that smacked of manufacturing was deemed necessary to stimulate the professional creativity that was the wellspring of innovation. The thinking behind science parks is similarly simple, and alarmingly linear: provide the right surroundings as an input to high technology and the output will be beneficial innovation. It is significant that public rather than private funds have provided most of these surroundings. It is policy—policy for the perception of change with which the middle-class, suburban voter feels most comfortable—that has deduced that if ducks and ponds stimulate research, then from ducks and ponds spring forth monoclonal antibodies and the riches therefrom. Reliance on the linear model is even more starkly evident when, as is very often the case, science and technology parks are located on university campuses. The reasoning is embarrassing: the scientific knowledge required for innovation resides in the university. Proximity will allow it to enter high-technology firms, where it will be converted into high-technology innovation. [24] This from those who would strenuously disavow any adherence to anything so discredited as the linear model.

Education and manpower

A perpetual complaint of industry is that it lacks the qualified scientists and engineers required to generate the innovation expected of it. Industry is generally pleased to regard such human capital as a public good to be produced at public expense. When shortfalls in quality or quantity arise, it is the government that is held responsible, blamed for failure to provide the means for firms to generate innovation and hence to compete internationally. Similarly, when demand for scientists and engineers is slack and they very sensibly respond by seeking jobs in other countries, what is the most natural of economic phenomena takes on the dimensions of a national disaster. There is talk of brain drain and selling the seedcorn upon which future prosperity depends.

Were it not for the linear model, neither argument would be tenable. Industry might well attract more and better scientists and engineers were it willing to pay more. The same response might rapidly reverse a brain drain. Were the problem to arise with accountants rather than scientists and engineers, this would be the response. The problem does not arise, and quite simply because scientists and engineers in the UK are expected to ply their trade, to stick to their last in a way that those with other qualifications are not. No eyebrows are raised when accountants enter general management: it is seen as a complete abandonment and betrayal of profession, a refutation of values and beliefs, a waste of human resources, an indictment of industry and education policy when scientists or engineers do precisely the same thing. Those with qualifications in science and engineering are expected, and expect themselves, to play a seminal role in innovation, to accept responsibility for creating the means by which wealth is generated. Such inflexibility meets its just deserts in the labour market.

The situation is exacerbated by education policy, at least by that considerable part of education policy directed to the enhancement of wealth rather than of intellect. It is expected that resources devoted to the education of scientists and engineers will yield returns in terms of innovation. When these returns are thought to be insufficient, there is pressure for greater specialization in the education of scientists and engineers that they may be the more productive. Thus is their flexibility further sacrificed to the belief that more resources applied at one end of a linear system will inevitably yield more innovation at the other.

INNOVATION FROM AN INFORMATION PERSPECTIVE

The expert witness syndrome

Simplicity being the essence of a model, complication reduces its effectiveness as a means of encapsulating and presenting a situation. This is of little consequence for those who are familiar with the situation, but it is of great moment for the uninitiated. They are dependent on the model for their grasp of the situation. Complication may sound impressive, but it does nothing to assist comprehension. To this add the expert witness syndrome, the preference of lawyers for expert witnesses who do not know a great deal about their subject, but are still knowledgeable enough to be accepted as experts. Such witnesses can truthfully provide simple and unequivocal answers to complex questions, whereas those who are more expert must be less definite if they are to be equally truthful. The juror finds the simple response easy to follow and its certainty convincing. The same issue arises when a simple model of change is opposed by one more complex. Yet, what is readily comprehensible and convincing does not necessarily promote understanding. There is need for a model which does advance the understanding of change and innovation, and which does not resort to the neatness and simplicity of process and linearity.

Of packages and patterns

It is quite possible, and actually quite useful, to perceive what is done, and the way in which it is done, as an information package. A whole bevy of bits of information is required to do even the simplest things. Much of the information required is tacit information, derived from distant experience and deeply embedded. Some of the information is explicit, the stuff of which operating manuals and blueprints are composed. The whole comprises an information package on which accomplishment of the task is dependent. If part of the package is missing, the task cannot be completed. If there is to be change in the way things are done, or in what is done, an addition is required to this information package. Put another way, an addition to the information package means that new things can be done or old things done in new ways.

This package model has its uses; for example, it accommodates the notion that learning by doing runs dry without the fillip of invention. [25] Yet the package model of change is not enough; it is patently unsatisfactory to picture what is done and how it is done as some sort of bag steadily filling with loose bits of information. How these bits relate to each other is clearly crucial. It is much more satisfying to picture the package as a pattern of bits of information so that what is done and how it is done becomes dependent not simply on collecting ever more bits of information, but on fitting them together into a pattern. Only when the pattern is complete can the task be accomplished. In such a model, minor change—typical in incremental innovation —would involve only a small alteration in the pattern: major change quite radical alteration (Fig. 2.4).

Product and process innovation

If this notion of packages and patterns does encapsulate change, it may seem more appropriate for process innovation than for

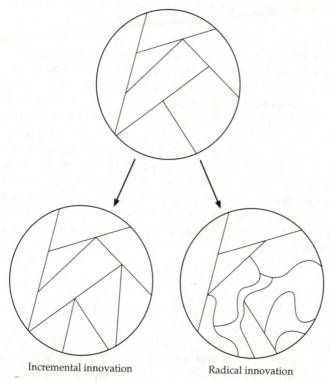

Incremental innovation   Radical innovation

FIG. 2.4   Information for change

product innovation. A clear distinction is normally made between
the way things are done and what is done, between the way
things are made and what is made. It is a distinction which originates in manufacturing industry, whence comes, in the opinion
of many, the only real wealth, and consequently the only real
innovation. There is no trouble at all picturing manufacturing innovation as a new sort of gadget, shiny in its polystyrene
packaging and quite separate from the noise and machinery
that produced it. As if to emphasize the distinction, factories
customarily keep examples of their innovations, glass-cased in
Reception, for visitors to admire before—or to obviate—their
descent to the factory floor.

The distinction between process innovation and product
innovation is less clear in the service industries. Here product is

process, the end result being scarcely distinguishable from the way in which it was achieved. An insurance policy is called a product, but the agreement between company and customer is only a formal acceptance of complex actuarial calculations and organizational procedures for indemnifying loss. The distinction is also seen to break down in some manufacturing industries. Take semiconductors: the characteristics and performance of the product are entirely a function of how it is made. [26] Changes in process are changes in product. The integrated circuit, for instance, was a process innovation (to permit the batch manufacture of discrete transistors) before it was ever a product innovation. Extend this example, if you like, to the computer, a conjunction of tangible hardware and intangible software. It is unrealistic to see the innovation that takes place in one as being in some way quite different from the innovation that takes place in the other.

Change and uncertainty

It may be that existing ways of looking at change and innovation are unsatisfactory, but does an information perspective offer any improvement? In that it regards change as a matter of information, it would seem better able than other approaches to cater for uncertainty. To see change as process, especially a linear process, as a learning experience, seems to ignore uncertainty. An information approach not only depicts uncertainty as inherent in change, but also accommodates the uncertainty resulting from change. Indeed, the approach has some trouble distinguishing between change itself and the impact of change, simply because both the impact of past change and the predicted impact of future change make an information contribution to current change. The notion of cause and effect makes little sense when effect can also be cause.

The information approach also copes comfortably, in a way that other approaches do not, with random change. It is quite understandable that an information package not fortified and defended may be penetrated by stray bits of information, and that some of these bits may happen to fit within a pattern. Even the routine of the nunnery is not sacrosanct from such intrusion. As for learning to change, normally perceived as replicating the patterns created by others, that becomes the deliberate acquisition of new bits of information for addition to the package and fitting within the pattern. [27] Evidence suggests that, whether through learning or more passive acquisition, these bits emanate from a vast range of sources and are conveyed by a variety of means. The information perspective has no trouble with this reality. In contrast, other approaches tend to view learning to change as an instructional process, often an organizational process, whereby those who are to change can be tutored in what they must do. [28] Add linearity and learning to change is perceived to follow a determined path; it takes on the characteristics of a production line processing information in the manufacture of change. Two examples of this mode of thinking will be more than enough.

Change will occur when $K \times D \times V > C$, where:
  K represents Knowledge of first practical steps
  D represents Dissatisfaction with the status quo
  V represents the desirable Vision of the future
  C represents the Cost (material and psychological) of movement. [29]
Change will occur when $C \times V \times L > I$, where:
  C represents significant pressures and arguments for change in the inner and outer Context of the organization
  V represents the presence of Visionary leadership
  L represents the perceived Legitimacy of change proposals
  I represents the organizational Inertia sustained by the current dominant ideology. [30]

But it is the linear model itself which contrasts most vividly with the information perspective and which perhaps best illustrates the advantages of the perspective. The linear model's deficiencies are legion and widely acknowledged, yet it survives to undermine understanding and to create massive misunderstanding of change and innovation. It cannot cope with the complexity of reality; the observation, for example, that the impetus for innovation can come just as easily from other activities in the organization as from R&D, and that there is no predetermined order in which these activities must make their contribution. [31] Indeed, the notion of an information package accommodates nicely the observation that sources outside the organization must be exploited for the new bits of information that change is likely to require. While a focus on research suggests the importance of creating new information for change, emphasis on information suggests that very little information is actually created and that very much is gathered—even in research. [32] Even where external information is not exploited and change is dependent on information already contained within the organization, the information perspective still copes. Change is then dependent on either the discovery and incorporation in the information package of bits of information which have lain neglected within the organization, or—much more likely—on the rearrangement of the bits the package already contains to form a new pattern. [33] A jigsaw is a helpful analogy, though some sort of pattern, be it ever so elementary, always exists before rearrangement, and there is never any ultimate, definitive pattern. In this sense, all innovation is incremental, it builds on what existed before. The idea of a pattern is also useful in that it suggests that alternative patterns may be formed, not only by adding new bits of information, but by discarding old bits. So entrenched is the view of change as improvement wrought by disciplined accumulation that the importance of forgetting is itself forgotten. [34] An information perspective accommodates forgetting as easily as it accommodates learning.

Where an information perspective fails dismally is in its ability to prescribe. It may well aid understanding of how change comes about, but it has little to say on how to bring about that change. Other perceptions of change and innovation have much to say on this matter. This does not mean that they are correct, of course, though they are definitely reassuring. They present change as an ordered process which can be controlled. The importance of control is paramount, and it is for this purpose, not for understanding, that order and process are sought. An information perspective may be an aid to the understanding of change and innovation, but it offers no assurance whatsoever of order and process, no ready means of control.

REFERENCES

1. See Carmel Maquire, Edward Kazlauskas, and Anthony Weir, *Information Services for Innovative Organizations* (AP Professional, San Diego, 1994).

2. There is a useful overview of the arguments in Mairead Browne, *Organizational Decision Making and Information* (Ablex, Norwood, NJ, 1993), 11–17.

3. Ernest Braun, *Wayward Technology* (Frances Pinter, London, 1984).

4. Dorothy Leonard-Barton and W. Kraus. 'Implementing new technology', *Harvard Business Review*, 63:6, 1985, 102–10. See also W. Kip Viscusi and Michael Moore, 'Product liability, research and development, and innovation', *Journal of Political Economy*, 101:1, 1993, 161–84.

5. Stuart Macdonald and Tom Mandeville, 'Reflections on the technological change debate', *Australian Quarterly*, 52:2 (1980), 137–48.

6. e.g. Peter Robertson, Darryl Roberts, and Jerry Porras, 'Dynamics of planned organizational change: assessing empirical support for a theoretical model', *Academy of Management Journal*, 36:3 (1993), 619–34.

7. J. March, L. Sproull, and M. Tamuz, 'Learning from samples of one or fewer', *Organization Science*, 2:1 (1991), 1–13.

8. e.g. W. Rostow, 'The fifth upswing and the fourth industrial revolution', *Economic Impact*, 44 (1983), 58–63.

9. D. Kelleher, P. Finestone, and A. Lowry, 'Managerial learning: first notes from an unstudied frontier', *Group and Organization Studies*, 11:3 (1986), 169–202; P. Senge, *The Fifth Discipline: The Art and Practice of the Learning Organization* (Century Business, London, 1992).

10. Sten Jonsson, 'The changing role of knowledge bases in organizations and the significance of knowledge for competitive performance', paper given to a workshop on strategic change, University of Venice, May 1991.

11. Bengt-Ake Lundvall and B. Johnson, 'The learning economy', *Journal of Industry Studies*, 1:2 (1994), 23–42.

12. L. Girifalco, 'The dynamics of technological change', *Economic Impact*, 42 (1983), 54–9.

13. Peter Lilley, *Innovation: Competition and Culture* (Department of Trade and Industry, London, 1991), 5.

14. The development of the argument can be followed in Dorothy Leonard-Barton and Everett Rogers, *Horizontal Diffusion of Innovations: An Alternative Paradigm to the Classical Diffusion Model*, Sloan School of Management Working Paper 1214, 1981; Roy Rothwell, 'Innovation and re-innovation: a role for the user', *Journal of Marketing Management*, 2:2 (1986), 109–23; Eric von Hippel, *The Sources of Innovation* (Oxford University Press, New York), 1988.

15. Joseph Schumpeter, *Business Cycles* (McGraw-Hill, New York, 1939), 84. Quoted in Devendra Sahal, 'Invention, innovation and economic growth', *Technological Forecasting and Social Change*, 23 (1983), 213–35.

16. See L. Greiner and L. Barnes, 'Organization change and development', in G. Dalton and P. Lawrence (eds.), *Organizational Change and Development*, (Irwin-Dorsey, Homewood, Ill., 1970), 1–12.

17. See G. Foxhall and J. Tierney, 'From CAP1 to CAP2: user-initiated innovation from the user's point of view', *Management Decision*, 22:5 (1984), 3–15.
18. Ernest Braun, *Wayward Technology*.
19. e.g. Pari Patel and Keith Pavitt, 'A comparison of technological activities in West Germany and the United Kingdom', *National Westminster Bank Quarterly Review*, May 1989, 27–42.
20. See Margaret Sharp and Keith Pavitt, 'Technology policy in the 1990s: old trends and new realities', *Journal of Common Market Studies*, 31:2 (1993), 129–51.
21. Edwin Mansfield, 'How rapidly does new industrial technology leak out?', *Journal of Industrial Economics*, 34:2 (1985), 217–23.
22. Stuart Macdonald, 'Theoretically sound: practically useless? Government grants for industrial R&D in Australia', *Research Policy*, 15 (1986), 269–83.
23. Albert Rubenstein *et al.*, 'Management perceptions of government incentives to technological innovation in England, France, West Germany and Japan', *Research Policy*, 6 (1977), 324–57.
24. See David Storey and Adam Strange, 'Where are they now? Some changes in firms located in UK science parks in 1986', *New Technology, Work and Employment*, 7 (1992), 15–28.
25. Alwyn Young, 'Invention and bounded learning by doing', *Journal of Political Economy*, 101:3 (1993), 443–72.
26. Ernest Braun and Stuart Macdonald, *Revolution in Miniature: The History and Impact of Semiconductor Electronics* (Cambridge University Press, Cambridge, 1982).
27. See Stuart Macdonald, 'Learning to change: an information perspective on learning in the organization', *Organization Science*, 6:2 (1995), 1–12.
28. e.g. C. Argyris and D. Schon, 'Organizational learning', in D. Pugh (ed.), *Organizational Theory* (Penguin, Harmondsworth, 1984), 352–71.
29. David Gleicher as quoted in David Buchanan and David Boddy, *The Expertise of the Change Agent* (Prentice-Hall, New York, 1992), 59.
30. Andrew Pettigrew as interpreted in Buchanan and Boddy, ibid. 68.
31. e.g. I. Gazdik, 'Stimulation enhances inventiveness on the shopfloor', *Technovation*, 4:2 (1986), 131–41; G. Sawyer, 'Innovation in organizations', *Long Range Planning*, 11:6 (1978), 53–7.
32. Herbert Simon, 'Bounded rationality and organizational learning', *Organization Science*, 2:1 (1991), 125–34.
33. See I. Isabella, 'Evolving interpretations as a change unfolds: how managers construe key organizational events', *Academy of Management Journal*, 33:1 (1990), 7–41.
34. Lundvall and Johnson, 'The learning economy'.

3

Sources of Information for Change and Innovation

If innovation is a new pattern of bits of information, it is legitimate to ask whence come these bits, how they make their way from their source, and how they are formed into a new pattern. The last two matters are major issues and the subject of the next two chapters. The first is the subject of this.

Even the most uncompromising interpretations of the linear model do not insist that research provides absolutely all of the information required for innovation; merely the first and most important bits. The remainder apparently come from succeeding activities of secondary importance, secondary because, though their contribution to innovation be minor, it is still apparently inadequate. Thus, failure of a firm or an industry or a nation to innovate is normally attributed to deficiencies in design, or production, or marketing; any of a large range of activities—except, of course, research. If any deficiency in research is admitted, it is in the amount and not the quality of the research performed. Research quality, like scientific fact, is taken to be absolute. Research quantity is always insufficient. The argument that it is possible to spend too much on research, though thoroughly plausible, is rarely voiced. One consequence of this perception is that not a few countries are pleased to look upon themselves as naturally inventive and ingenious—a sentiment supported by patent statistics, or citation analysis of academic publications, or numbers of Nobel laureates—but slow to seize the advantage this should present for innovation. The unhappy but revealing expression used is that they have trouble turning invention into innovation. The British certainly see themselves in this way, but then so do the Australians, and so do the Peruvians. The Japanese reputation for being strong in innovation and weak in research is really quite exceptional.

Our modern history is littered with examples of inventions that were first developed in Britain but which had to go abroad to find companies willing to manufacture the final product. [1]

Forty years ago, Japanese technology was held in low esteem. It was considered derivative, unoriginal. Stories abounded of Japanese touring the world's factories *en masse* to pick up every scrap of information they could find. The world obliged, perhaps in much the same way that British companies opened their doors to curious foreigners during the Industrial Revolution, confident that while potential competitors might copy a specific change, they could not match the continuing pace of change. British entrepreneurs of the eighteenth century were generally quite correct, at least for their foreseeable future, but in picking up whatever they could, the Japanese managed not just to match but to exceed the pace of change. A country which was once renowned for its cheap metal pressings, labelled 'Empire Made', is now much better known for innovation in a range of industries that is envied by competitors in other countries, and to which the huge increase in Japanese prosperity is largely attributed. Yet, legend had it that the Japanese capacity to innovate was based on copying what others did and not on domestic research. With the Japanese rapidly catching up with the world's leaders in innovation and unable to invent, it seemed inevitable that the Japanese innovation machine must run out of steam when it could no longer be fuelled by foreign inventions.

Even now there are those who console themselves with this belief. Others choose to see Japanese innovation as a continuing threat. The Japanese myth has been so useful in stimulating and directing both technology policy and technology strategy in the West that there has often been little incentive to examine the reality. [2] This is basically that the Japanese have elevated the many other activities that contribute to the organization's innovation to a prominence they have rarely achieved in the West. Conversely, research has simply never been accorded the dominant, seminal role in Japan that is claimed for it in the West. That foreign observers have for so long focused on perceived deficiencies in research as the chief characteristic of the innovation they fear and admire is tribute to the pervasive strength of the linear model. That this has been changing is less attributable to revisionist attitudes towards Japanese innovation than to an interest in transferring Japanese management methods to the West. These have been sought not specifically to improve the capacity of Japan's chief competitors to innovate, but to increase their competitiveness, especially through higher quality. If innovation is required, it is as a means rather than an end, a supporting role which innovation has not normally been allocated in the West. Much of the reverence for Japanese ways in management is fad. Western management has imposed—superimposed—many a technique Japanese in little more than name, sanitized to suit Western tastes. At least some of these techniques originated in the West in the work of Drucker and others, and in the West they were summarily rejected. [3] Not surprisingly, the most fundamental use of Japanese management methods in the West has been by the Japanese themselves in their own subsidiaries.

The adoption of Japanese management methods may not have been much stimulated by interest in Japanese innovation methods. Even so, it has helped to counter the argument that Japanese methods of innovation were irrelevant as a model for the West because they could work only amidst a whole host of other Japanese ways. At least some of these other ways have now been imported, and with them the context in which Japanese innovation makes sense. At long last, Japanese innovation is accepted as relevant to Western industry not just as threat, but as example of how innovation happens and perhaps even of how it can be managed. [4]

Part of the explanation for Japanese strength in innovation lies in the ability to gather information from a wide variety of activities within the organization, each of which is deemed to make a contribution every bit as important as that from research. What has been characterized negatively in the West as innovation despite weak research is more accurately and more positively innovation based on the strength of many other organizational activities. But no matter how well they are performed as discrete activities, their contribution to innovation would be spasmodic and haphazard were it not for the interest taken by Japanese managers in activities beyond those for which they are immediately responsible. In part, this is attributable to the

Japanese system of giving managers wide experience in many departments; in part to management by consensus. Thus, Japanese managers not only have personal experience of what goes on elsewhere in the organization, but also feel themselves responsible for these activities. This has sometimes been represented as a system by which information is pooled and shared: it is perhaps more realistic to see the system as one in which information is traded, not in open barter, but as part of a tradition in which obligations are recognized and honoured. [5] The consequence is that information from one part of the organization is readily made available to other parts, a situation which an information perspective suggests is highly conducive to change and innovation. This situation does not exist in many Western organizations. A survey of competitive intelligence programmes in US firms found an appreciation that all employees acquired information and that these discrete bits had to be combined with others before they could be used. It also found that employees had no incentive to contribute their information mite: 'How do we motivate employees to contribute data without being asked?' [6]

There can be a problem when innovation must spring entirely from information available within the organization, Japanese or any other. Obviously, the larger the organization, the more information it is likely to contain, and the more information available to contribute to innovation. But be the organization ever so large, the information within is there not to rattle round pointlessly until the day when it might make a contribution to innovation, but because the organization has some use for it. Basically, the information inside the organization supports what the organization is already doing. To be sure, there will be information lying neglected in some remote corner that may be brought into the information package that is innovation; and innovation may well be wrought by rearranging the bits of information in existing patterns to form new patterns. Learning by doing, from experience on the job, is almost entirely the latter. An example of the former might be the model of an integrated circuit which emerged from the physics cupboard at the Telecommunications Research Establishment at Malvern in 1957. Though the device never worked and was rapidly returned to its cupboard in the UK, it may have made a small and extremely indirect contribution to radical innovation in the United States. Innovation derived entirely from the organization's internal information is unlikely to be radical; it tends to produce small changes, though they are often numerous. Most innovation is of this steady, incremental sort rather than the radical innovation on which fortunes, firms, and whole industries are occasionally built. Indeed, in as much as the former is a product of the organization, of its own information and systems, and causes little disruption, it is often preferred to radical innovation—so much so that it can be a major obstacle to major change. [7]

In this company, which is big, the sailing ship effect is very large. The production division will carry on doing what they have done and do it a little better because they have large technological resources and if you come with a new invention they will be against it. These fellows will say, 'Oh well, we can probably do it by tweaking our existing processes'. And they will do that until they make a better [product] than you can make with a revolutionary idea, because in the beginning you aren't high up on the learning curve. So you don't win and it takes a long time, until everybody is really screaming that the new will take over. [8]

Fig. 3.1 is an attempt to depict the problem facing the organization: bits of information are contained within its boundaries, but there are many more outside. While the bits within have simpler shapes than those outside, and will easily fit together, the addition of some external bits is required for change. The greater the contribution of these external bits to the information packages within the organization the more radical its innovation. Not only are these of less regular shape and hence much harder to fit with other bits of information, but there is also an infinity of them from which to choose.

OBVIOUS SOURCES OF INFORMATION

Radical innovation, and even the continuation of more modest incremental innovation, demands new information, which generally means information from outside the organization. Whence comes this information? The vast majority of external information will assuredly be new to the organization, but there is an awful lot of it and most is quite incompatible with the information inside the organization. No matter how willing and how great the effort, most cannot be squeezed into the organization's existing information packages. It simply does not fit and can

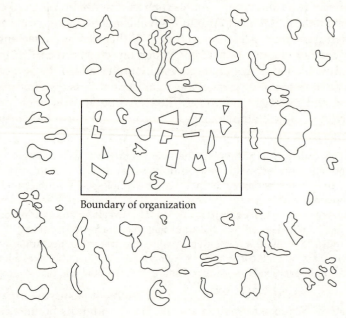

Boundary of organization

Fɪɢ. 3.1   Information bits

make no contribution to information patterns already in use. The firm making tractor wheels has no place for information about the manure most beneficial for the growing of leeks, or the ice-cream flavour most favoured by Indonesian youth, or the astro-logical configuration considered most propitious by Amenhotep. A more practical alternative to searching the haystack in the hope of finding a needle or two is to look where needles are likely to be found, sources that can be relied upon to have information that fits. For the firm, this might mean a trade association, a responsible government department, a research association or university department involved in similar work, collaborators in the same industry, specific classifications of patent applications, and so on. Though internal information would fit more easily still, obvious external sources provide information that fits far more readily than that from the huge variety of other possible sources. [9] The role of the consultant is less to find external information of use to the client than to find external informa-tion that will fit with the client's information and still be of use.

A trade-off is apparent: it is between the information that is easiest to use, and easiest to find, but which can make only a small contribution to change, and that which is much harder to use, much harder to find, but which can make a major contribution to change. If there is any single issue that is central to the management of change, it is this. While the management of change is normally seen as a matter of encouraging the organization to welcome and accept change, much more is required of management than exhortation and the following of recommended procedures. The task of deciding where the balance lies between ease of fit of information and its contribution to change is one requiring judgement and discretion in conditions of massive uncertainty and where there is no right or wrong approach. This demands the most fundamental of management skills.

THE NIH SYNDROME

Resort to any external source of information, even when it yields bits that fit nicely in a new information pattern, presents further problems. One of these is particularly evident in what is known as the not-invented-here (NIH) syndrome—the resistance of organizations to developing, manufacturing, and marketing what has been invented elsewhere. This is nothing more than a sober reaction to a hopelessly linear expectation, yet the NIH syndrome is widely castigated as mindless rejection of any external influence on internal change. That the syndrome exists is irrefutable; that there is considerable justification for its existence is less appreciated. Even where the problem of finding external information relevant to the activities of the organization has been solved, the very fact that it is torn from a context different from that prevailing inside the organization means that it may not fit. Relevance by no means ensures compatibility. What seems to those outside like a sensible approach for the organization may seem less sensible to those inside, perhaps because it has been tried previously, because it is incompatible with something else the organization is planning, or perhaps simply because an influential individual is committed to an alternative approach. The external source is unlikely to be aware of such internal circumstances, to have access to the mass of secondary information which supports and preserves the organization's information packages. An information perspective suggests that, in as much as the NIH syndrome appreciates the difficulties of assimilating external information, it is actually sympathetic to innovation.

It is hard not to conclude, however, that the NIH syndrome is much more a product of organizational demands than of any appreciation of the information demands of innovation. This is apparent in the cursory dismissal of external information that cannot contribute to the organization's innovation, but it is transparent in resistance to external information that can. Such Luddite reaction is not at all uncommon. In part it is explained by an understandable aversion to the uncertainty and disruption that accompanies change, but a further explanation is that any admission that external information is of value to the organization can be interpreted as an indictment of the organization's own information resources. Accompanied by the belief that new information is created rather than gathered, and that the process of creation is an organizational task, the indictment is especially damning. The NIH syndrome will be considered in some detail later on (in Chapter 6). An information perspective shows it to hide as many of the obstacles to innovation as it reveals.

EXTERNAL INFORMATION AND CONTROL

No matter how inadequate for innovation the information within its boundaries, the organization does at least exercise control over its own information. This is not the case with external information. Control is important to the organization; its structure and power balance are maintained through control. To invest resources in a project of which a crucial part belongs to someone else may seem at best imprudent and at worst thoroughly irresponsible. This is often precisely how the organization sees its situation if it does manage to find external information it can put to use. Indeed, the greater the contribution to innovation made by information from such a source, the more exposed the innovating organization is likely to feel. Thus, it is thoroughly understandable that the innovating organization will do what it can to reduce its exposure. When it insists on independent inventors having patent protection for the inventions they offer, the patent system is being used not just as a screening device, but also as the means by which the organization rests assured that it can control this external information. In much the same way, collaborative agreements set down the terms under which information from other parties may be used. Membership of research and industry associations brings with it assurance that all other members have agreed to such conditions. Formal agreements may also have been reached with such long-standing and obvious sources of information as university departments, but even where these are absent, as they may be with government departments, tacit understanding has probably been established over the organization's rights to use information.

While management can feel reasonably sure of the organization's entitlement to use information from the obvious external sources, no such assurance accompanies information from less obvious sources. The less obvious the source of external information, the less assurance the organization is likely to have of its rights. In as much as obvious sources yield obvious information, and less obvious sources less obvious information, this will constrain the rate and degree of the organization's innovation. Those whose primary concern is technology transfer have often underestimated the importance of control to the organization, interpreting demands for ownership of information as resistance to innovation or as failure to understand the nature of information. These elements may be present, but so too is the need for the organization to control whatever it does.

SEARCHING AND SCREENING

Management faces an impossible task if it attempts to search all external information for those bits that might fit into the organization's own information patterns. The temptation is strong to avoid the task altogether and to rely exclusively on internal information. This not only confines the search to manageable limits, but also allows the use of the organization's own information systems to screen information. The hierarchy which establishes who reports to whom, and procedures which determine membership of committees, circulation of papers, and recipients of reports, exerts a powerful influence on what information is made available for specific activities. But these systems are geared to internal information, not external. If external information is to be sought, even from obvious sources, additional screening mechanisms must be installed to separate the information which might fit from that which will not. Because existing mechanisms are integral to the functioning of the organization, these additional screening mechanisms tend to be kept quite separate, and usually quite modest. There might be a committee formed to review inventions offered to the organization by independent inventors, or another to monitor information being acquired from a collaborator. Often this screening task is performed by a single individual, as when a manager is given responsibility for liaison with universities.

But how to find and screen information from less obvious sources, where the search must always be much more extensive and the need for screening very much greater? There is certainly no easy solution to this problem, and it may be that it is beyond the power of any organization to resolve. A common organizational response is to avoid the problem altogether, and hence the need to find a solution. Another is an incidental approach whereby the usefulness of information from less obvious external sources is judged in terms of the relationship between the organization and the source. Where it is clear to the organization's managers that sources must be using information similar to their own, as when the source is in the same industry, then the relationship itself, the common interest, promises that information from the source may fit with that used in the organization. Where the relationship is closer still and some of the organization's activities are in some way integrated with those of the source, the fit is even more likely. Many producers have just this sort of integrated relationship with their suppliers and customers, made the closer and the more necessary by the application of such management techniques as just in time, and by computer and telecommunications technology. [10] Information from a supplier who is accustomed to delivering precisely what the producer wants when it is wanted and to co-ordinating his supply with the producer's demand is much more likely to fit with the information already used by the producer than information from a supplier with whom there is no such close relationship. Of course, it could be argued that the integration which gives some assurance that information will fit also reduces the variety of sources from which external information is available. When the information provided by external sources is little different from that already in use within the organization, although fit may be easy, the information is unlikely to contribute much to innovation. [11]

LESS OBVIOUS SOURCES OF
EXTERNAL INFORMATION

It should cause no surprise when surveys reveal that dominant among the external sources of technological information found most important by managers are suppliers, customers, and competitors. [12] These are sources where relationships and integration perform the screening function that allows the organization to use the information they provide, but which are still sufficiently unlikely sources to provide the sort of information that will make a major contribution to the organization's innovation. The easier the screening, the less the likely contribution to change. Clearly there must be a point at which the costs of finding and screening information from external sources outweigh the benefits from its incorporation in innovation, but it is not clear that the location of this point is best determined by the practicality of screening rather than by the potential value of information. There is, of course, no way of knowing the latter before screening. Yet it is assumed that information which cannot be easily found and screened must be of little value. In fact, this is no more than what is not known not being apparent. This is the more interesting in the light of the parallel assumption that the means by which organizations find and screen information from even obvious sources are so imperfect that government intervention is required. Hence governments commonly subsidize research associations and institute programmes to improve the links between universities and industry.

It is hard to believe that the information market fails only when sources of information are obvious. In fact, other forces are at work, most notably the belief that information is created rather than gathered, that it is created to be used rather than transmitted and mixed with other information, and that information will inevitably be lost to others in the process. This logic supports public funding of R&D on the grounds of market failure, but it also supports the belief that information is to be found only where specific efforts are made to create it. Consequently, there are no grounds for expecting external information that may be of use to the firm to be anywhere other than where it is being deliberately created. This attitude, common among managers and policymakers alike, as well as among those who are attributed with responsibility for creation, is not one which encourages radical change.

It is, then, with some surprise that revelations of what are actually the sources of most significant information are greeted. They are not disbelieved, for they are in accord with personal experience, but they are often ignored, largely because they are inconvenient. It does not suit managers to acknowledge their dependence on competitors, nor does it suit policymakers to accept that intervention directed by market failure arguments and the linear model of change is not especially conducive to creating the innovation they crave. While the grounds for government intervention in R&D, and even for management itself treating R&D as a non-market activity, an overhead, are well established, the justification cannot be extended to the acquisition of external information. Another justification, based on acceptance that there is particular failure in the information market, that information cannot be bought and sold like other goods, could well serve were it not that the organization's ability to acquire information in the market is seen as having a direct impact on its competitiveness of rather more significance than any indirect impact through innovation. So, government policies to improve access to the external sources of information that organizations deem important for innovation must always aim to benefit all firms in an industry. They take the form of dissemination and demonstrator programmes displaying what is taken to be best practice, of subsidized consultancy to explain to laggards what adopters are doing, of collaboration initiatives to share information. The idea is that the best information should be available to all firms so that they can compete more effectively on an equal footing. If there is any bias in such policy, it is towards small firms, the argument being that these contain less information than large and must, therefore, be more dependent on external information.

As if there were not already enough ranged against recognition of the importance of less obvious sources of external information, there is yet another factor. By definition, there are no organizational, formal, institutional channels of communication between these sources and the organization. Given the difficulties inherent in market transactions in information, how is the information to travel? It would seem that personal and informal means are important, yet firms and government departments are often at a loss to know how to encourage these means. It is commonly accepted, for example, that much more is learnt from chatting over a drink at the conference bar than from listening to the conference papers. Yet, while government programmes or industry associations might subsidize the conference, they would balk at subsidizing the beer.

It can be argued—and will be—that this constraint is fortuitous in that any official intervention would rapidly erode informality and nullify the advantages it provides in the transfer of information. But recognition of the importance of informal information flow for innovation falls far short of intervention. In the absence of even acknowledgement, it is hard for managers and policy-makers to concede that less obvious sources of external information have any major part to play in innovation. It follows, then, that internal sources of information and obvious external sources do.

If the Japanese have any other advantage in innovation, it may be that the Japanese system of industrial organization does acknowledge the importance of informal information flow. Amidst a tradition in which lifetime employment is common, though not general, with the clear risks this brings of isolation from external sources of information, there is general recognition of how essential are the informal and personal connections that link industry to universities and to government departments.

In the Japanese network organization the exchange of information involves intense interaction among network members. Consequently, a large amount of resources is needed merely to maintain such human networks, which form the basis for information gathering. However, in most cases a price is not paid for each individual transaction.... Information exchange ... has traditionally been a long-term bilateral exchange in kind (information), rather than an economic transaction with monetary compensation.... This type of information exchange devoid of direct payment has in the past provided a hidden source of Japanese competitiveness in manufacturing. [13]

It is the recognition of these connections which has allowed the Ministry for International Trade and Industry (MITI) to act as a facilitator in a way that would have been difficult for government departments in the West. Indeed, MITI's role has been widely misunderstood in the West as a consequence of the assumption that governments can exert such influence only through direct intervention. [14] At the organizational level, recognition of the role of the informal is perhaps most marked in the expectation that Japanese employees will gather external information relevant not only to their own activities, but also to those of others in the organization. What is normal behaviour in Japan is seen as quite exceptional gatekeeping behaviour elsewhere. The Japanese who were scouring the world for information for innovation forty years ago were gathering not just for their own purposes, but for those of colleagues as well. It is institutional accommodation of this informal activity that allows the easy development of loyalty to organization, teamwork, quality circles, and decision-making by consensus. In the West, where there is clear demarcation between the informal and the institutional, it is much harder for the organization to accommodate the informal, for the informal to be accorded official recognition. [15] This is evident in the need to impose Japanese management practices from above, but also in an inability to exploit the informal means by which less likely sources of information for innovation may be tapped.

REFERENCES

1. *Winning for Britain: Labour's Strategy for Industrial Success* (British Labour Party, London, 1994), 13.
2. Brian Oakley, 'Idle thoughts of an old hand', paper presented to the conference 'Management of Collaborative European Programmes and Projects in Research, Education and Training', University of Oxford, Apr. 1994.
3. 'Gingrich's future', *The Economist*, 23 Jan. 1995, 48–50.
4. Consider, for example, the information perspective of Hiroyuki Itami, 'Learning and technology accumulation by Japanese firms and the

concept of "ba" (interactive field)', Faculty of Commerce, Hitotsubashi University, July 1994, mimeo.

5. Ikujiro Nonaka and Tim Ray, *Knowledge Creation in Japanese Organizations: Building the Dimensions of Competitive Advantage* (National Institute of Science and Technology Policy, Science and Technology Agency, Tokyo, 1993).

6. John Prescott and Daniel Smith, 'The largest survey of "leading edge" competitor intelligence managers', *Planning Review*, 17:3 (1989), 6–13 (p. 13).

7. Stuart Macdonald and Ernest Braun, 'The invention barrier', *National Electronics Review*, 13:6 (1977), 112–16.

8. British industrial scientist as quoted in Ernest Braun and Stuart Macdonald, *Revolution in Miniature: The History and Impact of Semiconductor Electronics* (Cambridge University Press, Cambridge, 1980), 154.

9. Alan Macpherson, 'Innovation, external technical linkages and small firm commercial performance: an empirical analysis from Western New York', *Entrepreneurship and Regional Development*, 4, (1992), 165–83.

10. Stuart Macdonald, 'Too close for comfort? Implications for strategy and change arising from getting close to the customer', *California Management Review*, 37:4 (1995), 1–20.

11. Stuart Macdonald, 'Information networks and the exchange of information', in Cristiano Antonelli (ed.), *The Economics of Information Networks* (North Holland, Amsterdam, 1992), 51–69.

12. Eric von Hippel, *The Sources of Innovation* (Oxford University Press, New York, 1988) and 'Users as innovators', *Technology Review*, 80 (1978), 30–9.

13. Ken-ichi Imai, 'Potential of information technology and economic growth in Japan and associate policy problems', ICCP Committee Background Report (OECD, Paris, Dec. 1987), 28.

14. See Charles Edquist, *Technology Policy — Social, Economic and Political Aspects*, TEMA-T working paper, Department of Technology and Social Change, Linkoping University, Nov. 1990.

15. Christopher Bartlett and Sumantra Ghoshal, 'Changing the role of top management: Beyond strategy to purpose', *Harvard Business Review*, Nov./Dec. 1994, 79–88.

4

The Flow of Information

No matter how rich external sources of information, no matter how vital for change the information they contain, nothing at all can happen unless the information is transferred from its source to where it is to be used. There are only two ways by which information can exist in any location—either it was created there, or it was transferred there from somewhere else. Reinventing the wheel is a slow, uncertain, and tiresome business, and nearly all information is transferred. Consequently, this transfer, this information flow, is of some importance. It is ironic, then, that so much attention is paid to information creation, so little to information transfer, and hardly any to the information transactions required to effect information transfer.

The initial contention of this chapter is that the nature of the transfer is misunderstood. It is often assumed, perhaps for the sake of convenience, that information is transferred from a single source as a complete package, a finished innovation. There is, of course, no such thing as a final innovation; all innovation is a contribution to yet more innovation. Rather than a complete package delivered from a single source, transfer is much more likely to be of a variety of bits of information, flowing from several sources by different means. A further and more fundamental contention of this chapter is that the transfer of information is not distinct from the use that is made of the information. Transfer and use are united by transaction, but there is another link beyond this trinity. There are good grounds for supposing that the means by which information becomes available, rather than just availability, affect the use that is made of information. Yet, corporate strategy tends to treat the acquisition of external information and its exploitation within the firm as two quite separate steps. Government programmes for technology transfer are also just that; intervening in the transfer of information, but not in its use by the organization, a demarcation justified by a linear view of innovation and compatible with a linear reluctance to interfere in near-market activities. Their distinction is quite artificial: the way in which information is transferred from sources is integral to the role it plays in innovation. The next chapter will consider the relationship between the way information is acquired and the use that the organization makes of this information. First, though, it seems sensible to look at the influence of the way information is acquired, the way it flows, on what information is available for the organization to use. That is the subject of this chapter.

BITS AND PIECES

Just occasionally, a complete package of information may find its way from a single source to a destination where it may be used intact without the contribution of additional information from the using organization or from other sources. One thinks of the 'turnkey' factory exported complete from a developed to a less-developed country and requiring only doors to be unlocked and switches to be thrown for production to commence. At least, that is the theory: in practice, even the most turnkey of factories requires other information before it can operate; for instance, from a workforce sufficiently literate to read the instructions on the machinery. Even a turnkey factory demands the addition of infrastructural information, in this case from the educational system. Most information packages cannot aspire to be turnkey. Information is transferred in the expectation that the destination has created or acquired the extra information needed to fill the package, to complete the information pattern. The painful reality tends to be that just as information at the destination is required to select the information to be transferred, so the transferred information is required before further information can be selected. Iteration is essential.

No package of information could be more neatly wrapped and apparently complete than a patent specification. Legal fiction maintains that all the information needed to re-create the invention is contained in the patent specification. The fact is that the

specification is forced to refer again and again to other information, information that is in the public domain, which means that
it is available somewhere but must be acquired from these sources
before the information in the specification can be used. Much of
this other information will be tacit and uncodified information, the
sort that is often acquired through education or training, that is
often embodied in individuals, and that cannot easily be expressed
in a document. Efforts to transfer technology by licensing patents
make clear the need for such tacit information. [1] A licensing
agreement refers only to the information in the patent specification, explicit information which in itself is insufficient for the
reproduction of the invention. In theory, the licensee should be
able to find the other information required in the public domain:
in practice, the transaction costs of finding and acquiring this
information are great and the licensee is dependent on the patentee to supply a variety of tacit information. The expectation and
obligation are often expressed in a know-how agreement incorporated in the licensing agreement. That know-how should be
additional to the information contained in the patent specification is revealing; that it is transferred in a quite separate way
even more so. That the whole lot is not bound up in one large
information package is not for want of trying on the part of the
legal system; there is no lack of incentive to render proprietary
as much information as possible. The problem is that information cannot easily be sold unless the buyer has some assurance
that he will be able to use it. This the buyer cannot generally
have unless he is able to acquire additional information from
other sources, or additional tacit information from the seller. In
the first case, the value of the seller's information depends on
the buyer's ability to acquire information from elsewhere. In the
second, its value is dependent not so much on what information the seller owns, but on what else he is able to transfer to
the buyer. In either case, transfer of information is clearly dependent on complex transactions involving information over and
above that which is contained in the information package. [2]

THE EPIDEMIC MODEL OF DIFFUSION

As an alternative to the pretence that all the information required for change is generated within the organization in which

the change takes place, the notion of diffusion of change, of information spreading from one place to another, is a substantial advance. It is also an acknowledgement of reality; the wheel is not constantly reinvented. Much of the initial academic interest in diffusion was displayed by those concerned with matters spatial, by geographers fascinated by the new locations of change brought about by its diffusion. [3] For these geographers, the information transferred to make change possible and the change itself were one and the same, a neat confusion of cause and effect. Change was both what occurred in the new location and also what travelled there. Consequently, an epidemic model of diffusion suited the geographers' requirements nicely, providing some understanding of the rate and direction of diffusion.

Epidemiology provided the obvious framework for this geographic thinking. A disease is not likely to arrive in parts from multiple sources; what is transmitted is what arrives, and all that is required to be known about its transfer can be deduced from the location and timing of its further incidence. The epidemic model supports notions of diffusion which envisage but a single change, a complete and absolute transformation, a transition from not being to being. This traditional model makes no allowance for incremental or subsequent innovation, and is static in that no further interest is taken in the adopter once change has occurred, an event which happens suddenly and, it would seem, immediately on receipt. Adoption and adaptation are one.

From here, it was no great leap to investigation of the adopters of change. Anthropologists and sociologists found themselves well qualified to participate. [4] Were they small firms or large? run by their owners or by managers? new firms or old? domestic or foreign? and so on. Those who adopted change early were called 'leaders'; those who delayed 'laggards'—emotive terms which suggested there was something worthy about the adoption of change, and consequently about change itself. The bell-shaped curve of progressive adoption and the S-shaped curve of cumulative adoption became symbolic indicators both of the receptivity of the population exposed to change and also of the impact of the change. The steeper and higher the curves, the greater their significance. No one bothered much with shallow curves.

While this work yielded some fascinating insights into who was adopting change and where, it did little to explain why (except by associating the characteristics of adopters with their rate of adoption), and less to explain how. Interest in diffusion was almost entirely in what went where; how it got there was not seen as important. If change occurred in a new location, then transfer had obviously been successful and could be ignored: if change did not occur, then there was nothing to measure and the issue of transfer did not arise. Transactions, of course, were never considered.

Efforts have been made to build on this diffusion research, but by an assortment of economists and scholars interested in technology policy and management, rather than by geographers and anthropologists. This miscellany of minds exploited diffusion theory, not to develop the theory further, but to uncover empirical evidence of innovation. So, the population surveys from which the diffusion curves were drawn were extended to discover more about adopters (and even non-adopters), the primary purpose being to establish causal links between their characteristics and the adoption of change. Almost incidentally the opportunity was taken to discover the source of the information that contributed towards change, and—even more incidentally— the way in which the information was transferred. This empirical fishing, unencumbered by any responsibility to develop the theory of another discipline, has produced an enormous, and surprising, catch.

This sort of diffusion model of change is basically the obverse of the linear model: it focuses on where change fetches up and cares not a fig how change came about. But obviously the change that diffuses must first have been created. In their failure to consider how this happens, diffusion models bestow credibility on linear models. They are complements rather than alternatives to linear models. Together they may be imagined to provide a complete picture of change, from the creation of information for innovation to the adoption of an innovation created elsewhere. The two may certainly be forced together, but there is something distinctly wrong with the resulting picture. The bit in the middle is missing, the bit which explains how the information necessary for innovation reached the adopters. If the hypothesis advanced in previous chapters is correct, this part should be of particular importance both in itself and also for the light it throws on every aspect of the way change occurs.

DISSEMINATION AND WATER

For those who would acknowledge the economic importance of information without delving too deeply into details, it is convenient to see information as a universal lubricant, essential if everything is to work, but otherwise taken for granted. Oil is the simile. For those concerned with the flow of information, with dissemination, the simile is inevitably water. As water is essential for life, so information is essential for change—a necessary requirement, though not sufficient. Like water, the availability of information is perceived to be more significant than any differentiating characteristics. Both water and information are esteemed for their generic, rather than their particular, qualities.

The natural allocation of water is determined by forces beyond the control of man. Water may be redistributed by man, of course, and vast projects—from irrigation schemes to community sewerage systems—are undertaken to do just this. Once the channels are dug, though, the pipes laid, gravity will do the rest—with the aid of a little pumping. And so it seems with information: there are information channels to be laid along which information will flow quite naturally—with the aid of a little pumping where necessary. The analogy is profoundly misleading. The creation of information channels does not ensure that information will flow along them, no matter what pressure is provided. The forces which control the flow of information are not at all akin to gravity and pumping.

It is certainly the case that much information is as universally available as water. Thus it is that the dissemination models can search for understanding of what is happening in the characteristics not of information flow, but of the adopters of change. To assist this differentiation, the information they acquire is assumed to be uniform, constant over time, and from a single source—much like water. Government programmes to stimulate the adoption of innovation by making information widely available to potential adopters also assume information to be uniform. A flood of information about best practice is thought to be effective in encouraging best practice. The diffusion of change is seen as analogous to the ripples resulting from a stone tossed into a pond. Once the stone plops, the rest is automatic and only obstacles interfering with the perfectly concentric are worthy of interest. The same aquatic analogy extends to the cascading of information within organizations, whereby information is sent tumbling from one level to the next, unchanging in its descent. Much as technological change was once seen as a constant having a variable impact wherever it was adopted, the uniform information which is sent cascading down the organization is expected to have a variable impact, measured—believe it or not—by 'splashback'.

Much information certainly is cast on the waters, obviously by the media, and such information may often be a vital component of the information package that is innovation. However, the information which can contribute most to change is unlikely to be the information that is broadcast to all, perhaps because it is specialized and of interest to few, perhaps because an owner wishes to sell it, or simply because it is unknown to those who broadcast information. More fundamentally, there is a world of difference between information being available and information being acquired. The Internet is example enough of that. It does not follow that the most widely available information, even were such information sufficient for change, is the information that is acquired. There is simply too much information available. Selectivity is essential. Earlier chapters have sought to show that sifting through the global supply of information is impractical, but they have also argued that information must somehow be sought. The information required for change is not delivered unbidden to the factory gate. Given the enormity of the selection task and the uncertainty imposed by the characteristics of information, it is generally necessary for selection to be guided by the source of the information. This is very different from the acquisition of information through dissemination; it is acquisition through transaction, an information transaction. A watery metaphor is totally inappropriate for information flow by such means.

TRANSFER AND TRANSACTIONS

Indiscriminate transfer of information is easy enough, but is akin to shouting from the rooftops; transfer of the right information at the right time to the right place is actually rather difficult. [5]

There are those who subsume such difficulties within the considerable problems involved in using information; a nice point, but only sometimes valid. If pie manufacturers demand apples and receive oranges, it would be perverse to assume that the problem must lie in their inability to manufacture orange pies. Demand for specific information, just like demand for anything else, is satisfied by means of a transaction. Because of the characteristics of information, it is a rather awkward transaction.

The problem is, of course, that those who want information cannot know what it is they want. If they did, they would no longer want it. Conversely, potential buyers of information cannot be allowed to know what it is they might purchase, otherwise there would be no need for them to buy. Even once they have bought, buyers cannot secure complete transfer of their property because information is inevitably retained by the seller. Even if buyers were allowed to check the goods before purchase, this would not allow them to ensure that the acquired information was fully compatible with what they already own. As will be argued in the next chapter, they really need to be able to take new information home before they buy, to see how it fits, to try it out for a while. This sellers cannot permit, it being impossible for dissatisfied buyers to return the goods without also keeping them. Finding information that will fit without being allowed to know its characteristics presents obvious problems, and they are not to be solved simply by improving ability to use whatever information happens to arrive.

NETWORK EXCHANGE AND INFORMATION FLOW

Market transactions to effect the transfer of information are fraught with difficulties. Exchanging information, rather than buying and selling it, overcomes a good few of these difficulties. [6] The problem with exchange, though, is that it really requires a network. [7] Restricted to two parties, information exchange would hardly satisfy the information needs of either for long. A network allows multilateral exchange. Some would argue that the more extensive the network, the more likely it is that the information requirements of any individual can be satisfied, and that there will be demand for an individual's own information. [8] Not necessarily so; if information exchange is to occur, it is fundamental that each participant in the network has some appreciation of the sort of information the others have to offer in order to evaluate their contributions before delivery, or at least know that others in the network can evaluate them. [9] No one is going to give information without the expectation of something—most commonly information—in return. [10] Free riders soon find themselves ostracized from information networks. Here, then, is a major distinction between an information network and a telecommunications network: bigger is better in telecommunications because more information can be transferred to and from more points. From a telecommunications perspective, this transfer is all that is required of an information network; from an information perspective, transaction is also required. [11]

Exchange of information overcomes some of the problem of pricing information. It also overcomes much of the uncertainty inherent in information transactions. The common interest of those in the network ensures relevance of information without the need for codification. Over time, the value to the individual of information received must be at least as great as his perceived value of the information he supplies. Everyone must be able to estimate that he is getting value for information. Those who feel short-changed will just as surely desert the network as those who are inadequate in their contributions will be eased out of it. This is not to say that information networks are a means for the common pooling of information. Far from it; information is given only to specific individuals who realize full well that this supply will cease unless they, or others to whom they themselves have supplied information, reciprocate. The network functions as a mechanism for information exchange precisely because —much more effectively than intellectual property rights—it allows information to be private property, not because information becomes a public good. Despite organizational exhortations for teamwork and collaboration, those who take information seriously do not share. They deal in information for their own benefit and, indirectly, for that of their employers.

What's in it [sharing information] for people is the drive we have put on recently to insist we are a global business and that we have got to work together and that if we don't work together, you are in the wrong company. . . . It may not necessarily be in the best interest of you and of your budget or your bonus, and I don't expect absolute altruism—that's probably unrealistic because we do drive people for results—but they cannot refuse to help. That's unacceptable behaviour. [12]

INFORMAL INFORMATION FLOW

Many information networks are formal. All organizations contain them. [13] They exist to transfer information from those whose job it is to acquire, store, and process information to those who must use the information to make decisions. Costs are covered by the firm and individual payments are rarely made for specific bits of information. [14] Information exchange may occur, but generally only by prior agreement. Such formal networks can also exist among organizations, as when there are joint ventures or other forms of collaboration. [15] In such cases, extensive monitoring of information transfer is required by each participant so that no one supplies too much or receives too little. Formal accounting for information is an onerous task, and the more thoroughly it is attempted, the more likely it is to impede what it is trying to monitor. An alternative is to make all information freely available to all members of the group on payment of a standard subscription. Professional associations try to function in this way, though there may be little incentive for those who know most to share information with those who know least. Rewards may come in other ways, such as raised status, rather than as new information.

Basically, information exchange works best where there is no insistence on formal accounting for transactions. These informal information networks are very often personal networks, [16] partly because organizations, by their very nature, have difficulty accommodating the informal, but mainly because of the inability of most individuals to distinguish between their own information and that of organizations to which they belong. Once acquired, and particularly once used, information melds with personal skill and experience. It cannot also be retained in a totally separate mental file. Inevitably, it becomes personal information to be exploited to the individual's advantage, just like any other resource he might possess. Individuals engaged in information-intensive activities in which new information is highly valued by others are particularly well placed to exploit an information advantage. Thus, key employees in high-technology industries tend to be active members of information networks. So copious is the information such individuals obtain, and so valued is it by firms in these industries, that the physical transfer of the individual often becomes the most efficient means of conveying information. [17] With the relocation of what is virtually a human container of information comes tacit information, especially difficult to transfer in any other way. In high-technology industries, personnel mobility is high, and always there is recognition that no firm, no matter how large, can compete without access to the information of other firms. [18] This recognition extends to firms appreciating that access is achieved through personal and informal networks, and making quite sure they do nothing to impede the functioning of these networks. [19]

In other industries there is a certain reluctance to allow employees to trade in information they acquire in the course of their employment, to use as they see fit. This use is not necessarily detrimental to the firm, a point likely to be appreciated by individuals active in information exchange networks, if not always by their employers. Individual standing is a prerequisite for membership of the information network, and reputation is determined by ability to supply and use regularly information unlikely to be available from non-network sources. The network will not include those whose information is of value solely because it is confidential. Anyway, as will become evident from the discussion of espionage in Chapter 7, disclosure of this sort of information hardly requires the sophistication of an information network. Where mobility is great and human containers are a major vehicle for the transfer of information in the network, an inability to be discreet is likely to weigh heavily with potential employers. The major problem for the individual, then, is not whether to disclose confidential information, but determining what information, especially what mix of information, is genuinely confidential. Clearly, some judgement is required, judgement which is out of the hands of employers and which must rest with the individual.

INFORMATION NETWORKS IN PRACTICE

There is an extensive literature on information networks, but one which understandably concentrates on those industrial sectors where they are most evident. These are basically the high technologies, where very obvious networks transfer a type of information—technological information—sufficiently discrete to be identifiable. There has been little interest in information networks associated with more mundane areas of endeavour, except by sociologists, who tend to be concerned with the relationships of the participants rather than with the information they transfer. Economic History suggests that information networks have been of some importance, especially in the transfer of the technologies of the Industrial Revolution. [20] Yet, these studies often assert that while such informal methods were appropriate for the transfer of craft technology, they were progressively replaced by more formal methods as the technology became increasingly sophisticated. [21] The conclusion is ironic—and an excellent example of how unyielding disciplinary barriers can be—in as much as the most sophisticated of modern industries are now renowned for reliance on informal information networks. [22]

Nevertheless, the supposition accords well with conventional understanding of the growth of industrial research and development since the late nineteenth century. Technological information was to be created by and for the firm, and this was best done in the firm's own R&D laboratory, properly staffed by professionals. In the quarter century following the Second World War, R&D came to be regarded as the essential first step in a linear process which culminated in innovation, the major competitive weapon in a world of accelerating technological change. So esteemed were R&D and the proprietary information it produced that expenditure on R&D was accepted as a valid indicator of future competitiveness for firms and nations alike. By the mid-sixties, 3 per cent of GNP was considered a desirable level of spending on R&D for developed countries. Later, as the enthusiasm of many firms for big R&D in big research laboratories began to wane, government policy sought to increase the level of industrial R&D by means of grants and other incentives. The justification for such largesse was that, try as they might to secure information for their own exclusive use through increased internal security and by rigorous use of intellectual property legislation, firms would still find that much information from their R&D would inevitably leak out to other firms. Thus they would be discouraged from performing as much R&D as they would have done had they been able to appropriate all the information created. [23] Leakage, then, was entirely undesirable and justified compensation from public funds.

So much for recognition of the importance of information exchange and of the networks which facilitate this process. Government policy, supported by selective use of economic theory, has encouraged firms to believe that information is property which should be jealously guarded, certainly not something to be eagerly exchanged for other information. [24] But are firms convinced? Many probably are; even if they do appreciate that information is different from other economic goods, they still find difficulty devising systems to treat it differently. If the organization's machines cannot be given away in order to receive superior machines some day in return, then it seems axiomatic that neither can the organization's information. This conviction and its implications have been examined in some detail in Chapter 1. But now to the use of information, particularly by the organization, a task which an information perspective sees as the mixing of information.

REFERENCES

1. Lawrence Welch, 'The technology transfer process in foreign licensing arrangements', in S. Macdonald, D. Lamberton, and T. Mandeville (eds.), *The Trouble with Technology* (Frances Pinter, London, 1983), 155–68.
2. See Eric von Hippel, 'The impact of "sticky data" on innovation and problem-solving', Working Paper 3147–90-BPS, Sloan School of Management, MIT, Apr. 1990.
3. e.g. T. Haggerstrand, *The Propagation of Innovation Waves*, Lund Studies in Geography, Series B, 4 (Lund, 1952).
4. e.g. Everett Rogers and F. F. Shoemaker, *Communication of Innovations: A Cross-Cultural Approach* (Free Press, New York, 1971).

5. Eric von Hippel, ' "Sticky information" and the locus of problem solving: implications for innovation', *Management Science*, 40:4 (1994), 429–39.
6. Everett Rogers, 'Information exchange and technological information', in D. Sahal (ed.), *The Transfer and Utilization of Technical Knowledge* (Lexington Books, Lexington, Mass., 1982), 105–123.
7. Eric von Hippel, 'Cooperation between rivals: informal know-how trading', *Research Policy*, 16 (1987), 291–302.
8. See John H. Harwood III, 'The importance of a competitive international marketplace for value-added network services', *Pacific Telecommunications*, 9:4 (1989), 27–8.
9. See John McCrone, 'Promises, promises . . .', *Computing*, 12 May 1988, 20–1.
10. See D. C. Mowery, 'Collaborative ventures between US and foreign manufacturing firms', *Research Policy*, 18 (1989), 19–32.
11. Stuart Macdonald, 'Notions of network: some implications for telecommunications of differences in perception', in G. Madden, S. Macdonald, and M. Salamon (eds.), *Telecommunications and Socio-Economic Development* (Elsevier, Amsterdam, forthcoming).
12. Senior manager quoted in Stuart Macdonald, 'Information, strategic change and the international firm', in Don Lamberton (ed.), *International Communication and Trade: Essays in Honour of Meheroo Jussawalla* (Hampton Press, Cheltenham, 1996), 59–80.
13. See E. Daniels, 'Information resources and organizational structure', *Journal of the American Society for Information Science*, 34:3 (1983), 222–8.
14. 'A model of information network costs', *Computer Economics Report*, 10:4 (1988), 1–3.
15. Helen Lawton Smith, Keith Dickson, and Stephen Lloyd Smith, ' "There are two sides to every story": innovation and collaboration within networks of large and small firms', *Research Policy*, 20 (1991), 457–68.
16. See Sidney Passman, *Scientific and Technological Communication* (Pergamon, Oxford, 1969), 66–72; L. Jauch, W. Glueck, and R. Osborn, 'Organizational loyalty, professional commitment, and academic research productivity', *Academy of Management Journal*, 21:1 (1978), 84–92.
17. Elizabeth Bell, 'Some current issues in technology transfer and academic–industrial relations: a review', *Technology Analysis and Strategic Management*, 5:3 (1993), 307–21.
18. Stuart Macdonald, 'Headhunting in high technology', *Technovation*, 4 (1986), 233–45.
19. See Michael Tushman, 'Technical communication in R&D laboratories: the impact of project work characteristics', *Academy of Management*

Journal, 21:4 (1978), 624–45; and 'Managing communication net-works in R&D laboratories', *Sloan Management Review*, Winter 1979, 37–49.

20. David Landes, *The Unbound Prometheus* (Cambridge University Press, Cambridge, 1969), 147–50; Nathan Rosenberg, 'Economic develop-ment and the transfer of technology: some historical perspectives', *Technology and Culture*, 11:4 (1970), 550–75.

21. J. R. Harris, 'Industrial espionage in the eighteenth century', *Industrial Archaeology Review*, 7:2 (1985), 127–38; Sidney Pollard, *The Industrialisation of Europe 1760–1970* (Oxford University Press, Oxford, 1981), 147–8; Charles Wilson, 'The entrepreneur in the Industrial Revolution in Britain', *Explorations in Entrepreneurial History*, 7:3 (1955), 129–45.

22. An outstanding exception to this generalization is R. C. Allen, 'Collective invention', *Journal of Economic Behavior and Organization*, 4:1 (1983), 1–24. See also Stephen Hill and Tim Turpin, 'Cultures in collision: the emergence of a new localism in academic research', in Marilyn Strathern (ed.), *The Uses of Knowledge: Global and Local Relations. The Reshaping of Anthropology* (Routledge, London, 1995), ch. 7.

23. See Stuart Macdonald, 'Theoretically sound: practically useless? Government grants for industrial R&D in Australia', *Research Policy*, 15 (1986), 269–83.

24. See Stuart Macdonald and Tom Mandeville, 'Innovation protection viewed from an information perspective', in William Kingston (ed.), *Direct Protection of Innovation* (Kluwer Academic, Dordrecht, 1987), 157–70.

5

The Mixing of Information

The boundary of the organization seals in internal information as much as it repels external information. It bounds an information regime, or series of regimes, which contain information relevant to the activities of those within. The whole organization, especially if it is a small firm, may comprise a single information regime; or the organization's structure, hierarchy, and reporting requirements may determine smaller regimes, based on individual departments or people working together on common tasks. [1] A regime may also consist of a group of individuals within the organization with common interests which are not captured by organizational structure. A company sports team would be a trivial example; a trades union, or professional contact among engineers working in different departments on different sites, more substantial examples. Some organizations take pains to help create such regimes by bringing together employees who are normally separated by organizational structure, but have common interests among their responsibilities. The use to which e-mail and local area networks are put has helped demonstrate just how diverse and widespread are common interests in large organizations, and how they have been kept apart by organizational structure. [2]

It is customary to see relationships based on common interests as conducive to information flow. In as much as an information regime is a concentration of a certain sort of information, information relevant to a common interest, it is as much defined by the absence of this information elsewhere as by its prevalence within the regime. Just as the information network is exclusive, permitting transactions only among its members, so the information regime tends to exclude those who do not share the common interest. An e-mail system may be a network in which information transactions take place, or it may be a regime, providing a link among those who share interests. In either case, it obviously excludes those who are not physically or psychologically connected to the system, even those who do not constantly consult their terminals. While it is accepted that information regimes outside the organization can be exclusive, that even the Women's Institute can be masonic, it is often assumed that the exclusivity of information regimes within the organization is diluted by the loyalty of all employees to the organization and its goals, and by the structure of the organization itself. This may not be the case. Indeed, if information flow is facilitated by the exclusivity of networks, it may be that exclusivity in an information regime assists the easy use of the information the regime contains.

The exclusivity of information regimes bestows particular advantage on those who are members of several, especially when these individuals also occupy positions at the junction of overlapping networks. Research on external technological networks suggests that public servants, at least in the UK, may sometimes occupy this crucial position. [3] They seem to be important members of information exchange networks, yet are not sufficiently knowledgeable to make much personal contribution to these networks. Network theory would have them drummed out of the network, and yet they are regarded as important by other network members. It may be that the public servant is using his status in information regimes to facilitate information transactions between, and even within, networks. The public servant may not know himself, but he may be aware of someone who, because of his position or associations, should know. This is quite different from knowing someone who does know, for that degree of assurance would qualify the public servant for full network membership. In this role, the public servant is facilitating information transactions rather than participating in them.

GATEKEEPERS

It seems that the gatekeeper may also occupy an enviable position within several information regimes and on the edge of information networks. The gatekeeper is an employee existing at the boundary of the organization who brings in information from the wider environment for use within the organization. A large part of the gatekeeper's value lies in his ability to distribute the external information he acquires to those parts of the organization best able to use this information. Some of this activity, and the acquisition of some external information, may involve network transactions, but these are not characteristic of gatekeeping. [4] The gatekeeper may trade in information within the organization, but he is more likely to trade the external information he has acquired for something else altogether. Such trade is not unlike that in which the archetypal 'operator' in the Army engages, and equally allows him entry to regimes which would otherwise be exclusive. It is important to remember that this part of the gatekeeper's activity is as informal as other parts: had the gatekeeper a functional responsibility to deliver the information he acquires to the most appropriate destinations within the organization, his ability to operate would be much impaired. An official function would deny him access to many of the information regimes, and certainly to the networks, in which he operates.

The gatekeeper's use of information within the organization contrasts with that of the expert. Both acquire external information, but the expert so that he may use the information himself, and the gatekeeper primarily so that he can pass on the information he acquires for others to use. The gatekeeper is no polymath, adept at putting to use information from many fields; indeed, he may well benefit from ignorance. It is the advantage of the ignorant that they must ask childish questions in order to understand. Thus, the newspaper reporter who knows little about the topic he is assigned must first grasp the basic points himself. His success in conveying information to a lay audience is in large part dependent on an ignorance which allows him to acquire only this information. The expert, burdened by a welter of information on the subject, is less well placed to distinguish major from minor matters. His own understanding isolates him from those who do not understand.

THE EXPERT

Although breadth of knowledge—membership of many information regimes—is widely admired, society reserves its greatest incentives and rewards for specialization, the honing of expertise.

The 'best' scientists are not those who are prominent in several disciplines, but those who excel in one. In order to reap greater economic benefit from the educational system, it is argued, greater specialization is required, an argument endorsed by those who have specialized themselves. The greater the participation in the educational system, the more employers demand educational qualifications; and the more education is expected to have a direct economic benefit, the more employers feel entitled to require qualifications specific to the job. Some educational institutions tailor their courses so closely to the expressed demands of particular employers that it is difficult to discern much distinction between education and training. [5]

This quest for expertise, and consequent reverence for the expert, is perhaps most pronounced where it is least evident. The higher echelons of the British civil service are filled largely by non-experts, traditionally classicists from Oxbridge who cannot hope to apply their expertise in public administration. Because they know little of direct relevance to that which they administer, it can be assumed that they can handle everything with impartiality, that they are unbiased, influenced only by the arguments presented and by prevailing political circumstances. In its unworldly dottiness, the British judiciary shares some of the same tradition, as did British management before the MBA created an elite, apparently expert at managing anything. Public services elsewhere, even where governments are based on the Westminster system, are less scrupulous, often finding it appropriate that those who administer know something about what they are administering, and even encouraging the development of expertise in these areas. In Australia, for instance, it is not uncommon for public servants to contribute papers to scholarly journals. One consequence may be that links between government and business are closer elsewhere than they are in the UK. While close links facilitate information flow and exchange of personnel, there are obvious reasons why they can be viewed with suspicion. The value of the non-expert in the British system is explained by a curious conviction that expertise in one area must surely mean deficiency in others. Those who know too much about one subject must obviously know too little about others. The same assumption is implicit in the caricature of the absent-minded professor: he cannot cope with ordinary matters precisely because his mind is on the subject about which he knows most.

It is hardly to be wondered that experts, whether individuals or organizations, resist change. [6] Certainly the value of their expertise is reduced by change. The more specialized their information, the more difficult they will find blending this with other information. Modern skill and training specializations are as much information regimes as the industrial trades of the seventies with their demarcation disputes that proved so disruptive to British industry. [7] When headhunters are hired by high-technology companies—companies which depend on rapid innovation for their very survival—to find key employees, their first task—some would say their major task—is to discover what sort of individual the company really requires. This is rarely the sort the company thinks it needs. Those who employ others display a pronounced tendency to hire individuals much like those already employed, people much like themselves, people who will fit in easily, carrying information that will fit in just as easily. [8] They are reluctant to recruit misfits, and yet these are just the sort of individuals able to bring into the firm the new information required for essential innovation. Similarly, while firms expect new recruits to bring their resources into the organization, these are not usually seen to include the individual's own information networks. Recruits are expected to adapt to the organization's networks. [9]

Once desirable characteristics have been agreed with the client, the headhunter's task is to find them in a single individual. Headhunters are not hired to search for expertise; there is screening aplenty in the educational system, in professional organizations, in peer review which readily identifies the expert. From an information perspective, expertise is cheap and there is no need to employ a headhunter to find it. Instead, the headhunter searches for individuals who contain uncommon blends of information, typically technological information and commercial information. [10] Though the contribution to innovation of such ready-mixed information is evident, it is less clear why such extreme measures must be taken to find the individuals who contain it. The cult of expertise is largely responsible. It is also to blame for the encouragement that is given to academics to remove their expertise from universities to start their own small firms, encouragement given in the full knowledge that such expertise is quite inappropriate for coping with the commercial challenges of the real world. Always these academics are to have technological expertise, to which they will somehow add commercial information: never are they envisaged as commercial experts who might acquire technological information. There is obviously a linear explanation for this attitude, but it is complemented by a disregard for the problem of mixing information. The reality is rather different: high-technology headhunters are often commissioned by venture capitalists to find young firms worthy of their investment. This is largely a matter of assessing the individuals running the firms. Investment in the chosen few is generally conditional on removing any academics, it being argued that their expertise is incompatible with the change in the firm that investment will engender.

It is commonly observed that technological expertise alone is insufficient to produce innovation. The usual explanation is that business flair and entrepreneurial skills are also required. [11] What is less common is much appreciation that these very different sorts of information do not mix well; indeed, they often seem to repel each other. Were this otherwise, there would hardly be much need to encourage those with the required flair and skill to search out those with technological expertise, and there would be rather less demand for headhunters, at least in the high-technology industries.

Though universities extol the virtue of inter- and multi-disciplinary approaches, and firms the advantages of teamwork, collaboration, and integration, it would be a mistake to assume that they take a catholic view of information mixing. What they mean is that each unit, be it the individual, the department, or the whole organization, should be as specialized as possible, but should also work with other units equally specialized in other areas. This has a certain theoretical neatness, but it poses problems in practice. Similar sorts of information are much easier to mix, but the result is a pattern little changed from what existed before. Very different sorts of information, although they blend much less readily, can produce a much-changed pattern. Consider a dinner party at which the guests are a physicist, a plumber, and an accountant, each an expert in his field. Dwell on the challenge of integrating their expertise in conversation. Proximity—at the dinner table, in the department, on the science park—is far from sufficient to ensure the mixing of information. It is horribly common to discover what is going on just down the corridor not from those who work there, but from others in a different organization altogether. As was suggested in the last chapter, this is partly a characteristic of information flow, or rather the lack of it. But beyond this there is another problem: it would seem to be quite possible for two people, each with half the answer to a question, with half the bits of information required to form a pattern, to work together on a solution and still not find it. Now why is this?

CHALK AND CHEESE

The NIH syndrome emphasizes the resistance of organizations to external information, which, in the absence of any information transaction, is unlikely to fit with the information already in use within the organization. But information that is already within the organization may be just as difficult to mix with other internal information, and for the same reason—the absence of transactions. In the days when it was fashionable for large companies to locate their R&D activities on greenfield sites far from the distraction and mess of manufacturing, employee researchers found themselves as isolated as independent inventors from the internal information with which their own had to be mixed before innovation could result.

The information of which change is composed is different from that which is currently in use. The difference is achieved through the addition to the current package of other information. The more similar this other information to what is already in the package, the easier it is to mix, but the smaller the change that results. The more at variance the information added, the greater the change, but the more difficult the mixing. Once again —as so often in the consideration of change from an information perspective—there is a trade-off. The judgement of management would seem to be required. In fact, it is rarely exercised, simply because very different sorts of information do not often come together. All transactions in information—formal or informal— balk at the obstacle of trading in information that is totally unfamiliar, and information regimes quarantine information that is different from information in other regimes. Peer review for academic publication, for example, may well simply reject new

ideas from other academic regimes. [12] Only in extraordinary circumstances are very different sorts of information forced together,
as when wartime exigencies force departments to accept totally
novel responsibilities, or—a better example still—when individuals from vastly different backgrounds find themselves thrust
together to solve a common and urgent problem. Under such circumstances, there is no time to create new information nor much
opportunity to search out and gather appropriate information
elsewhere. Yet the demand for innovation is intense. It must be
satisfied largely with the information resources to hand. When
widely divergent packages of information are forced together by
such extreme circumstances, the range of radical innovation which
emerges can be quite extraordinary.

Similar circumstances can arise without the necessity of war;
for instance, when a major innovation undermines and topples
the system of expertise designed to yield gradual improvement
in an industry's product. Firms in some industries judge such a
situation not to be in the interest of any of them, and may take
collusive steps to avoid it. If it arises anyway, all the industry's
firms, no matter how great their previous expertise, are suddenly amateurs on a level playing field. Thus, when large US
electrical companies could work up no more than reluctance to
develop the transistor in the 1950s, small, new firms scurried
to seize the advantage. Apart from the information that had
been created and gathered in the large companies, there simply
was no transistor expertise, there were no complete packages.
Consequently, these new firms were forced to search widely for
scattered bits of information which might be relevant to the task,
and to fit the bits into some sort of pattern.

Most of the people who were key people in the development of the
transistor did not have their training in solid state physics. In fact, the
single largest group involved in the development of the transistor were
nuclear physicists, by far. They certainly outnumbered engineers and
it turns out that other groups, like biologists, were quite important. [13]

The results of their endeavours in terms of significant economic and social innovation speak for themselves. The innovation which is the subject of Part II is not quite of this decisive sort.
Quite enough has been written about successful innovations on

the grounds that others can learn by imitation. The subject of each of the following chapters is perspective, and the object to reveal what an information perspective can contribute to prevailing views of innovation. So, Part II is as much concerned with policy and strategy for innovation as with innovation itself. It is certainly more concerned with failure than with success. Failure is always so much more revealing.

REFERENCES

1. Lars Lindkvist, 'Accounting in hierarchies: a TCA interpretation of internal reporting', *Scandinavian Journal of Management*, 9:1 (1993), 45–66.
2. Lee Sproull and Sara Kiesler, *Connections: New Ways of Working in the Networked Organization* (MIT Press, Cambridge, Mass., 1991).
3. W. L. Giusti and L. Georghiou, 'The use of co-nomination analysis in real-time evaluation of an R&D programme', *Scientometrics*, 14:3/4 (1988), 265–81.
4. Stuart Macdonald and Christine Williams, 'Beyond the boundary: an information perspective on the role of the gatekeeper in the organization', *Journal of Product Innovation Management*, 10 (1993), 417–27.
5. See 'The flawed education of the European businessman', *The Economist*, 4 June 1994, 89–90.
6. Rebecca Henderson, 'Underinvestment and incompetence as responses to radical innovation: evidence from the photolithographic alignment equipment industry', *Rand Journal of Economics*, 24:2 (1993), 248–70; Stuart Macdonald, 'Technological change and the expert', in W. Ward and M. Bryden (eds.), *Public Information: Your Right to Know* (Royal Society of Queensland, Brisbane, 1981), 53–9.
7. Tim Brady, *New Technology and Skills in British Industry* (Manpower Services Commission, London, 1984).
8. Alistair Mant, *The Rise and Fall of the British Manager* (Macmillan, London, 1977), 54–69.
9. Denise Welch and Lawrence Welch, 'Using personnel to develop networks: an approach to subsidiary management', *International Business Review*, 2:2 (1993), 157–68.
10. Stuart Macdonald, 'Headhunting in high technology', *Technovation*, 4 (1986), 233–45.

11. e.g. Bruce Ross, 'Strategic commitment, unknowledge and the nature of entrepreneurial activity', *Prometheus*, 6:2 (1988), 270–84.
12. J. Scott Armstrong, 'Peer review of scientific papers', *Journal of Biological Response Modifiers*, 3 (1984), 10–14.
13. Harvey Brooks as quoted in Ernest Braun and Stuart Macdonald, *Revolution in Miniature: The History and Impact of Semiconductor Electronics* (Cambridge University Press, Cambridge, 1978), 73.

PART II

Information and Practice

6

Resistance to Information:
The Organization and the Independent Inventor

The organization copes much more easily and comfortably with its own information, that which it already contains and controls, than with information from beyond its boundaries. Consequently, organizations display a tendency to reject external information in favour of internal. So pronounced and common is this tendency that it has been given a name—the not-invented-here (NIH) syndrome. The title derives from what is taken to be the absolutely classic case of the organization's resistance to external information. It has been observed that the invention produced by an independent inventor, someone who invents on his own behalf rather than with or for an organization, nearly always requires the resources of the organization if it is ever to become an innovation. Realizing this, the independent inventor approaches the organization for its assistance and encounters immediate and complete dismissal. Indeed, rejection may well be determined by corporate policy rather than by any assessment of the invention's potential. [1]

Investigation of the syndrome commonly reveals three explanations for this behaviour:

1. although an individual who has no connection with the organization just might produce the sort of information package unlikely to come from an employee, the costs of screening mountains of dross for the occasional nugget are too high to be worth contemplating; [2]
2. acceptance of the value to the organization of external research, especially from a source with few and primitive resources,

would be an indictment of the organization's own, much more sophisticated research; and

3. ideas produced in ignorance of the organization's own systems and activities can be accommodated by the organization only with extreme difficulty.

Certainly these explanations are prominent among the reasons organizations give for rejecting the inventions of independent inventors out of hand. Moreover, they are very far from mere excuses; they are presented with conviction and they are convincing. An information perspective is sympathetic to all three, but particularly to the last—the problem of fitting external information with that already in use within the organization is horrendous. What, then, feels wrong with the not-invented-here syndrome?

While independent inventors are understandably rather annoyed by the dismissive attitude of organizations towards their inventions, it is hard for those concerned with the much broader issues of innovation and change in the organization to share their despair. Despite the enthusiasm of some commentators for the contributions of independent inventors, and the official encouragement such inventors occasionally receive from government programmes, there is probably little economic or social gain from their activities. One can sympathize with the independent inventor who lamented the cost of the British government not developing and adopting his aeroplane navigation system in 1939, but it is hard to follow his logic.

To a number of people it was quite well known during the war that, due to the lack of precise navigation equipment, the effectiveness of the RAF's bombing raids was much reduced, and the hoped-for damage to the German war effort and hence an early victory was not achieved. As a result, many more British soldiers (and civilians) died needlessly, or suffered in German p.o.w. camps. Also, probably a million inmates of concentration camps might have been saved. [3]

So who cares if organizations instinctively reject the inventions of independent inventors? Little would seem to be lost. Inconveniently, the same might be said of the results of most other research. This is simply because the contribution of research to innovation is usually rather small. Other activities seem to put much more information into the total innovation package. Yet it would be a nonsense to suggest that innovation would proceed just as well without research as with it. Small the contribution of research may be, but it is obviously important. Small the contribution of the independent inventor certainly is, but it, too, may sometimes be significant.

A syndrome is a number of symptoms which, taken together, indicate a particular disease. It is odd to regard automatic rejection by the organization as a syndrome, for it is just a single symptom. If diagnosis of disease on the basis of one symptom—rejection—is hard to justify, the prognosis which follows the identification of the syndrome should be presented as extremely speculative. Just the opposite tends to be the case: the NIH syndrome is commonly presented not as a model to help explain why firms are less innovative than they might be, but as the explanation of why they cannot be more innovative and of the fate that awaits such intransigence.

In fact, the organization's ready rejection of the independent inventor involves no syndrome at all. A syndrome might well be involved were organizations to welcome unreservedly the inventions of independent inventors. There would then be curiosity aplenty to identify the symptoms of receptivity. Consider the massive interest in the characteristics of organizations which are especially quick to adopt innovations. But the NIH syndrome is concerned with the rejection of ideas which consequently played no part in the organization's innovation. Summary dismissal is its only characteristic, and there is no interest in the ideas themselves, or in how they came to be rejected.

Acceptance of the NIH syndrome, then, is analogous to the syndrome itself: just as organizations show no interest in the inventions of independent inventors, so thinking in terms of the syndrome discourages any real interest in what actually happens. The experience of the independent inventor at the hands of the organization may be of little moment to anyone who is not an independent inventor, but the NIH syndrome is widely used to explain organizational reaction to all external influences just because they are external. Now this is a matter of moment. If there is a syndrome at work here, it is important that it be recognized and understood. Current use of the NIH syndrome is as dismissive of this as the organization is supposed to be of the independent inventor.

This chapter takes a step or two towards this recognition and understanding by exploring the NIH syndrome in its very basic form. It investigates independent inventors, not to estimate the paucity of their contribution to organizational innovation, nor to speculate on what might have been had organizations been more receptive to their ideas, but to try to discover why it is that organizations encounter such difficulties exploiting the ideas of these inventors. The aim is not particularly to encourage smoother transactions between organizations and independent inventors, but to apply an information perspective in order to gain some comprehension of the processes at work which result in the organization's rejection of external information. Much of the evidence presented comes from surveys of independent inventors and research units of organizations; quotations from respondents to these surveys are used throughout to illustrate the argument.

THE INDEPENDENT INVENTOR

First to the independent inventor, the source of the external information. Conveniently, he is as unsullied a source as any could be. The independent inventor's isolation from the sources of information that normally contribute to research is profound, and so the information package he delivers to the organization is likely to be at least different from that available from any other research. Independent inventors rely on books and newspaper articles to supplement their own experience. [4] The local library is as much their laboratory as the garden shed. It is hardly surprising, then, that a frequent criticism of independent inventors is that their inventions are obvious and unoriginal.

There are now several machines similar to this invention commercially available. [research unit]

In general most private inventors who come to us are unfortunately trying to produce a product or concept which is already in the public domain. [research unit]

If nothing else, the patent system is a test of novelty and independent inventors make heavy use of it. In Australia, where the survey work on which this chapter is based was carried out, nearly three-quarters of all the 1978 patent applications from

Australian domiciles came from independent inventors. To be sure, this dominance is not reflected in their share of patents granted, and is even less evident among the group of patentees who assiduously continue to pay the annual fee required to maintain a patent. [5] Also, in most countries it seems that there has been a progressive decline in the relative use of the patent system by independent inventors. [6] Even so, independent inventors remain significant users of a system which certainly tests for originality, and which provides a handy screening device for those who would study the attitude of organizations to external information.

GOVERNMENT POLICY FOR INDEPENDENT INVENTORS

Many, perhaps most, Western governments run occasional programmes intended to help independent inventors. The importance of independent inventors in the patent system makes them hard to ignore and modest assistance is unlikely to annoy any political constituency. Indeed, it is likely to bring some pleasure to all those with a romantic attachment to the notion that individual perseverance will occasionally triumph where organization fails. [7] As one American report concluded, 'The independent, basement inventor and the small firm are the fair-haired boys of politics; they can do no wrong, and must be encouraged'. [8]

Although public resources allocated to the assistance of independent inventors are not sufficiently extravagant to warrant much attention, the use to which they are put is significant. It is governed almost entirely by acceptance of the not-invented-here syndrome. The argument is that the resources of the organization are required to develop, manufacture, and market the inventions of independent inventors. If their inventions do not yield major benefits, and are rejected by organizations, it must be that they do not yield major benefits because they are rejected by organizations. This market failure can be rectified, it is assumed, by making independent inventions better known to firms and thus overcoming the barrier presented by the NIH syndrome. Selection by government committee or by public competition serves as much to make certain inventions more prominent as to spot those that are most promising.

The supposition that a committee of worthies will be able to identify those inventions of most value to individual firms is an odd one, suggesting that the application of any criteria at all is preferable to the NIH syndrome's universal damnation. The conviction that anything is better than that also helps justify paltry funding of programmes and casual administration. The Australian Inventors' Assistance Scheme provided chosen inventors with grants to develop their inventions in order to make them more attractive to firms. It failed to make any grants whatsoever during its first year of operation, a situation which attracted the rancour of independent inventors somewhat less than when, seven years later, the Scheme was overwhelmed by submissions and simply ran out of funds. [9] It had spent considerably more on administering itself than it had ever bestowed in grants. In the Australian Inventions Advisory Committee, independent inventors felt that they faced an unreasoning and inert obstacle even more insuperable than that which they encountered in firms. In fact, what they met was the NIH syndrome in a particularly pure and simple form: members of selection committees showed no interest in learning from independent inventors, in discovering what lay behind the NIH syndrome.

[This invention] is the kind of ratbag nuisance I suffered for a long time when I was a member of the New Zealand Inventions Development Authority. The few inventors who came to our department are of the same kind, with all kinds of perpetual motion machines for making water or solving the energy crisis. Invariably they have no technical background and a healthy disregard for basic economics. Frankly, they are a bloody nuisance. [research unit]

But paltry grants to a few independent inventors aside, government programmes are concocted not so much to provide public resources as to encourage industry to contribute its own. Once committees of public servants, scientists, and senior managers have selected from among the many inventions submitted those that would somehow be best for industry, the task is then to stimulate industrial interest in these inventions. One Danish scheme, for example, provides advice and facilities to make prototypes which look as if they have come from a production line rather than a garden shed and whose means of manufacture will be instantly recognizable to factory managers. Another Australian scheme encourages independent inventors to accompany the invention they present to industry with a business plan. In the United States, there are private-sector firms which act as brokers between independent inventors and the organizations which might turn their inventions into innovations. While their intervention may counteract the NIH syndrome, it does not guarantee innovation, a failure which exposes such firms to the wrath of inventors and government alike.

CHARACTERISTICS OF THE INDEPENDENT INVENTOR

Much of the information in this chapter is based on responses from 601 independent inventors who had applied for an Australian patent in 1978. [10] Given the general predisposition to regard all independent inventors as cranks, the characteristics of this group of individuals are not unimportant. Of the 601, all but 21 were male. Women, it seems, rarely invent, or if they do, rarely apply for a patent. These inventors were somewhat older than the population at large, though typically aged between 35 and 60 rather than in their retirement or dotage. They were very much better educated than the general Australian population, with a strong bias towards qualifications in science and engineering. Of this group, 71 possessed a bachelor's degree, a further 15 a master's degree, and 17 more had a doctorate. Just under half were self-employed, either full- or part-time, often running their own small—usually very small—businesses. Nearly three-quarters were professional, technical, or administrative workers. Most had had a go at patenting before, and therefore at inventing, but they were hardly inveterate inventors; some 40 per cent had no experience of the patent system, and those who had dozens of patents ('to their credit' as some see it) were exceedingly rare. In short, rather than according with the starkly simple stereotype—the pestering crank—which best fits the NIH syndrome, the characteristics of independent inventors suggest that many might actually be rather interesting and perhaps even complex people.

But why do they invent? Table 6.1 gives some idea. Most important is the desire to solve problems they have personally encountered, though a range of other motivations is also important, including simply having fun.

TABLE 6.1   Why Independent Inventors Invent (% of Respondents)

To solve specific problems	70
To make money	56
To be useful to society	44
To satisfy natural curiosity	30
For fun	20

Total responses	1,295
Total respondents	586

TABLE 6.2   Why Independent Inventors Want a Patent (% of Respondents)

To make money from the invention	77
To prevent others making money from the invention	39
To justify inventive activity to themselves	27
To determine whether the invention is any good	21
To inform the public of the invention	20
To assist application for development funding	11
To justify inventive activity to friends and relatives	11

Total responses	1,176
Total respondents	569

THE INDEPENDENT INVENTOR AND
THE PATENT SYSTEM

I am still inventing and like many inventors know of problems which could be solved to form an invention. [independent inventor]

The motivation for inventing is not at all the same as that for wanting a patent (Table 6.2). The vast majority of independent inventors clearly patent to make money out of their inventions, though making money is not their primary reason for inventing. Note that there is also a host of subsidiary reasons for wanting a patent, indicating purposes for which the patent system was certainly never designed. For many independent inventors, the patent provides justification to others, and to themselves, that their time and effort have not been wasted after all. The NIH syndrome suggests that the only real obstacle faced by the independent inventor is the obduracy of the firm he wishes to develop his invention: in reality, he encounters the self-doubt of the self-employed, and faces the tolerant opposition of all who know about his activities.

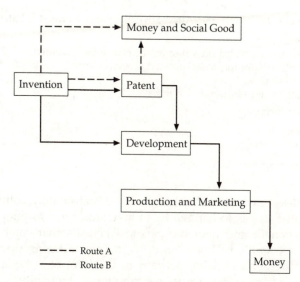

FIG. 6.1 Alternative perceptions of the route to innovation

The attitude of independent inventors to the patent system provides a reasonable indication of how they perceive the innovative process. Without a doubt, it is linear in their minds, but the line is short. It starts with their invention and ends soon after with an innovation and accompanying financial rewards, probably—but not necessarily—taking in the patent system on the way. In the view of independent inventors, difficulties lie not in the creation of innovation, but in reaping their rightful share of the rewards.

My inclination is to solve a problem—primarily for myself—but where the benefit flows on to the community I like recognition—where benefit is commercial I seek reward. [independent inventor]

Fig. 6.1 provides a graphic interpretation of this perception. Everything starts with invention—their invention—and should end with gain. Even for those who are particularly concerned with improving the lot of their fellow man—and many independent inventors fall into this category, the problems they strive to solve being social rather than commercial (Table 6.1)—money is somehow inextricably associated with the social good they feel will come from their invention. For these individuals,

TABLE 6.3 Preferred Alternatives to Being Granted a Patent

Group A

Cash award based on value to society of the invention	221
Token recognition to acknowledge significance of the invention	75
Right to recognition and publicity	80
Total in group	304

Group B

None of these	277
Total respondents	581

regardless of whether they patent, there is absolutely nothing of moment that has to happen to an invention for it to pour forth public benefit and then the personal benefits that come from public recognition. This is Group A in Table 6.3, a group which feels it deserves acclaim, perhaps in the form of a medal or a television appearance, for its contribution to humanity.

ATTITUDE OF INDEPENDENT INVENTORS TOWARDS ORGANIZATIONS

Many of these independent inventors (those in Group A) believe not only that the world should beat a path to their door for their inventions, but that the door has only to be opened for the invention to bring benefits. Those in organizations are all too aware of the impracticality of this approach.

Individual inventors can play a significant part as a source of new ideas. However their [sic] is usually a large investment in time and money necessary to take the invention from the original concept to rough prototype stage to a fully tested saleable product. Most inventors do not fully appreciate this. [research unit]

With rare exception, individual inventors are unaware of the market's real needs and the marketing process. Emotion generally prevents the proper functioning of objectivity. [research unit]

Many inventors have no conception of the mark-up on manufacturer's costs to cover marketing, distribution, profit, etc., and their usual claims of enormous savings and profit margins are generally nonsense. [research unit]

Individual inventors tend to be motivated by *their* perceived need for some improvement. Many of their ideas are excellent but have not been researched from the *market's* perceived need.... We tend to look at market needs *before* we conduct research. We get fewer misses that way [emphasis in original]. [research unit]

But many independent inventors (those in Group B) are decidedly more worldly. They seem to appreciate a hard and uncertain, though linear, haul from invention to innovation. These inventors also seem ready to accept that there is an important role for organizations in what they perceive as a process. Few in even this group, however, would accept the proposition that the organization must make a vastly greater contribution than their own if innovation is to result. They do appreciate, though, that they must either develop an innovation, and then manufacture and market it themselves, or persuade someone else—an organization—to do this. [11] Most would much prefer to undertake the task themselves, but lack the skills and resources.

I think unless you are lucky enough to come across something which is cheap enough and simple enough to begin building and marketing yourself then the time and costs involved in getting someone interested are much too great. [independent inventor]

It would appear to me that the person most likely to gain from invention is the person who invents and manufactures himself. The pure inventor who wants someone else to take up his invention mostly fails. [independent inventor]

To the independent inventor it seems not at all unreasonable to expect these organizations to put their resources where the independent inventor himself would put his own, if he had them. Among the miscellany of reasons perceived by independent inventors as responsible for the failure of a successful innovation to emerge from their inventions, the paucity of resources to prove the potential of the invention is most prominent. Also marked is a tendency to blame the patent system rather than any inadequacy of their own or of the invention, as if a properly working patent system should transform inventions into innovations. Amidst the analysis in Table 6.4 of what went wrong, there is certainly some indication that organizations are less than enthusiastic to take on their inventions, but this is clearly only one obstacle among many. The predominance of the NIH syndrome

TABLE 6.4 Obstacles Encountered by Independent Inventors in Realizing Gains from Inventive Activity (% of Responses)

Lack of funds to prove potential of inventions	21.5
Cost of patenting	17.5
Poor marketing skills	14.6
Manufacturers not interested in inventions from independent inventors	14.0
Manufacturing too costly for existing market	9.5
Complexity of the patent system	9.5
Inadequacy of the invention	4.6
Problems associated with scaling up inventions	3.5
Lack of co-operation from Patent Office	1.7
Lack of co-operation from patent attorneys	1.5
Failure to be granted patent	1.2
Potential or actual costs of dispute over ownership	1.1
Total responses 1,332	

in discussions of organizational innovation would suggest that in these of all circumstances it should be paramount. In fact, there is more evidence here of what might be called a 'patent syndrome', to which is attributed the failure of inventions to become innovations.

Although friends and relatives are a source of disparagement for independent inventors, they are also the usual source of external funding. In defiance of the NIH syndrome, most development funding actually comes from industry. Banks, the obvious source of such funding, provide very little, and that generally in the form of personal loans. Although independent inventors should encounter the NIH syndrome when they present their inventions to organizations which might develop, manufacture, and market these inventions, they would seem to experience a more total rejection when they approach their local bank manager.

Bankers and financiers are absolutely naive about what is required to make money. They can only understand existing profitability with figures supplied. They have no ability whatsoever to assess the potential of a new enterprise. The Bank did not have an *Engineer* but relied on an *Accountant* to assess the future of our business [emphasis in original]. [independent inventor]

But only 85 of these inventors had ever received any funding from any source: 499 had had none at all. It should be remembered that Group A never even thinks in terms of development funding and that many in Group B, although they appreciate its essential part in innovation, would really rather get back to inventing something else.

[M]any inventors would like simply to see someone take up the idea, if it is proven good; and simply get something back so that the inventor can get back to inventing. [independent inventor]

BIG SCIENCE, BIG TECHNOLOGY, AND THE LITTLE INVENTOR

Complementing the conclusion that the NIH syndrome results from the complexity of modern organizations and their consequent inability to accommodate the solicitations of independent inventors is an observation on the sophistication of modern technology. Independent inventors, it is reasoned, might have had something to contribute when industry was craft-based and industrial technology dependent largely on personal experience. But those days are long gone; the simple discoveries have all been made; technology is now science-based, its further development dependent on the combined efforts of professionals, organized and directed in vast—and expensive—R&D laboratories. [12] Thus, the independent inventor, pottering alone in his garage, can hardly be expected to have much to contribute. [13]

The inventor is full of good intentions but a scientific foundation is lacking. The dental and medical professions are full of inventors but few inventions are of significance or commercial value. [research unit]

Most ideas worth considering come from organizations or at least professionally qualified individuals. [research unit]

In general individual inventors do not have sufficient technical support, expertise and knowledge to produce highly technical products. In our experience, research and development in modern chemical technology requires a multi-disciplinary team backed up by fundamental research, experimental development, manufacturing and marketing expertise. [research unit]

Our particular areas of research often require expensive equipment e.g. large scale reactors etc. which means individual inventors are most unlikely to contribute in this area. [research unit]

This Big Science accompaniment to the NIH syndrome is common, and plays its part in discouraging examination of what actually happens. It is also fortified by the syndrome. Those who value the trappings that Big Science (and Big Technology for that matter) affords feel the more secure if it is widely accepted that all modern technological change emanates from their endeavours. This is a linear view, of course, and because it is no longer acceptable in its crude form to non-scientists, it has required some defending of late. In this defence, models of innovation which do not allow the seminal function of science to be confused with self-interest are valued highly. The NIH syndrome is perfect for the purpose. It presents the organization, not science and technology, as automatically rejecting external information. Science and technology can be seen to remain—as they must— open and receptive to all ideas, even the pathetic notions of cranks. Widespread acceptance of an NIH syndrome has helped protect the institutional structure and professional organization of science and technology from the accusation that they, too, prefer internal information to external.

It is not, of course, the case that all innovation springs from research in huge corporate R&D laboratories, and that science is the fount of all this new technology. The argument, once taken very seriously by scientists and engineers, no longer convinces and is rarely presented in isolation. But it gains strength, and may even be believed, in the context of the NIH syndrome: if information from cranks is associated with organizational rejection of information, then the institutional contribution of professional scientists and engineers can be more readily associated with organizational acceptance of information. In short, there are sectoral interests which promote the acceptance of the NIH syndrome, a factor that helps explain how wide and uncritical this acceptance has been. Further investigation into the actual relationship between the independent inventor and the organization is warranted.

THE RESEARCH OF THE INDEPENDENT INVENTOR AND THE RESEARCH OF THE ORGANIZATION

Examination of patent classifications reveals that independent inventors concentrate their activities in areas of technology neglected by organizations. Over 40 per cent of all patent applications made by independent inventors in Australia are in the patent categories of agriculture, personal and domestic objects, and health and amusement. Less than 10 per cent of applications from Australian firms are in these categories. Many independent inventors, then, are active in areas in which organizations are probably not concentrating their research. This does not necessarily mean that their work is incompatible with the interests of organizations.

The investigative activity of 56 independent inventors who had succeeded in being granted patents (as opposed to merely applying for them), and who held these patents in 1983, was compared with organizational research activities. [14] The object of the exercise was to match patent abridgements with the declared research interests of a large number and wide range of Australian organizations. Despite considerable effort, no organizational interest could be found which in any way related to six of the inventions (a hydroplane boat hull, a soil level, an electric guitar, a bed support aid, a wheelchair, and a kite). Some 50 patented inventions remained which did seem to be relevant to the declared research activities of organizations, and often to those of more than one organization. This allowed 233 research units in government, industry, and higher education to be sent patent abridgements (and full specifications if more information was required) to see what they made of them. Some 147 usable responses were received (93 from industry, 33 from government research units, and 19 from higher education).

In essence, this exercise replicated the attempts of independent inventors to find organizations interested in their inventions. Consequently, it was tempting an NIH response. The team used every resource at its command, from published directories to personal suggestions, resources which far exceed those of independent inventors. They also appeared to exceed those used by organizations themselves to discover what is going on outside: the majority of research units working in these areas was unable to identify any other institution engaged in similar research. Australia, of course, is a small country, at least in terms of research resources, and often there simply was no other related research activity. The corollary is that in such a small country it is easy to be aware of whatever is going on.

TABLE 6.5 Contact of Research Units with Independent Inventors
(% of Research Units)

Research unit approached
never	12.9
rarely	32.7
several times	38.1
many times	16.3

Research unit provided research advice in previous five years
never	27.2
rarely	31.3
several times	33.3
many times	8.2

Research unit collaborated in previous five years
never	44.2
rarely	27.9
several times	25.9
many times	2.0

Total research units   147

Although many of these research units had had experience of independent inventors in the past, they had hardly been pestered (Table 6.5). The NIH syndrome suggests they should have been and would draw strength from the revelation that only 2 per cent of research units had collaborated frequently with independent inventors over the previous five years. Yet, only 16 per cent had been approached many times, and only 8 per cent had often been called upon to provide research advice. Although a few independent inventors receive unsolicited enquiries from large organizations which screen patent applications, it seems that nearly all contact between these research units and independent inventors is initiated by the inventors.

Of the 147 research units, 72 confirmed that they were, or had been, working in an area closely related to that of the patent abridgement they had been sent. These covered 35 of the 50 patented inventions. For the remaining 15 inventions, no related research work could be found in any organization, which, given the exhaustiveness of the search, strongly suggests there was none to be found. To this group of 15 should be added the six for which no similar research activities could be discovered. Consequently, it would seem that there is a substantial proportion of independent inventors who cannot possibly contribute to the research of organizations simply because research in that area is not being carried out. When such inventors approach organizations, it is incumbent on them to present a complete package, ready to be manufactured; they cannot expect the organization's research to be able to make good any deficiency. Given the limited resources of the independent inventor, such inadequacies are very likely to exist. But what is apparent here is simply that the inventions of many independent inventors are irrelevant to the activities of organizations. This is hardly evidence of an NIH syndrome.

Neither did the response of the research units to the remaining 35 inventions reveal much evidence of any NIH syndrome. Those employed to research inside the organization did not look down on the efforts of those outside the organization not employed to research. Those inside often felt that they shared research interests with those outside, and that they faced with them a common obstacle in the attitude of the rest of the organization towards research and change. Research units were obviously anxious to share with independent inventors—almost as colleagues—their vastly superior experience of the commercial realities of life.

We tested the unit described and found it worked well was clever and obviously would have had some success in the Australian market. However the market size is small. Productionising the unit would be expensive and such a device has many competitors in international markets. Product life of the design is limited to around 5 years and in balance a decision was made not to take the matter further. [research unit]

Staff members in this department have collaborated with the inventor of this unit to develop a prototype and assess performance. Technically this proved difficult and a combination of cost overruns and staff resignations have caused shelving of the project. [research unit]

The invention described is too complex for commercial application. High complexity results in high cost which makes this invention impractical. [research unit]

This shared research interest did not mean that independent inventors had come up with just the solution to the research units' problems. Far from it; just over half of the research units swore that they had devised something similar in the past, and 84 per cent declared themselves technically capable of producing the same thing. It might, then, seem reasonable to conclude that the research units considered the inventions of independent inventors old hat. Maybe, but it was much more important to them that the inventions were relevant. The linear view of innovation, redolent in the NIH syndrome, sees invention as playing a seminal role in research and so emphasizes the information-creation function of research. The reality of research, appreciated by independent inventors and research units alike, is that it is largely an information-gathering exercise. Relevance tends to be of more consequence than novelty. Consequently, that others have done or could do what the independent inventor has done is not necessarily the indictment that the NIH syndrome suggests. Research units were decidedly sympathetic towards independent inventors whom they saw as duplicating other research.

Occasionally we are approached by individual inventors with ideas or products in our field. Where applicable we will either purchase or come to an appropriate arrangement with the inventor. Where not applicable we will assist the inventor in the right direction if possible. Individual inventors' activities in our area tend to be 'bright idea' oriented rather than research oriented. [research unit]

The invention may have some application to our organization in that we are involved in the assembly of nut and bolt like devices although on a more automated scale. [research unit]

The other impeller is supposed to rotate freely on some kind of bush. This will be a point of high wear necessitating frequent maintenance and it was judged by our group to be very important in deciding not to take up the offer of manufacture. [research unit]

The research units regarded most of the inventions submitted to them as fairly obvious, and also as of little commercial value (Table 6.6). This would be totally in accord with the NIH syndrome had not nearly 60 per cent of these research units declared that they would possibly or definitely have taken out a patent themselves had they produced the same inventions. The patent system is not an institution to be entered into lightly. It would seem that their assessment of the value of inventions from independent inventors is much more a reflection of the uncertainties of research than a rejection of external information.

I believe that industry does not take advantage of individual inventors to solve problems that are not dependent on specific industry knowledge. [research unit]

TABLE 6.6 Research Units' Opinions of Inventions of
Independent Inventors (% of Research Units)

Technical ingenuity

fairly obvious	62.9
clever	31.4
ingenious	4.3
brilliant	1.4
Total research units	70

Potential commercial value

none	20.6
small	64.7
considerable	14.7
worth a fortune	0.0
Total research units	68

Such inventions provide a stimulus to our efforts to try and produce something of a similar stature. [research unit]

The [company] have purchased several of the ploughs from the inventor and have found them to be all that has been claimed of them. [research unit]

THE PATENT SYSTEM

It also transpired that 20 per cent of the research units had at some time taken out a licence from an independent inventor, and that a further 12 per cent may have done so. Considering that most of these units patented rarely and some not at all (the 72 research units had been granted 142 patents in the previous five years, but 80 per cent of these had been awarded to just five units), this is actually quite remarkable. About a quarter regularly consulted patent specifications, and yet something like half of the research units were already aware of the invention whose patent abridgement they had been sent. How, if most do not check new patents regularly and they are rarely approached by independent inventors (Table 6.5)? It would seem that informal networks may be in operation. Yet, as has been discussed, there is some evidence that research units are not particularly aware of what research other organizations are undertaking. It would be ironic indeed if informal mechanisms allow research units to be more aware of the research going on outside other organizations than of the research going on within them.

Other work has demonstrated the importance of the patent system as a screening mechanism for firms dealing—or trying to avoid dealing—with independent inventors. Some evidence was found among these research units of the patent system being used in just this way.

Individual inventors seldom have any worthwhile ideas in the products my firm is interested in and we try to discourage approaches by insisting they have patent protection before listening to their idea. [research unit]

Let the patent system provide some preliminary screening and then the organization can deal with those inventions which pass through on a proper, institutional basis. This view accords totally with the NIH syndrome, but reality may be rather more complicated. The NIH syndrome assumes that organizational research is the professional user of the patent system and that independent inventors are no more than amateurs making occasional use of it. In fact, most of these research units made little use of the system themselves, and that highly selective. The independent inventors were relatively experienced in taking out patents: the research units were the amateurs.

Generally patents would only be sought if there were considerable novelty and commercial possibility. [research unit]

Generally feel that individual inventors are excessively encouraged— by patent attorneys—to seek protection (spend money) for 'inventions' of dubious originality and unlikely commercial benefit. [research unit]

This does not mean that the research units were unfamiliar with the uses to which the patent system can be put. They were quite unabashed in their confession that the patent system gave no real protection to independent inventors, or to others for that matter.

Most commercial patents (mechanical) can be designed around . . . In the agricultural equipment manufacturing ind., the bigger the company —the fewer the patents. [research unit]

Our company has very few patents as it considers a patent only worth while if it has reasonable commercial value over competitors in Aust. or overseas. . . . Rather than get involved with owners of patents, we design around patents. [research unit]

The suspicion of independent inventors—often interpreted as paranoia—that organizations will not respect their intellectual property would seem to have some justification. This disregard for, and often abuse of, the patent system is important, especially when independent inventors feel that they must patent if their inventions are ever to be taken seriously. It is important because much of the reaction of research units to the patent abridgements and specifications they were sent should possibly be interpreted as reaction to the patent system rather than to the inventions themselves. Their observation was commonly that the invention should never have been patented, not that it should never have been made or brought to the attention of research units.

Because of the abundance of similar designs similar to that described, we do not believe that the patent would be held to be valid. [research unit]

We were surprised to find that a patent had been taken out for something that is, at least in our production, used daily. [research unit]

The invention described is really an extension of prior art and not very innovative in my opinion. [research unit]

It is quite fascinating that what is more likely to be a lack of faith in the patent system has been assumed to be condemnation of the inventions patented. It is acceptance of the NIH syndrome that has led to this assumption. Once again, in their opinion of the same patent system, independent inventors show common cause with research units.

The patent office is full of rubbishy non-commercial inventions. [independent inventor]

As an inventor I feel privileged to say this: I think the average inventor is a hopeless, irresponsible trusting idiot. Came to this conclusion after spending some hours checking through Patent applications at Brisbane patent office. Became almost hysterical after reading of an inventor's portable 18 hole golf course. [independent inventor]

Would like to express the lack of cooperation, assistance in obtaining patent by attorney, their only purpose has been various ways to obtain moneys. [independent inventor]

[T]he patent attorney I used made sure he drained the last dollar out of me on my invention. [independent inventor]

After almost 12 months of repeated rejections, by the Patents Office Canberra, of my Complete Specifications, on the grounds of incorrect grammar, irrelevant to the invention, I gave up in frustration. [independent inventor]

The patent system offers a codification of information. In theory, this should assist the organization in dealing with the information: in practice, it is quite inappropriate to attempt the codification of the information produced by many independent inventors. The information package they put together is generally too messy and incomplete. The patent system denies this inadequacy, with the consequence that its codification is considered inappropriate by independent inventors and research units alike. Functioning in this manner, the patent system poses a barrier between the independent inventor and the organization at least as great as that attributed to the NIH syndrome. It is, though, a barrier which acceptance of the syndrome does much to disguise.

THE DO-NOT-DISTURB SYNDROME

It could just be that, in its separation from the other activities of the organization, the research unit often finds itself as isolated as the independent inventor. This would explain something of their community of interest. It would then be less important that invention did not take place within the organization than that any invention—indeed, anything new—is resisted by the organization, whatever its source. The NIH syndrome, in drawing attention to the organization's rejection of the new because it comes from an external source, implies that the organization welcomes new ideas when they come from an internal source. The organization may prove obdurate in its intercourse with the outside world, but this is a cost to be paid if it is to function efficiently as an organization. This may be why senior managers are quick to acknowledge the NIH syndrome as an unfortunate characteristic of organization, but slow to throw up their hands in horror and swear that efforts will be made to counter it. The reality, of course, is that the research units encountered just as much resistance to their ideas as independent inventors encountered. The only difference is that the research units met this resistance from their own organizations. Consequently, they sympathized entirely with the problems faced by independent inventors, seeing them as a product of organizational attitude towards change in general, and towards research in particular.

Research—if it can be called that—at this establishment is process not product oriented, but we hope to change this in the future. [research unit]

My apologies for the negative replies, but, as a manufacturing area, our main thrust is quick and varied utilisation of existing technology. [research unit]

It is inevitable that such a machine will be developed and I see no reason why the principles outlined should not be effective when fully developed. [This] research unit . . . is no longer effective as local design of hydraulic equipment . . . has ceased, all hydraulics with exception of some old designs being totally imported. [research unit]

Our research efforts are directed towards products which have a high expectation of acceptance by our major Original Equipment Automotive Industry customers. These are extremely rare at present due to the overbearing adoption of overseas technology. [research unit]

It is probable that most Australian vehicle manufacturers would be more interested in the application of *proven* systems to their products rather than commit extensive resources for the development of an invention that may subsequently prove ineffective. This would certainly apply to all of the inventions that have been submitted to this company during recent years [emphasis in original]. [research unit]

For consumer products, design aesthetics would normally be a more compelling selling point than the energy saving advantages—the invention falls short in this regard. The creativity of individual inventors is to be applauded, however, many inventions fail because often what is practical is not commercially attractive to industrial or domestic consumers. Our research is totally commercially orientated. [research unit]

This is not to argue that there is no such thing as an NIH syndrome. There is; there is institutional rejection of external information as typified by the organizational response to the inventions of independent inventors. But rejection of this information would seem to be not so much because it is external as because it is new. External information is, of course, much more likely than internal information to be new to the organization. These research units, which might have been expected to be resentful of amateur interference, were anything but; they were genuinely interested in what the independent inventors had produced. It is really quite fanciful to imagine them feeling threatened by these independent inventors. A more satisfactory explanation of the NIH syndrome might be that the independent inventor has assembled a rather small information package in isolation from the information already available within the organization. This is most evident in his frequent replication of what the organizational research unit has already done. But replication is not frowned on by scientists and engineers as much as it is by economists and accountants.

The information package that the independent inventor is able to contribute to the organization, because it has been assembled in isolation from all the other activities of the organization, is unlikely to be compatible with what is already being done in production or marketing, or with what is being planned in the boardroom. The evidence presented here confirms that this is the case, but also indicates that this organizational reaction to new information may be experienced just as much by the organization's own research unit as by the independent inventor. The divide between research and the other activities of the organization is hidden by the traditional notion of the NIH syndrome. In concentrating on the boundary between the organization and the outside world—a boundary which is of no small importance —the assumption is made that the organization is a homogeneous whole, with all parts sharing the same interests and fully aware of what is going on elsewhere in the system. This is not a realistic model of the organization. Among the parts most likely to be isolated from the rest of the organization, to be most remote from the seat of power, is R&D. The NIH syndrome suggests a blind, instinctive reaction to external information by those in the organization who have most to lose by change, or who feel most discomforted by the uncertainty and disruption it engenders. Those in the organization's research unit are more likely to be at odds with this group than part of it. From an information perspective, the not-invented-here syndrome looks much more like a do-not-disturb syndrome.

REFERENCES

1. Gerald Udell and Michael O'Neill, 'Technology transfer: encouraging the non-corporate inventor', *Business Horizons*, 20:4 (1977), 40–5; Adrian Hope, 'It's a wonderful idea, but . . .', *New Scientist*, 1 June 1978, 576–81 and 'The death of an idea', *New Scientist*, 13 Sept. 1979, 294–7.

2. L. J. Hartnett, *Little Wheels, Big Wheels* (Lansdowne Press, Melbourne, 1964), 140. This is not, of course, to suggest that the nuggets are never found. See W. F. Mueller, 'The origins of the basic inventions underlying Du Pont's major product and process innovations, 1920 to 1950'; J. L. Enos, 'Invention and innovation in the petroleum refining industry', in National Bureau of Economic Research, *The Rate and Direction of Inventive Activity: Economic and Social Factors* (Princeton University Press, Princeton, 1962), 323–46, 299–321; J. Jewkes, D. Sawers and R. Stillerman, *The Sources of Invention* (W. W. Norton, New York, 1969); P. S. Johnson, *The Economics of Invention and Innovation* (Martin Robertson, London, 1975), 59–63.

3. Heinz Lipschutz, 'Confessions of a frustrated inventor', *Electronics and Wireless World*, 94 (1988), 276–8.

4. Stuart Macdonald, 'The patent system and the individual inventor', *The Inventor*, 24:1 (1984), 25–9.

5. See Jacob Schmookler, 'Inventors past and present', *Review of Economics and Statistics*, 39 (1957), 321–33.

6. See S. Encel and A. Inglis, 'Patents, inventions and economic progress', *Economic Record*, 24 (1966), 582; F. M. Sherer, *Industrial Market Structure and Economic Performance* (Rand McNally, Chicago, 1980), 440.

7. e.g. Leonard de Vries, *Victorian Inventions* (John Murray, London, 1971); Edward de Bono (ed.), *Eureka! How and When the Greatest Inventions Were Made* (Thames and Hudson, London, 1974); Leo Port, *Australian Inventors* (Cassell, Stanmore, NSW, 1978).

8. US Congress, Joint Economic Committee, *Invention and the Patent System* (US Government Printing Office, Washington, DC, 1964), 132.

9. Stuart Macdonald, 'The individual inventor in Australia', *Australian Director*, Feb. 1983, 44–51.

10. For details see Stuart Macdonald, 'Australia—the patent system and the individual inventor', *European Intellectual Property Review*, 5:6 (1983), 154–9.

11. See Chris Freeman, *The Economics of Industrial Innovation* (Penguin, Harmondsworth, 1974), 69–72.

12. J. A. Schmookler, *Capitalism, Socialism and Democracy* (Allen and Unwin, London, 1947), 131–4; J. K. Galbraith, *American Capitalism: The Concept of Countervailing Power* (Houghton Mifflin, Cambridge, 1952), 90–5.
13. Joseph Rossman, *Industrial Creativity: The Psychology of the Inventor* (University Books, New York, 1964), pp. xv–xvi.
14. For details see Stuart Macdonald, 'The distinctive research of the individual inventor', *Research Policy*, 15 (1986), 199–210.

7

Information Intrigue:
Controlling the Flow of Information

TECHNOLOGY AND WORLD DOMINATION

Between the end of the Second World War and the collapse of the Soviet Union, the Western allies sought to deny the Soviet bloc Western technology likely to increase its military strength. Export controls were the primary instrument, employed originally to wage virtual economic war against the Soviets, and then to appease through some relaxation during the period of *détente* of the seventies. During the eighties, export controls were adapted to deprive the Soviet bloc of dual-use technology, that which was judged to have civilian as well as military application. Critical technologies were identified and it was this information of which the Soviet bloc was to be deprived. Controlling the flow of technological information rather than the flow of equipment posed some problems. An information perspective provides some insight into these problems.

There were two export control systems: the unilateral system enforced by the United States, and that agreed multilaterally by the NATO allies and Japan, arranged through the Co-ordinating Committee (CoCom) in Paris. [1] CoCom never had an official existence, which obviated the need for governments to make public defence of their membership. Their delegates met every Tuesday to decide the fate of applications to export equipment exceeding the performance range specified on lists administered by national governments. Updating these lists was also a responsibility of CoCom, but as member governments varied enormously in the latitude they allowed their own firms, both this and the application procedure often took some time. Delays, uncertainty, and the suspicion of bias infuriated firms trying to export, and CoCom would probably have fallen victim to its own incompetence had it not been for the United States. Most of the funding for CoCom came from the US, as did the pressure for countries to join and to make the unanimous decisions that CoCom rules required. CoCom was always a ramshackle organization held together by the United States; it struggled to deal with regulating the export of hardware and was never able to cope with regulating the export of information.

The unilateral controls of the United States were another matter altogether. Throughout the eighties, the US really did try to control the flow of technological information from the West to the Soviet bloc. The problems it encountered are wonderfully illustrative of the difficulties inherent in a task which is the inverse of the normal concerns of technology transfer. The whole episode also gives some idea of the opportunities available to those who try to control the flow of information, and of the impact on innovation that their efforts may have.

The real irony is that Western export controls probably caused the West much more trouble than they did the Soviet bloc. [2] The Soviet economy existed almost in isolation, with all the inefficiency and independent robustness that that implies. No external influence, neither technology transfer nor its prohibition, could be expected to have much impact on such an economy.

[I]nternational technology transfer has not been a vehicle for Soviet 'overtaking', and in fields of rapid change it is not even sufficient for 'catching up'. [3]

The dominant view among specialists is that the aggregate impact of the transfer of Western technology on Soviet industry . . . is likely to be rather modest (and the impact on the Soviet economy as a whole, of which industry is only a part, even more so). [4]

This was not unappreciated in the West, any more than the hollowness of the Soviet Union's threat of world domination was unappreciated, which makes the energetic enforcement of export controls all the more intriguing.

The most charitable view of the policy is to suppose that no one in the United States seriously believes in its efficacy as a means of stemming the flow of technology to the East. [5]

THE BUCY REPORT AND THE DEPARTMENT
OF DEFENSE

The Bucy Report is just 39 pages long, but its brevity belies its importance. [6] The report appeared in 1976, the product of a task force chaired by Fred Bucy of Texas Instruments, and set up by the Department of Defense (DOD) to consider the relative effectiveness of the means by which Western technology was being transferred to the Soviet bloc. The report is scarcely exhaustive—certainly not in the same league as later reports from the National Academy of Sciences [7]—and yet its influence has been fundamental. It observed that export controls would have to address technology transfer mechanisms to be effective, especially the most efficient mechanisms, and that controls should concentrate on those critical technologies that would provide the most significant advance to the receiving nation. It did not consider information transactions, an omission which increased the freedom with which the report's recommendations could be interpreted, and also the severity of the consequences arising from their application.

Bucy has since had occasion to reflect that his recommendations were not implemented quite as his report intended, [8] and that the Militarily Critical Technologies List (MCTL)—the attempt by the Department of Defense to define categories of critical technologies as recommended by Bucy—had grown rather long.

The MCTL is the size of the New York phone book and worth a lot less. It's a bastardization of the concept of critical technology. The bureaucrats have taken a clear concept and turned it into a two inch document that's absolutely worthless. [9]

Others of the report's recommendations were also to come to pass in ways that were probably unintended. The turf battle that ensued between Defense and the Department of Commerce is one example. Defense originally had little more than an advisory role in export control matters; Commerce was responsible for what goods left the country, and State took the lead in CoCom. Bucy recommended that Defense should play a more prominent role.

While Defense does not have the primary responsibility for control of technology export, . . . the initiative for developing policy objectives and strategies for controlling specific technologies are their responsibility. [10]

No one could possibly accuse the DOD of having been inact-
ive in this area in the years since 1976, and much of the lever-
age it has applied has been gained through an uncommon ability
to recognize and exploit certain of the characteristics of information. Defense went to some lengths to expose as graphically and
publicly as possible the failure of Commerce to enforce export
controls. Fines imposed on some offenders were ridiculed by
comparison with the penalty for taking a deer out of season in
Maine, and Commerce was deliberately embarrassed by being
forced to admit that while there had been no recorded infringements of the grain embargo on the Soviet Union, only one officer
had been checking. [11] Commerce had long held an equivocal
attitude towards export controls—essential in principle, but a
deterrent to trade in practice—and Defense was not slow to expose
this ambivalence by creating yet more damaging information.

In response to the plea by Commerce that it simply could
not afford more enforcement, Defence provided $30 million to
Customs to fund Operation Exodus, a move bound to provide
fresh evidence of infringements and to make an ally of the
Commissioner for Customs.

The Defense Department has the experts on what items have military
applications. That Department is a great supporter of the Customs
Service and I'm a great supporter of the Defense Department. Therefore,
the more involvement that the Defense Department has in the decisions
to license high-technology exports, the happier I am. [12]

Over the next few years, the public and politicians in the
United States were exposed to a barrage of dramatic examples
of how the export control system desperately needed tighten-
ing. Perhaps the most notorious of these seizure cases was the
one involving Richard Mueller, whose plans to export DEC
VAX 11–782 computers to the Soviet Union via South Africa,
Germany, and Sweden were frustrated by dozens of agents
leaping aboard ships and planes. The spoils from these *Boys'
Own Magazine* adventures were triumphantly displayed for press
inspection in a large hangar at Andrews Air Force Base, and the

conclusion invited that the Soviet Union had been deprived of the wherewithal to assemble an entire factory for high-speed integrated circuits. [13] The technical press ridiculed the assertion, [14] but went unheard amidst the fanfare orchestrated by the Department of Defense.

At a background briefing for reporters following the public press conference, top Pentagon officials, who spoke on condition they not be identified, said the seizures pointed out flaws in the US export control system, particularly in the way the Commerce Department handles export licensing applications. [15]

It was in the most simple and exciting of ways that DOD chose to present the export control issue to the public. The argument for controlling information was too esoteric for mass appeal and would have been likely to arouse mass suspicion anyway. For popular consumption, a myth was deliberately created by elements within Defense that technology was being stolen by the bad guys, who had to be stopped by the good guys. What was fed to the media—often in private briefings—were stories with a simple and consistent plot: dual-use technology just about to leave the country, intercepted in the nick of time by energetic agents of justice, replaced with sand or gravel or concrete before being sent on its way, often with an obscene note.

Prankish federal agents decided to send along the Soviet-bound parcels —sort of. They filled the crates with 700 lb of concrete, and, inside one, tacked a two-word note, in plainest English: 'F . . . you!'. [16]

US Customs agents seized two shipments, removed the contents and repacked them with concrete in a 'sting' operation to trap a supplier of American scientific equipment to the Soviet Union, the Pentagon says. [17]

In early 1982, according to US Customs, McVey sent a computer on a private plane from Southern California to Mexico, where it was put on a jetliner bound for Amsterdam. When the plane stopped in Houston, Customs inspectors found the container, removed the computer and replaced it with a load of sand. [18]

[Customs agents] removed the silicon baking equipment, which was labelled an industrial oven, and substituted sand and a four letter message to be sent on to Moscow. [19]

While the crates were in the USA, customs officials removed $150,000 worth of Century 20 and Century 21 computers. Convinced that the sophisticated electronic equipment would find its way to the Soviet Union, the Americans replaced the computers with an equal weight of sand and concrete. [20]

What is fascinating about this campaign is that it presented technology as merely equipment, as something contained in a crate. Yet, Defense was really interested in preventing the export not of hardware, but of information. The myth helped provide the public and political support for the authority Defense needed to interfere with the flow of information.

Almost as a preamble to its consideration of technology transfer mechanisms, the Bucy Report discusses the importance of information. Information—or 'know-how' as Bucy thinks of it— is seen as the very heart of technology.

[C]ontrol of design and manufacturing know how is absolutely vital for the maintenance of U.S. technological superiority. Compared to this, all other considerations are secondary. [21]

[T]here is unanimous agreement that the detail of *how to do things* is the essence of the technologies. This body of detail is hard earned and hard learned. It is not likely to be transferred inadvertently. But it can be taught and learned [emphasis in original]. [22]

Now, to Fred Bucy, with a background in semiconductors, a field in which the intangible is infinitely more important in innovation than the tangible, the significance of information must have been so obvious as scarcely to warrant the assertion. In the context of export controls, the matter had hardly been considered. Certainly the Export Administration Act of 1969 had bestowed authority to control data and technical information, but virtually all practical interest had been in restricting exports of equipment—and in the era of *détente* even this emphasis had been distinctly muted. In stating what is really no more than a truism from which there can be no convincing dissent, Bucy was unwittingly opening a can whose worms are wriggling still.

CONTROLLING INFORMATION

There must have been many in the Department of Defense who failed to see the potential significance of Bucy's observations on information. Richard Perle (Assistant Secretary, International

Security Policy until 1987) was not one of them. There can be no doubting the provenance of his own reasoning on the subject.

> On the whole, the best way to prevent the Soviet Union from acquiring Western technology is by concentrating on protecting manufacturing know how rather than products. By focusing on basic know how, we can hope to slow the pace at which the Soviets are able to field new weapons. It needs to be emphasized that it should be the state of the art in the Eastern Bloc, not in the West, that serves as a guideline for what may or may not be transferred. [23]

As Congressional aide in his days before joining the Department of Defense, Perle had participated in drafting the legislation that became the Export Administration Act of 1979. [24] The new Act, although actually much more liberal than its predecessor, was also much more specific about the need to safeguard information, and included the requirement that DOD develop a critical technologies list with emphasis on know-how (the MCTL). This was an ambitious task, the result of which was to require constant updating, and which was never to be compatible with the Commodity Control List of proscribed goods—not technologies —maintained by the Department of Commerce.

Whereas the 1969 Act had limited control of the intangible to technical data (and had left the term undefined), the Regulations accompanying the 1979 Act defined technical data very widely as unclassified information of any kind relating to any industrial process, including services. [25] What remained unchanged, however, were the basic mechanisms by which exports of technology, including information, were to be controlled. Precisely the same regulations and licensing procedures were to be applied to exports of information as to exports of hardware. Information was to be treated just like any other good.

The usual aim of technology transfer policy is to stimulate the flow of technological information so that best, or at least better, practice may be brought to laggard firms or developing nations. Because of the nature of information, it is a task which often encounters failure, but the inverse—preventing the flow of information—is even more problematic. It would be a mighty challenge with tools specific to the task: mechanisms intended to prevent the export of equipment are not suited to the task. Other legislation and regulation also attempt to control information by inappropriate means. Copyright laws, investing property rights for half a century, are really not appropriate to the transient value of computer software; the patent system is not suited to the pace of high-technology industry; privacy legislation struggles to cope with computer databanks and data transfer by telecommunications. There was certainly no lack of precedent for the clumsy application of legislation and regulation to technological information. This is not to suggest that elements within the Department of Defense naïvely applied inappropriate mechanisms to the control of information. It is to suggest that these elements may well have been aware of just how inappropriate the mechanisms were, and of the advantages that lay in being able to reinforce them precisely because they failed to control information, this being justified by the ostensible success of the same mechanisms in the control of equipment. The export control saga is remarkable not so much for demonstrating failure to control information—for this was inevitable—but as an example of the costs and benefits which this failure, and continuing attempts to remedy it, bestowed on so many.

PROBLEMS IN IMPLEMENTATION

All governments find it necessary to classify some information. This may be morally distasteful, but that is not the issue here. In the United States, the Invention Secrecy Act of 1951 allows the Patent and Trademark Office to claim for the government information contained in patent applications. No explanation need be given to inventors and any compensation must be sought in the courts. In fact, fewer than 300 secrecy orders are issued annually, though defence agencies did review about 5 per cent of patent applications filed in 1979, [26] and DOD has since argued that the Act empowers it to exploit any sequestered patents. [27] The Atomic Energy Act of 1954 also allows the government—this time the Department of Energy—to classify information pertaining to nuclear weapons and atomic energy. Then there is the Arms Export Control Act of 1976, under which the State Department may try to control the export of information relating to items on the Munitions List. Just occasionally, the government's constitutional powers to restrict free speech are challenged on First Amendment grounds, usually with the conclusion that concessions are necessary for the sake of national security. Though there is some administrative discretion over what action may be taken, this range of legislation does, at least, limit this action to patent, nuclear, and munitions information.

Restrictions on the export of information under the Export Administration Act of 1979 have no such limitation. [28] They can be applied to any information relating to any industrial process, and transmitted in any way, including orally. Moreover, the limitations to executive discretion built into the Act are largely ineffectual. For example, although information may not be subject to controls if it is already available overseas—a circumstance which may be hard to prove when exact equivalence is demanded—the President may decide that controls should be enforced anyway on the grounds that there is risk to foreign policy or national security. Similarly, while the President is entrusted to consider the impact of controlling information on foreign policy, on the attitudes of other countries, and on the competitiveness and reputation of American industry, and must consider even whether controls are enforceable in practice, he is bound to do no more than consider and, having considered, may then do what he likes.

The basic legislation of 1979, amended in 1985, provided administrators with the means and the authority to work through regulation without recourse to further legislation. Faced with inevitable uncertainty about what information should be controlled, cautious bureaucrats quite naturally chose to exercise their authority widely, an authority which had been growing anyway in response to recognition that existing regulations could not cope with the problems presented by information.

[S]ome government administrators and policy makers believe that knowledge should be hoarded and traded like any other commodity . . . this kind of thinking is wrong because it mistakes the profound practical differences between controlling traffic in information ideas and controlling traffic in commodities. [29]

While equipment can be exported in only one way—by physically transporting it—information can travel by many means. In the form of books or blueprints—or even equipment (in as much as hardware may reveal information about its construction)

—it may be physically transported, but it may also be transferred through telecommunications, in people's heads, in the media, by means of lectures, or simply in conversation. Such a plethora of means of communication presented those who administered controls on information with enormous difficulties, and perhaps with enormous opportunities. Their efforts allowed interference in a wide range of areas which would normally have been beyond the purview of any single department. To those with the authority to control any information relating to any industrial process, transmitted in any way, virtually nowhere is out of bounds. Moreover, their interference was justified on the strongest of all possible grounds—national security.

With the failure of successive attempts to control the export of technological information came pressure for greater powers to stanch the flow. With the application of these greater powers came growing complaint that while the flow of technological information to the East remained uninterrupted, considerable damage had been inflicted upon information channels within the United States and on information flow in high-technology industry throughout the West. In as much as Bucy's observation is correct—that information is the core of technology—and as innovation withers without information, it is indeed possible that Western, and particularly American, technological and innovative capacity were damaged.

In theory, controlling the flow of 'know how' is a much more powerful defense than controlling product exports. But every time we make that decision, by classifying the knowledge, we pay a high price in slowed innovation rate. [30]

CONTROL OF INFORMATION WITHIN
THE UNITED STATES

The nature of information means that US authorities could never recover illegal exports of information. Once it had left the country, it was lost for ever—though the United States still retained the information, of course. But information did not have to be exported to be irrecoverable; a change of medium within the United States could produce the same result. Thus, a foreign student or conference delegate might absorb information within the United States and export it with him on his departure. A DOD directive of 1984 is quite explicit in its recognition of the problem.

Because public disclosure of technical data subject to this Directive is tantamount to providing uncontrolled foreign access, withholding such data from public disclosure, unless approved, authorized, or licensed in accordance with export control laws, is necessary and in the national interest. [31]

The Export Administration Regulations deemed to be exported any information transferred to an alien within the United States or to an American intending to take it abroad. [32] So, foreigners and those who had dealings with foreigners had to be separated from proscribed information even within the United States. Conferences on a variety of technical subjects barred foreign delegates at the behest of the authorities, [33] and the occasional foreign delegate was led away in handcuffs. [34] Even allied nationals were refused entry to the President's special colloquium on superconductivity in July 1987 on the grounds that there was no guarantee that they would not disclose American information to undesirable aliens once they had returned home. [35] Visas were denied to those thought to be seeking technological information, [36] and communist diplomats were no longer allowed to enter designated high-technology regions. [37] Universities were pressed to refuse foreign students entry to some courses and access to some equipment, particularly awkward when a quarter of all American doctoral degrees in science, and 60 per cent in engineering, are awarded to non-citizens. [38]

These so called exchange students run around 35 years old, on the average, and they are always skilled in highly technical areas—electronics, physics, that sort of thing.... [American exchange students] average 22 years of age and are studying Russian history, the history of the icon, that sort of junk. [39]

Dr Bryen [deputy to Richard Perle], who directs the Pentagon's efforts to regulate the flow of strategically important high technology products, added, 'If you are not willing to sell the computers but give them access to the machines on your own soil, you have lost the whole export control battle in one swoop'. [40]

Not surprisingly, these procedures encountered some opposition. Foreigners were nonplussed and dismayed by what acquired

the sobriquet of the 'noforn' (no foreigners) policy. Most opposition, however, came from the American academic community,
a group which lives by creating, assembling, and disseminating
information. It argued, with surprising cohesion for such a
diverse multitude, that science is stultified by secrecy and that
national security is best served by using information rather than
by keeping it secret; that it is wiser to advance the leader than
to seek to delay the pursuer. Others among the academics had
been more pragmatic: in 1982, a committee of the National Academy of Sciences had conceded in the Corson Report that there
would always be some information that should be classified, that
grey areas were inevitable, and that co-operation with the authorities was in the best interest of all. [41] Interestingly, and significantly, the business community tended to echo the intellectual
objections of the academics: [42] secrecy in research is dangerous
in that it stunts knowledge growth and innovation, and, however limited initially, spreads inexorably and insidiously. The
foreboding of business was to prove well founded.

There was at least one field in which the need for secrecy was
widely accepted and in which there was compliance through
general co-operation. Perhaps because so much of their funding came from military sources, the cryptographers had been
fairly guarded in their objections to government seizures of their
patents and censorship of their conference presentations. They
adopted a voluntary code of practice whereby their research was
reviewed by the National Security Agency before publication. [43]
Distinctive as cryptography is—a perfect candidate for one of
Bucy's critical technologies—even it cannot be segregated from
other fields and civilian applications. Much less could biotechnology, and the Pentagon's interest in restricting information
flow in this whole subject area met with enormous opposition from the commercial world as well as from the academic
community. [44]

EXTENSION OF CONTROLS

The business and academic communities were right to fear that
controls on information would be contagious. In April 1982, Executive Order 12356 permitted government agencies to classify any
government-funded research, without having to identify a specific

risk to national security or to balance national security against public interest. [45] Unlike previous orders, this one urged classification whenever there was bureaucratic doubt, and it permitted indefinite classification, and reclassification of declassified material and material that had already been made public. The prospect filled even the historians with alarm. [46] In March 1983, National Security Decision Directive 84 forced government employees and contractors with access to certain categories of information to sign lifetime pre-publication review agreements. [47] Growing appreciation of the need to keep cats in bags brought mounting pressure for official review of research before publication and, even in areas of no obvious military relevance, for published research to be sanitized. The following comes from a research contract offered to Harvard University by the National Institute of Education and relates to research on housing issues.

The contractor shall not disclose any confidential information obtained in the performance of this contract. Any presentation of any statistical or any analytical material or reports based on information obtained from studies covered by this contract will be subject to review by the Government's project officer before publication or dissemination for accuracy of factual data and interpretation. [48]

Just as it was claimed that the commercial costs of export controls on equipment could not be of any magnitude because so few applications for export were actually denied, so it was argued that information flow within the United States and the West could hardly be harmed because so little information was actually classified. Thus, ran the argument, the vast majority of information flowed as it always did.

The US has been pictured as seeking to control the transfer of technology to Western nations by limiting attendance at open scientific meetings to US citizens. . . . These articles and reports have blown out of proportion a limited number of isolated incidents. . . . There are, depending on what one counts, some 3,500 major scientific and technical conferences held each year in the US. Over the last 5 years, we have been able to identify less than 20 such conferences from which non-US citizens were excluded either in whole or in part. [49]

But information is not like other goods and the incidence of classification is no indicator of the real impact of attempts to control information. There were opportunity costs—of research not tackled, of papers not published, of contacts not made,' of information not gathered and used. [50]

Now the technical societies are finding that scientists and engineers are bowing out of presentations at conferences just to avoid trouble, not because there is any real technology transfer problem. [51]

There was also a more subtle cost: information packages comprise bits of information that fit together rather than stray bits, and it is the gathering of bits of information and their assembly into packages that creates innovation. Defense declared that the Soviet bloc was employing what it dubbed a 'mosaic' approach to the collection of information, acquiring a bit here and a bit there and gradually assembling these bits to form a pattern. [52] This observation is remarkable for its demonstration of the grasp of information that Defense was beginning to acquire, and because this was precisely what the Soviet bloc was doing. In 1985, an unusual report was circulated in Washington; [53] the author is not named, but the report came from the CIA, which had somewhat belatedly received information from the French intelligence services following the defection of a Russian agent, codenamed—appropriately, it would seem, given his mysterious fate—'Farewell'. The report, released at the express insistence of the Director of the CIA, William Casey, presented in vast and authoritative detail Soviet systems for the collection of technological information in the West.

Over 3,500 specific collection requirements for hardware and documents were satisfied over the 12 industrial ministries ... About 50 per cent of more than 30,000 pieces of Western one-of-a-kind military and dual-use hardware and about 20 percent of over 400,000 technical documents collected worldwide in response to these requirements were used to improve the technical performance of very large numbers of Soviet military equipment and weapon systems. [54]

Sophisticated as these systems were, what was more remarkable was that nearly all of them were quite legal. The Soviet bloc was much less concerned with stealing information than with problems inherent in dealing with information, problems of matching supply to demand, of finding, acquiring, and fitting information that was already in the public domain. Only when these efforts failed was there resort to the illegal acquisition of information. In short, the Soviet bloc was at least addressing the issue of information transaction while the West chose to restrict its attention to information transfer. For example, while the Soviet bloc took vast trouble trying to ensure that the supply of Western information met specific demands, the West showed little interest in tailoring its controls to Soviet information requirements or to the abilities of Soviet industries to use the information. Calculations made by the DOD had the single purpose of proving how much the Soviet bloc would gain from Western technological information: had a sample of 79 licence applications not been refused in 1983–4, the Soviet bloc would have saved between $6 billion and $12 billion through improved automated production and control equipment alone, and would have been able to 'release' between 20 and 35 million workers. [55] Fig. 7.1, showing the targeting of US universities in response to Soviet demand for specific information, and Table 7.1, outlining the performance of the Military Industrial Commission (VPK) in acquiring Western technological information, give some impression of how much more considered was the procuring of information than the protecting of information.

It was to guard against computer power being used to piece together odd bits of information that the Soviet bloc was denied electronic access to the medical database, Medline, from 1982. [56] Even though the Freedom of Information Act does not permit access to classified information, and has not allowed foreigners access to sensitive information since 1985, [57] it was still considered by some to supply enough pieces of information to allow diligent construction into useful packages. [58] On the same grounds, the FBI asked public librarians to report frequent usage of specialist collections by suspicious aliens. [59]

The FBI has documented instances for more than a decade of hostile intelligence officers who have exploited libraries by stealing proprietary, sensitive, and other information and attempting to identify and recruit American and foreign students in American libraries. [60]

The assumption was that only the bad guys picked up stray bits of information, while the good guys somehow received their information whole. Action taken to prevent the Soviet bloc collecting bits of information also made innovation in the West more difficult. For example, all foreigners—not just those from

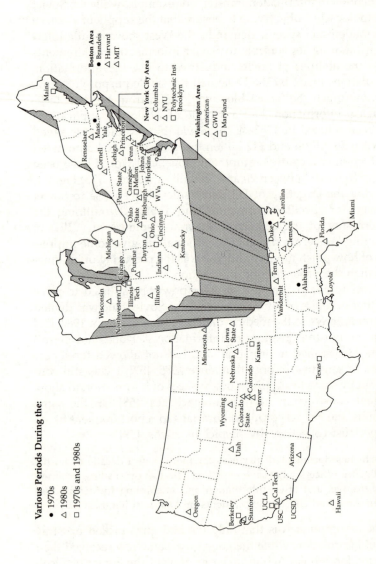

Various Periods During the:

● 1970s
△ 1980s
□ 1970s and 1980s

Boston Area
● Brandeis
△ Harvard
△ MIT

New York City Area
△ Columbia
□ NYU
□ Polytechnic Inst
   Brooklyn

Washington Area
△ American
△ GWU
□ Maryland

FIG. 7.1 Targeting of US universities

Source: Central Intelligence Agency, *Soviet Acquisition of Militarily Significant Western Technology: An Update* (Washington DC, September 1985).

TABLE 7.1 The VPK Acquisition Programme in 1980

Acquisition tasks in effect	3,617
Acquisition tasks completed	1,085
Material acquired	
samples	4,000
documents	25,000
Material studied	
samples	4,052
documents	25,453
Material found useful	
samples	3,167
documents	8,836
Material used in R&D, innovation, and production	
samples	2,152
documents	4,692
Economic effect of material found useful (million roubles)	407.5
New R&D and experimental design projects started because of material found useful	200
R&D and experimental design projects improved because of material found useful	3,396
Projects or stages of projects eliminated or accelerated because of material found useful	1,458

Source: Philip Hanson, *Soviet Industrial Espionage: Some New Information*, Royal Institute of International Affairs, Discussion Paper 1 (London, 1987), 31.

the Soviet bloc—came to be denied access to many reports held in the world's largest technology repository, the National Technical Information Service, and even to some of the Ph.D. theses collected by University Microfilms. With guile and perseverance, such obstacles to the acquisition of information could often be overcome, but at the risk of transgressing US law, a serious matter for those in the West outside the United States, but of little consequence to those in the Soviet bloc.

IMPLICATIONS FOR INNOVATION

The threat to academic freedom aroused some interest in the United States, but nothing compared with the more prosaic concern for the competitiveness of American industry, and especially its capacity to innovate. The Department of Commerce argued that export controls imposed costs on US industry and

Basic Technologies	US Superior	US/USSR Equal	USSR Superior
1. Aerodynamics/Fluid Dynamics		•	
2. Computers and Software		←—•	
3. Conventional Warhead (including all Chemical Explosives)		•	
4. Directed Energy (Laser)		•	
5. Electro-Optical Sensor (including Infrared)	•—→		
6. Guidance and Navigation	•—→		
7. Life Sciences (Human Factor/ Genetic Engineering)	•		
8. Materials (Lightweight, High Strength, High Temperature)	•—→		
9. Micro-Electronic Materials and Integrated Circuit Manufacturing	•—→		
10. Nuclear Warhead		•	
11. Optics	•—→		
12. Power Sources (Mobile) (Includes Energy Storage)		•	
13. Production/Manufacturing (Includes Automated Control)	•		
14. Propulsion (Aerospace and Ground Vehicles)	•—→		
15. Radar Sensor	•—→		
16. Robotics and Machine Intelligence	•		
17. Signal Processing	•		
18. Signature Reduction (Stealth)	•		
19. Submarine Detection	•		
20. Telecommunication (includes Fibre Optics)	•		

FIG. 7.2 East–West technology gap

Source: Richard Dehauer, *The FY 1985 Department of Defense Program for Research Development and Aquisition* (Washington DC, 1984).

was anxious to minimize these costs. Defense argued that the costs in terms of national security of not having effective export controls were so huge that US industry simply had to bear whatever was imposed on it. A study commissioned by Stephen Bryen, for which Richard Perle wrote the introduction, estimated that, without effective export controls, US defence expenditure would have to be increased by between $20 billion and $50 billion a year. [61] The calculation and argument were unequivocal: the transfer of US information ensured its transformation into Soviet hardware; unless this was prevented, the technology gap essential for national security could be maintained only through vastly greater R&D spending. Fig. 7.2 gives some idea of just how entrenched was this mercantilist attitude towards information.

US industry was not convinced. In high-technology industry, with its dependence on the rapid gathering and assembly of information, concern was especially acute. Bobby Inman, some-time Admiral, Deputy Director of the CIA, and Director of the National Security Agency, the man who had coined the cliché 'haemorrhage of technology' in his rush to fuel the export control debate, and who argued for review of research not only before publication, but before projects commenced, [62] rapidly changed his attitude towards constraints on information when he entered high-technology industry as Director of the Micro-electronics and Computer Technology Corporation. Inman became a member of the panel responsible for the NAS report which, in 1987, gave the first detailed estimation of the commercial costs of export controls. [63] An industry survey and investigation of licence applications submitted to the Department of Commerce suggested that these costs amounted to $9.3 billion and 188,000 lost jobs in 1985. [64] Of these direct costs, only $1.4 billion was incurred through lost trade with the Soviet bloc: $5.9 billion was attributable to lost trade with the West as allied firms reacted to US extraterritoriality claims by 'designing out' American prod-ucts. The report was unable to quantify indirect costs, though its investigations did suggest that the costs of uncertainty and of disrupted information flow were likely to be high.

Essential to high technology is information flow, both within and without the innovating organization, and often along per-sonal and informal information channels. Consider the impact on the functioning of these information networks of, say, a cru-sade to ferret out high-technology spies, [65] or a 'walls have ears' campaign.

You have got to question about the validity of the firms you are deal-ing with, especially a foreign firm. Go to the FBI, ask questions. The FBI have recently sought to publicize their efforts in this problem in our particular area by putting up billboards similar to the World War II type of thing about walls having ears. [66]

Zealous officials determined that small high-technology firms were particularly likely to leak information, [67] and tried to prevent the very sort of information exchange that makes high-technology industry so very innovative.

Corporate executives and leaders of the business community must not only be understanding of the need for compliance and be supportive of the government's export control efforts, they must translate this state of mind into effective action by their company staff, managers and supervisors. [68]

Modern economies are information-intensive and are probably becoming more so. Their high-technology sectors are distinguished by a voracious appetite for information and a facility for information consumption. Yet the channels along which information flows both within and without high-technology organizations are delicate things, easily blocked and diverted, the networks distorted. Once again, it is not that vast quantities of information are likely to be stopped, but that the risk of stoppage and interference discourages information from flowing. And again, the absence of a single bit of information renders the information package incomplete and unusable. In the case of high-technology industry, so rapid is the pace of innovation that even the late arrival of a missing bit has precisely the same effect. [69]

It is correct, inevitable and regrettable that restriction of technology transfer must lead to restriction of technological information: technology *is* information. But we have some reason to be apprehensive about rules formulated in this area. So much technology lies in people's heads. Most foreseeable rules are going to ask them to put a fence down the middle of their minds and be careful at all times, know and remember to whom they are talking and just what they are supposed to know and not know. We have all had to do this in our time, but it is a mental burden. This is tolerable for limited numbers of people in limited circumstances. It becomes almost intolerable if spread over the vast range of people knowledgeable about dual-purpose technologies and it is an intolerable handicap to the kind of free-wheeling discussions over a beer which generate so many scientific and technical advances [emphasis in original]. [70]

Calculating the impact of restrictions on information flow involves trying to measure what is missing—whether it be information itself or the innovations that arise from its use. This is no easy task; it is easier to reveal damage to the means by which information flows than the absence of information itself. Perhaps the greylist is the best example of how export controls disrupted relationships among firms, and hence the transactions which underlie the transfer of information for innovation.

The 1985 Amendments to the 1979 Export Administration Act, already prolonged for two years under the President's emergency powers, extended the penalties for the contravention of export controls and gave Defense further responsibility for enforcement. [71] If it were not to lose all influence, Commerce had to become as hawkish as Defense in export control matters. Commerce was responsible for exacting penalties from infringing firms and individuals, ranging from hefty fines and imprisonment, removal of the right to export from the US, and inclusion on the List of Denials, a compilation of firms with which other firms were not allowed to trade on pain of incurring the same penalty. This blacklist never contained more than about 300 firms and was widely available. The greylist was longer and it was secret.

The Office of Export Administration [in the Department of Commerce] reviews every incoming licence application through a computerised process that flags the names of persons and companies on which the department has adverse information or other enforcement concerns. Literally thousands of such names are now contained in the department's computers. [72]

In true mosaic fashion, information for the greylist came from a multiplicity of sources, [73] but by far the most prolific was firms themselves. The Department of Commerce issued a Red Flag checklist of signs of perfidy for which licence applicants were to be on their guard when they were dealing with customers and trying to determine the end use to which their technology would be put (Fig. 7.3). Firms were expected to report any suspicions.

The Office of Export Enforcement [in the Department of Commerce] has fostered a relationship with the private sector which encourages extensive business community cooperation in identifying and preventing potential illegal export transactions . . . Many of our most significant cases are now developed as a result of leads given to Commerce by the private sector. [74]

The greylist affected thousands of firms directly, and indirectly every firm which had anything to do with advanced technology. Bits of information accumulated without a firm's

U.S. DEPARTMENT OF COMMERCE
International Trade Administration
Office of Export Enforcement
Washington, D.C 20230

INDICATIONS OF POTENTIAL ILLEGAL EXPORTS

Listed below are some of the "red flag" indications that signal possible illegal exports or diversions. The listing is not exhaustive; it is provided by the Department of Commerce, Office of Export Enforcement (OEE), as an aid to further public awareness and the private sector's effort to combat illegal exportation of U.S. commodities and technology.

- Customer's/purchaser's agent reluctance to provide end-use or end-user information

- Performance/design requirements incompatible with destination country resources or environment, or with consignee's line of business

- Stated end-use incompatible with the customary or known industrial applications for the equipment being purchased

- Stated end-use incompatible with consignee line of business

- Stated end-use incompatible with the technical capability of the consignee or destination country

- Customer's willingness to pay cash for a large value item or order

- Little or no customer business background information available

- Apparent lack of customer familiarity with the commodity's performance/ design characteristics or uses

- Customer's/purchasing agent's declination of installation or service contracts that are normally accepted in similar transactions

- Ill-defined delivery dates or the use of delivery locations inconsistent with type of commodity or established practices

- Use of freight forwarders as unltimate consignees

- Use of intermediate consignees(s) whose location/business is incompatible with purported end-user's nature of business or location

- Packaging or packing requirements inconsistent with shipping mode and or destination

- Evasive responses to questions regarding any of the above as well as whether equipment is for domestic use, export or reexport

> For further information or advice regarding enforcement of the Export Administration Act, contact your nearest OEE field office or the OEE Washington, D.C. Headquarters.

OFFICE OF EXPORT ENFORCEMENT FIELD OFFICES

Los Angeles (Burbank) (818) 904-6019   San Francisco (San Jose) (408) 291-4204
New York (212) 264-1365   Washington, D.C. (Springfield, VA) (703) 487-4950

OFFICE OF EXPORT ENFORCEMENT HEADQUARTERS

Washington, D.C. (202) 377-4608 or (800) 621-2990 (Toll-free)

FIG. 7.3   Red Flag checklist

knowledge, and sometimes mere hearsay, could be evidence enough for a firm to be greylisted. Ignorant of its new status, the greylisted firm would find that any licence application with which it was associated encountered difficulties; it would find

TABLE 7.2 Attitudes of European, Japanese, and Australian Firms towards the Greylist

	yes	no	don't know/ no opinion
Firm has been fined or punished by US export control authorities (103 firms)	3	98	2
Firm suspects it is on the greylist (104 firms)	4	96	4
Firm suspects suppliers or customers are on the greylist (101 firms)	18	78	5
Firm would refuse to do business with a firm it suspects is greylisted (103 firms)	60	10	33

business slowing down, and that other firms were increasingly reluctant to do business at all. Inexorably, word would spread that something was not quite right about the firm, that it was best avoided.

[I]t is quite difficult to elicit from my clients and members of the coalition that I represent hard evidence of the Gray list, because these people have a tremendous stake in the licensing system, and they, like we, do not want to shoot themselves in the foot by stepping forward and pointing fingers. Nonetheless, the Gray list is there, and I don't frankly know how you deal with the Gray List. I don't know how you deal with an unwritten insidious process that could be manifested in any number of ways on a day-to-day basis. [75]

Official acknowledgement of a greylist was rare; this, and its method of compilation, made complaints from firms rarer still. Yet, US firms which had anything to do with advanced technology knew all about it, and foreign firms rapidly came to find out. Table 7.2 is from a survey, conducted in 1989, of European, Japanese, and Australian firms involved with advanced technology. [76]

US CONTROLS ON INFORMATION OVERSEAS

The United States claimed jurisdiction over all information of American origin no matter where that information was, nor how

Export Regulations Apply to Everyone!

SO BEFORE YOU DECIDE THIS MESSAGE ISN'T FOR YOU, TAKE A LOOK AT THESE SITUATIONS:

- One Varian employee does a favor for a second by providing emergency first aid to a customer in another country whose equipment is down. He stuffs in his briefcase printed circuit boards and a 64K memory expansion device to make the repair and hops on a plane.

- A product engineer mails production specifications and blueprints to his counterpart in one of Varian's foreign manufacturing facilities.

- A research engineer presents a paper in Palo Alto containing Varian technical data at a conference attended by foreign nationals.

- A domestic field representative receives an order from a new customer who has no apparent need for the equipment.

- A manufacturing engineer discussing Varian production capabilities with a foreign national finds himself talking about basic design parameters of the equipment.

- A service engineer takes his service kit, which contains licensable components, into a foreign country.

varian

FIG. 7.4 Compliance leaflet issued to Varian employees
Source: Published with the kind permission of Varian Associates, Inc.

mingled it had become with other information. [77] It had no choice: there was no point prohibiting the export of information from the United States to the Soviet bloc if the same information was available to the Soviet bloc from other countries. Though many foreign firms (if rarely their governments) objected to the extraterritorial application of American law, the consequences of disobeying export control laws could be catastrophic and they could hardly afford not to comply. [78] For large firms, this frequently meant the introduction of their own compliance procedures, detailed in company manuals which guided employees through the licensing process and which explained the ways in which their behaviour and work practices had to comply with American law. Fig. 7.4 is part of a leaflet supplied by one firm to all its employees. US authorities inspected firms overseas to check that their compliance procedures were satisfactory and being implemented. The task was horrendous and its execution not wholly popular with foreign governments. Inevitably, US export control authorities conceded that they could not seek to control the flow of information directly. What they could do, though, was delegate this responsibility to firms, monitoring not the information itself, but the means by which it was handled. Failure to install and implement approved means was treated as evidence of reluctance or inability to protect information and was treated accordingly.

This buck-passing solved none of the problems inherent in trying to control the flow of information. Firms had no real idea how strictly they had to comply. Terrified of the punishment for non-compliance, many played very safe indeed. Take, for example, the assurance sought by Texas Instruments from its customers in Britain that they would reveal no more about TI equipment than appeared in the company's operating manuals.

We hereby assure Texas Instruments Limited that unless prior authorisation is obtained from the competent authorities of the Government of the United States of America, we shall not knowingly:

(i) re-export, directly or indirectly, any technical data (as defined in Part 379 of the Export Administration Regulations of the United States Department of Commerce) received from Texas Instruments Limited, or

(ii) disclosure [*sic*] such technical data for use in, or

(iii) export, directly or indirectly, any direct product of such technical data. . . . [79]

Or take the example of International Computers Limited, whose legal opinion was that even 1 per cent American content (rather than the 10 per cent or 25 per cent working level that the Department of Commerce tended to use) rendered British equipment subject to US export control legislation.

The U.S. will assert control over an end product, such as a computer built in the U.K., if such an end product contains a controlled U.S. origin component and the end product, had it been built in the United States, would have been subject to control. This means that, in theory, a large British-built computer containing components costing say, 1 per cent of the total would, nevertheless, be subject to U.S. re-export controls. A U.S. licence is required for the oral disclosure of U.S. origin technical data by a non-U.S. citizen to a Communist end user which occurs outside the United States. Such a situation could arise, for example, where a non-U.S. technical expert acquired controlled U.S. origin technical data as part of training in the U.S. or work on a joint venture with a U.S. company anywhere in the world. Such U.S. control is asserted even where U.S. origin technical data is 'commingled' with non U.S. data. [80]

There were other examples aplenty: students visiting Digital Equipment Corporation training courses in Britain had to sign undertakings that they would not divulge information gathered during their instruction; [81] and the IBM journal, *Technical Directions*, which was distributed to customers and employees, contained the stricture 'Recipients must be US citizens and residents of the United States'. [82] While in the United States it was the government that acted to keep foreign students from advanced equipment, precisely the same result was sought overseas through the commercial contracts imposed on universities by supplying firms. [83]

Even though export controls probably had a more serious effect on the flow of information within the United States than on its flow overseas, US extraterritoriality prompted policy responses that threatened to produce serious and costly distortion in the allocation of resources. It was argued that, as the allies could no longer rely on supplies of technological information from the United States, they must have their own research and development programmes and must strive for technological independence. [84]

Thus, for example, US export controls prompted the North Atlantic Assembly to encourage greater European co-operation in R&D, [85] they justified advice to the European Commission to produce its own supplies of the most critical integrated circuits (an interesting transference of the Bucy concept), [86] and they reinforced arguments presented to the British government for maintaining its own information technology programme. [87]

The argument was quite spurious of course: these days there is no such thing as technological self-sufficiency for nations or for firms. All are interdependent, reliant on flows of information that know neither natural nor national boundaries. Competitors are among the most important of sources and it is with their most serious rivals that many high-technology firms now forge their closest information links. [88] Sometimes this takes the form of vast national research efforts, such as Sematech in the United States or the Alvey Programme in Britain; sometimes the form of strategic alliances with firms across the globe. [89] Such initiatives are supported by a vast infrastructure of formal, semi-formal, and informal information networks, ranging vertically from suppliers through producers to customers, and horizontally from the distributed production systems of multinational companies to discussion among friends in Silicon Valley. Increasingly, these networks, even the local ones, are likely to involve telecommunications and computer links, a means of information transfer that posed an enormous challenge for export controls. The challenge did not go unaccepted. In October 1986, for instance, the Poindexter memorandum was issued under National Security Decision Directive 145 of September 1984, authorizing inspection of unclassified information in telecommunications and automated information systems used by the federal government. [90] The Poindexter approach was to control information before it entered telecommunications and computer systems, to prevent information ever reaching the databases. To do this, it was necessary to create an entirely new official category of 'sensitive' information, [91] a concept that can be traced to the grey-area notion of the Corson Report, and which Corson—yet another who came to appreciate the unfortunate implications of his contribution to the control of information—later referred to as 'creeping greyness'. [92] The concept seemed to have been abandoned in September 1985 with National Security Decision

Directive 189, but then revived in the light of the challenge to information control posed by new technology. [93] The Poindexter memorandum was rapidly rescinded, [94] but it is an interesting example of just how far the authorities were willing to go in their attempts to control information flow.

Once again it could be argued that only a tiny proportion of all information would ever have been classified as sensitive, that only minimal interference with telecommunications and computer systems was ever contemplated. Once again, that is not the point. While the Dresser case—Dresser (France) was refused all access to the corporation's own database in the United States during the pipeline dispute of 1982 [95]—is exceptional, much more common may be a reluctance of firms to rely on distant databanks and unimpeded telecommunications. More generally, in an age when firms depend on network organization to co-ordinate production with other firms, the export control episode is a useful reminder of how vulnerable are information systems which extend beyond the boundaries of the firm.

LESSONS UNLEARNT

In general terms, the policy of the United States government was to deprive the Soviet bloc of technological information while allowing its ready circulation in the West. Implementation of such a policy meant that more and more information became classified.

[A]s attractive and logical as the procedures may be in theory, it is quite easy for a sprawling bureaucracy such as DOD to bungle day to day implementation when the sensitivity of technical information is in the eye of the beholder. . . . it is inherently easier and safer for reviewing officials to overclassify, or place dissemination controls on unclassified information, than to recommend public disclosure. [96]

That interpretation is generous. It offers petty incompetence as an alternative to a grand conspiracy theory that the Department of Defense used an export control strategy to extend its power base. Neither rings quite true. It is evident that elements within the DOD (and occasionally elsewhere) exploited the export control issue and the opportunity it provided to operate in the cause of national security. It is likely that these same elements were alert to the capacity of an information dimension in export controls to broaden their influence yet further. It is much less likely that they were able to anticipate the inexorable progress of attempts to control information. Control was extended from exports of information to information used domestically, from classified to merely sensitive information, from the transfer of information to the means by which it was handled and processed. Inevitably, these attempts to control information met with little success, but each successive failure brought with it justification for a more extreme approach to the problem.

Underlying all the furore over export controls were two assumptions. The lesser was that high technology, however defined, was something of immense value which had to be protected at all costs. It is not unreasonable to see export controls as a branch of high-technology policy and enthusiasm for that is now greatly diminished, not so much because any fundamental lesson has been learnt as because policy for high technology failed to produce the immediate and immense returns that were promised. The greater assumption is evident in the notion of dual-use technology; this went far beyond the idea that certain technology had both civilian and military applications. The reality is that innovation in civilian technology has far outpaced that in military technology, especially by the time military technology is in service. The reality is also that national security is recognized as being as much a matter of economic strength as of military might. The technological decline of the United States in the eighties relative to Japan generated much concern that was nearly always expressed in battlefield terms. It is no coincidence that punishment of the Japanese firm, Toshiba, was among the most severe meted out by the United States. [97] Export controls were intended as much to address this problem—to reassert the technological dominance of the United States, or at least to reassure Americans of this dominance and hence of their national security—as they were to contain the military strength of the Soviet bloc.

In all this, the role of information was crucial. This is evident in the Bucy Report, of course, in the way that elements within DOD exploited the characteristics of information, in the protests of some academics, and eventually in the appreciation by firms of the damage being done to their own capacity to innovate. But

national security export controls were not regarded as an information issue in the eighties any more than they are now. Though
CoCom and the communist threat are no more, the United
States—and other nations—still apply such controls to deny
technological information to a vast range of destinations considered to be undesirable. As a commercial weapon, controls on
the export of dual-use technological information are as powerful as ever. They continue to influence information transfer and
transactions. It is important that the extent of this influence and
its implications are appreciated. An information perspective is
of some assistance in this appreciation.

REFERENCES

1. See Stuart Macdonald, 'Control, chaos and dear old CoCom', *Leaders*, 13:2 (1990), 164–6.
2. Stuart Macdonald, *Technology and the Tyranny of Export Controls. Whisper Who Dares* (Macmillan, London, 1990).
3. Philip Hanson, 'Western technology in the Soviet economy', *Problems of Communism*, 27:6 (1978), 30.
4. Morris Bornstein, *The Transfer of Western Technology to the USSR* (OECD, Paris, 1985), 135.
5. A. V. Lowe, 'Export controls: a European viewpoint', *International Journal of Technology Management*, 3:1/2 (1988), 71–85.
6. Department of Defense Science Board Task Force on Export of US Technology, *An Analysis of Export Control of US Technology—a DOD Perspective* (Bucy Report) (Office of the Director of Defense Research and Engineering, Washington, DC, Feb. 1976).
7. National Academy of Sciences, National Academy of Engineering, and Institute of Medicine, *Balancing the National Interest: US National Security Export Controls and Global Economic Competition* (National Academy Press, Washington, DC, 1987) and *Finding Common Ground: U.S. Export Controls in a Changed Global Environment* (National Academy Press, Washington, DC, 1991).
8. J. Fred Bucy, 'Revolutionary and evolutionary technology', *Vital Speeches of the Day*, 52:22 (1986), 698–701. *Cf.* J. Fred Bucy, 'Going, going, goooonnnnne', *New York Times*, 11 Sept. 1976.
9. Fred Bucy as quoted in Willie Schatz, 'The hitch in high tech trade', *Datamation*, 29:10 (Oct. 1983), 148–59.

10. Bucy Report, p. iii.
11. Permanent Committee on Investigations, Committee on Governmental Affairs, Senate Hearings, *Transfer of United States High Technology to the Soviet Union and Soviet Bloc Nations* (USGPO, Washington, DC, May 1982), 131.
12. Quoted in John Rees, 'William Von Raab', *Review of the News*, 25 Jan. 1984, 39–43, 45–8.
13. Orr Kelly, 'High-tech hemorrhage from US to Soviet Union', *US News and World Report*, 7 May 1984, 47–8.
14. See Geoff Conrad, 'The clowns are on at the US exports circus', *Datalink*, 30 July 1984.
15. Mark Hosenball and Jim Fallon, 'DoD to use CPU seizures to win more export control', *Electronic News*, 26 Dec. 1983, 12.
16. 'Too much', *Time*, 2 Jan. 1984, 59.
17. Richard Cross, 'Customs "sting" foils Soviets with high-tech switch', *Albany Knickerbocker News*, 21 May 1984, 1.
18. William Smith, 'The technobandits', *Time*, 23 Nov. 1987, 61.
19. Joseph Fitchett, 'US agents track high-tech smugglers along shadowy trail to Moscow', *International Herald Tribune*, 21 May 1984, 5.
20. Scott Sullivan, 'High-tech Soviet spies', *Newsweek*, 11 Nov. 1985, 30.
21. Bucy Report, p. iii.
22. Ibid. 3.
23. Richard Perle, 'The eastward technology flow: a plan of common action', *Strategic Review*, Spring 1984, 29.
24. Clyde H. Farnsworth, 'Pentagon's wider role on exports', *New York Times*, 21 Mar. 1984, D1.
25. Patrick J. Monahan, 'The regulation of technical data under the Arms Export Control Act of 1976 and the Export Administration Act of 1979: a matter of executive discretion', *Boston College International and Comparative Law Review*, 6:1 (1983), 169–97.
26. Stephen H. Unger, 'National security and the free flow of technological information', in Harold C. Relyea (ed.), *Striking a Balance: National Security and Scientific Freedom. First Discussions* (American Association for the Advancement of Science, Committee on Scientific Freedom and Responsibility, Washington, DC, May 1985), 29–46.
27. 'Army hopes to use technology in pending patents for DOD purposes', *Inside the Pentagon*, 10 July 1987, 2.
28. Monahan, 'The regulation of technical data'.
29. Mary Cheh, 'Government control of private ideas', in Relyea (ed.), *Striking a Balance*, 17.
30. Testimony of Lewis M. Branscomb before Senate Judiciary Committee Subcommittee on Technology and Law, 16 Mar. 1988.

31. 'Withholding of unclassified technical data from public disclosure', Department of Defense Directive 5230.25, 6 Nov. 1984, para. D2.
32. Department of Commerce, *Export Administration Regulations*, 1 Oct. 1984, pt. 379, p. 1.
33. 'Science and the citizen', *Scientific American*, July 1984, 66; 'Restrictions on technical papers raise concerns', *Aviation Week and Space Technology*, 17 Jan. 1983, 22–3; 'Pentagon blocks papers at scientific meeting', *Chemical and Engineering News*, 13 Sept. 1982, 6.
34. Colin Norman, 'To catch a spy', *Science*, 222 (25 Nov. 1983), 904–5.
35. Letter from Robert L. Park in *Issues in Science and Technology*, 4:2 (Winter 1988), 10.
36. 'Denying visas to stop technology export', *Science News*, 123 (14 May 1983), 310.
37. 'Silicon Valley off limits to Soviets', *San Jose Mercury*, 20 Nov. 1983, 1A, 24A; Steve Magagnini, 'Where Russians can't go', *San Francisco Chronicle*, 21 Nov. 1983, 2.
38. 'Embarrassment of riches', *Scientific American*, May 1988, 16.
39. Robert Gast as quoted in John Raess, 'Silicon Valley: a tempting espionage target', *Peninsula Times Tribune*, 12 May 1983.
40. David E. Sanger, 'U.S. to try to bar aliens from supercomputers', *New York Times*, 30 July 1985, A14.
41. National Academy of Sciences, *Scientific Communication and National Security* (NAS Press, Washington, DC, 1982). See also Rosemary Chalk, 'Commentary on the NAS report', *Science, Technology and Human Values*, 8:1 (1983), 21–4.
42. 'An ominous shift to secrecy', *Business Week*, 18 Oct. 1982, 138–42.
43. David Schwartz, 'Scientific freedom and national security: a case study of cryptography', in Relyea (ed.), *Striking a Balance*, 68–74.
44. See Stephen Budiansky, 'Administration hints at clampdown on biotechnology exports', *Nature*, 309 (31 May 1984), 389; David Sanger, 'Pentagon seeks curbs on biotechnology flow', *New York Times*, 11 July 1985, D1, D6.
45. 'Smothered, by a security blanket', *New York Times*, 12 Apr. 1982, A22; Dorothy Nelkin, 'Intellectual property: the control of scientific information', *Science*, 216 (14 May 1982), 704–8; Robert A. Rosenbaum *et al.*, 'Academic freedom and the classified information system', *Science*, 219 (21 Jan. 1983), 257–9.
46. Constance Holden, 'Historians deplore classification rules', *Science*, 222 (16 Dec. 1983), 1215, 1218.
47. John Shattuck, 'Federal restrictions and the free flow of academic information and ideas', *Government Information Quarterly*, 3:1 (1986), 5–29.
48. Academic contract offered by the National Institute of Education, quoted in John Shattuck, 'Federal restrictions and the free flow of

academic ideas and information, *Government Information Quarterly*, 3:1 (1986), 9.

49. 'US policies on scientific communication', memorandum from US delegation to OECD, Paris, 1 July 1985.

50. See 'Restrictions on technical papers raise concerns', 22.

51. William H. Gregory, 'The technology transfer mess', *Aviation Week and Space Technology*, 14 May 1984, 13.

52. See John Shattuck and Muriel Morisey Spence, *Government Information Controls: Implications for Scholarship, Science and Technology*, Association of American Universities working paper, Mar. 1988.

53. Central Intelligence Agency, *Soviet Acquisition of Militarily Significant Western Technology: An Update* (Washington, DC, Sept. 1985).

54. Ibid. 6.

55. Office of the Undersecretary of Defense for Policy, Department of Defense, *Assessing the Effect of Technology Transfer on US/Western Security—A Defense Perspective* (Washington, DC, Feb. 1985).

56. Harold C. Relyea, 'Shrouding the endless frontier—scientific communication and national security: the search for balance', in Relyea (ed.), *Striking a Balance*, 75–124.

57. An Amendment to the Defense Authorization Act denied foreigners access through FOI to sensitive unclassified information that would otherwise require an export licence.

58. 'Secret science', *Scientific American*, 258 (6 June 1988), 14–15.

59. Charles Bremner, 'Librarians shelve FBI demand to report on "spies"', *Times*, 26 May 1988, 9.

60. FBI Library Awareness Program, quoted in *New Yorker*, 30 May 1988, 23.

61. Office of the Undersecretary of Defense for Policy, Department of Defense, *Assessing the Effect of Technology Transfer*.

62. Bobby R. Inman, 'National security and technical information', in Relyea (ed.), *Striking a Balance*, 51–5.

63. National Academy of Sciences *et al.*, *Balancing the National Interest*.

64. For details of the consultants' calculations, see William Finan, *Estimate of Direct Economic Costs Associated with US National Security Controls* (Quick, Finan & Associates, Washington, DC, Dec. 1986); William Finan and Karen Sandberg, *Analysis of the Effects of US National Security Controls on US-Headquartered Industrial Firms* (Quick, Finan & Associates, Washington, DC, Aug. 1986).

65. Peter Dworkin, 'US warms up war on high tech spies', *San Francisco Chronicle*, 22 June 1983; 'FBI swoops in the valley of spies', *New Scientist*, 27 Oct. 1983, 251.

66. Testimony of Douglas Southard, Deputy District Attorney, Santa Clara County in Permanent Subcommittee on Investigations, Committee on Governmental Affairs, Senate Hearings, *Transfer of United*

States High Technology to the Soviet Union and Soviet Bloc Nations (USGPO, Washington, DC, May 1982), 153.

67. William Casey, 'The challenge of American intelligence', speech to Commonwealth Club of California, Palo Alto, 3 Apr. 1984.

68. Theodore Wu, 'The citizen partner: a key force in strategic export control', *Signal*, Aug. 1983, 106–8.

69. Hanns-Dieter Jacobsen, 'High technology in US foreign trade relations', *German Foreign Affairs Review*, 36:4 (1985), 405–17.

70. Raymond Appleyard, 'Intervention', in *Papers Presented at the Workshop on International Technology Transfer: Promotion and Barriers* (Six Countries Programme on Aspects of Government Policies towards Technological Innovation in Industry, Ottawa, May 1985), 6.

71. Lionel Olmer and Richard Elliott, *The US Export Control System: Overview, Trends and Practical Tips* (Paul, Weiss, Rifkind, Wharton and Garrison, Washington, DC, Sept. 1987).

72. Department of Commerce, *Enforcement of US Export Controls* (Washington, DC, Sept. 1986), 7.

73. See Stuart Macdonald, *Strategic Export Controls: Hurting the East or Weakening the West?* (Economist Intelligence Unit, London, 1990).

74. Department of Commerce, *Enforcement of US Export Controls*, 11.

75. John Liebman, evidence presented to House of Representatives Committee on Foreign Affairs, Subcommittee on International Economic Policy and Trade, *Hearings on National Security Export Controls* (USGPO, Washington, DC, 1987), 122–3.

76. The full survey results are presented in Macdonald, *Strategic Export Controls*.

77. Department of Commerce, *Export Administration Regulations*, 1 Oct. 1984, suppl. 1 to pt. 379, pp. 1–6.

78. Kevin Cahill, *Trade Wars* (W. H. Allen, London, 1987).

79. Form accompanying letter from Peter H. Hodge, UK Country Manager, Texas Instruments Limited, May 1984.

80. Jeremy Strachan, 'US trade law: the triple threat. The stifling of high technology business', ICL internal working paper, London, 1983.

81. 'Tech embargo', *New Scientist*, 17 July 1986, 17.

82. 'US policy on transfer of technology', UK Department of Trade and Industry memorandum, Nov. 1984.

83. Susan Watts, 'Why the White House won't play ball', *Computer Weekly*, 12 Dec. 1985, 12; Michael Read, 'US export restrictions hit university software', *Computing*, 17 Mar. 1988, 1.

84. A major exception to this stance is Jurgen Schulte Hillen and Beatrix von Wietersheim, *Analyse von Beschrankungen des Zugangs zu Aussergemeinschaftlichen Informationsquellen*, report to Directorate 13, European Commission (Cologne, June 1986). This found little evidence of actual damage in Europe and recommended extensive discussion of

the issue. The methodology and conclusions have been thoroughly condemned in Jorg Becker, 'Zugangssperren bei US amerikanischen Datenbanken', *Nachrichten fur Dokumentation*, 39 (1988), 21–8.

85. Scientific and Technical Committee, North Atlantic Assembly, *Interim Report of the Subcommittee on Advanced Technology and Technology Transfer* (Brussels, Nov. 1984).

86. Mackintosh International, *European Commodity Chip Requirements*, report to the Commission of the European Communities (Luton, Dec. 1985).

87. IT 86 Committee, *Information Technology — a Plan for Concerted Action* (Bide Report) (HMSO, London, 1986).

88. Shoichi Saba, 'The U.S. and Japanese electronics industries: competition and cooperation', *Issues in Science and Technology*, 11:3 (Spring 1986), 53–60.

89. Dorinda G. Dallmeyer, 'National security and the semiconductor industry', *Technology Review*, Nov./Dec. 1987, 47–55.

90. John Poindexter, 'National policy on protection of sensitive, but unclassified information in federal government telecommunications and automated information systems', White House, 29 Oct. 1986.

91. Michael Schrage, 'U.S. limits access to information related to national security', *Washington Post*, 13 Nov. 1986, A1, A29.

92. Evert Clark and Alan Hall, 'The Administration vs. the scientists: a dangerous rift over locking up sensitive data', *Business Week*, 4 June 1987, 79.

93. Shattuck, 'Federal restrictions'.

94. 'White House withdraws computer control plan', *International Herald Tribune*, 19 Mar. 1987, 6.

95. R. Brian Woodrow, 'Telecommunications and information networks: growing international tensions and their underlying causes', *Information Society*, 6:3 (1989), 117–25.

96. Stephen Gould, 'National security controls on technological information: in search of a consensus', in John P. Hardt and Jean F. Boone (eds.), *Proceedings of the CRS Symposium on US Export Control Policy and Competitiveness* (Congressional Research Service, Washington, DC, Apr. 1987), 129.

97. See Stuart Macdonald, 'Out of control? US export controls and technological information', in Jorg Becker and Tamas Szecsko (eds.), *Europe Speaks to Europe: International Information Flows between Eastern and Western Europe* (Pergamon, London, 1989), 309–38.

8

Information Innocence:
High-Technology Policy and Technology Parks

'High technology' is almost entirely a product of policy—the term, that is, rather than the activity. The perception of high-technology policymakers is that the difference between high-technology industry and ordinary industry is profound and absolute. Yet, those who work in whatever has been designated high technology tend to see their jobs as neither markedly similar to other high-technology jobs nor markedly different from jobs in industries which have not been designated high technology. There are differences of course, but these are differences of degree, basically degree of information intensity—a concept not always familiar to those responsible for high-technology policy.

During the 1980s, and especially the first few years of the decade, high-technology industries attracted the attention of policymakers throughout the developed world because they were declared capable of delivering prodigious and immediate benefits. [1] By the early 1990s, policy and public fervour for high technology had begun to subside, perhaps simply because enthusiasm cannot be sustained indefinitely, but perhaps also because there was no firm foundation for its support. It was not quite that high technology had failed to deliver the goods. The lack of any single definition of high technology meant that wherever benefits appeared they could always be attributed to high technology; wherever they failed to appear, clearly the technology was insufficiently high. Such flexibility is attractive to policymakers.

It is hard to take high-technology policy seriously, but for a good decade it was no laughing matter. It should have been. If nothing else, an information perspective applied to the decade of high technology provides a little amusement. But there is actually something to be learnt from so much naïve enthusiasm for high technology, something which the passage of time—and a little humour—make easier to appreciate.

DEFINING HIGH TECHNOLOGY

Everyone knows, instinctively, what high technology is: it is something to do with computers. Policymakers also failed to provide precise definitions. Those most commonly on offer concentrated on generous R&D expenditure, interaction between scientific and technical skills, the generation of new products and processes, and entrepreneurs with scientific or technological backgrounds. [2] These, of course, are indicators rather than definitions; they catch the flavour of high technology by identifying major ingredients, but they do not betray the recipe. [3] Reduced to standard industrial classification, they produce decidedly unsatisfying fare, excluding, for instance, virtually all industries in the tertiary sector because they are not considered to perform R&D. [4] But confusion was evident even within the manufacturing sector. One American study lists oil and rubber among the high-technology industries: [5] another categorically declares that 'High technology entrepreneurs are a breed apart from the entrepreneurs of traditional industries like steel, rubber, oil and automobiles.' [6]

All the policy concern over high technology during the 1980s never really produced a satisfactory definition of what it was. In practice, then, it came to be whatever happened to be the subject of high-technology policy. One Japanese author even concedes defeat and defines high technology as that which needs 'governments' close attention to its growth and development'. [7] Such catholic comprehension of high technology encouraged interest groups to interpret the activity to their own advantage, and so to add their own contribution to the confusion; this, for example, from the scientist heading the Australian government's scientific research organization:

[M]y definition of high technology is that which originates from science and scientific research—research derived through what we call the scientific method. [8]

Classifying industries by the purity of their research posed a problem, a problem never solved and, for that matter, never tackled.

High technology is high not because it is nearer to God than ordinary technology, but because it involves high risk and possibly high return, a high rate of change, and—especially—high information intensity. As a definition, this is as inadequate as any other—it could apply nicely to many sophisticated criminal activities—but it at least has the merit of stressing the utter dependence of high-technology industries on their ability to deal quickly with vast quantities of new information. Such a notion was, and still is, quite foreign to most definitions of high technology, except in as much as they included research as an information-creating activity. Their distinctive approach to information is the common factor among high-technology firms and what makes them different from the mass of firms engaged in most other industrial activity. Certainly high-technology firms have little else in common and referring to high-technology industry as if it were a single entity was always fanciful. High-technology industries are often composed of tiny firms alongside giant multinationals, all exploiting different technologies for different purposes, usually in conjunction with established technologies. To the extent that other industries rely on the products of high-technology industries, they too may share the essential information intensity of the activity.

HIGH HOPES OF HIGH TECHNOLOGY

High technology—whatever it is—was esteemed a rare and precious economic activity; understandably, because it was considered able to deliver prodigious benefits while imposing almost no costs at all. Even the programmes encouraging it were generally cheap to implement. With a benefit–cost ratio approaching infinity, high technology captivated those responsible for the economic management of whole nations, and whole regions, and whole towns, and whole villages. Such enthusiasm is just a little surprising: in the UK the 'white heat of the technological revolution' had brought little but chill wind, and technological change was still seen as the scourge of employment in most developed countries. But high technology was imagined to be quite different from ordinary technology and much could be expected of it. Too much was expected.

Most prominent by far among the benefits claimed for high technology was its ability to create employment, even in the depths of recession. In reality, high-technology industries do not employ vast numbers and there are no real prospects of them ever becoming large employers. [9] US employment in the fast-food industry is greater than that in high technology, and has grown faster both proportionately and absolutely—all without a sniff of policy to encourage the consumption of hamburgers. [10] Of course, it could be argued—it has been argued—that low-grade service functions create jobs mainly for the semi-skilled and unskilled, and do not make full use of human capital. Unfortunately, the same is true of much high-technology employment. That is why such a large proportion of the American industry, and of late the Japanese, is to be found in cheap-labour countries. Highly qualified professional employees may be more common in high-technology industries than in other industries, but the typical high-technology employee in the US is poorly paid, part-time, and female, with the daily prospect of tedious, repetitive work, with no union protection and no career structure. [11] There is even substantial and illicit 'back alley' employment in the very cradle of high technology, Silicon Valley. In the developing countries, the lot of the average high-technology worker is rather worse.

Whether the products of high technology help generate employment in industries adopting them is a moot point. It rather depends on how the technology is used and on the facility with which adopting organizations adapt to change. [12] Initial experience of using new technology to cut labour costs may lead to the realization that jobless growth is an easy alternative to any other sort. Certainly there was no justification for the bold assertion that high technology necessarily generates employment in the rest of the economy. [13]

A perpetual dilemma faces those whose political life cannot be guaranteed to extend beyond the time taken for policies to yield their benefits. With high-technology policy, the problem was deemed unlikely to arise because returns were imagined to be not only huge, but also immediate. While it is incontestable that some high-technology firms have been outstandingly successful, surpassing even the hopes of their founders, this is not at all typical. Many high-technology firms fail, most just linger (what the Americans call the 'living dead'), and only a very few find instant success. The few, however, were presented as typical. Policymakers saw high technology rising above such mundane matters as competitive advantage and corporate competence. They predicted that whole new industries would mushroom from the spores and manure of public policy, foresaw the wholesale capture of international markets, described new firms spinning off in geometrical progression from those which soared to success. In the promised land of high technology, there would be prosperity for everyone. Rarely has the public servant's imagination been so strenuously exercised.

We are concentrating on technology at this time because we have the tools and we have the need to apply them but we don't necessarily know where or how to apply them. [14]

[I]n the area of high technology industry, comparative advantage is not bestowed, rather created. [15]

Unlike the smoke-stack industries with which they were commonly compared, high-technology industries were reputed to be clean and healthy, a boon to their employees and to the environment. Just why comparison should always have been made with the older parts of manufacturing industry, which had come to provide relatively little employment, is something of a mystery. Comparison with other growth sectors, with office or even fast-food employment, would have been more meaningful, though less impressive. But the smoke-stack industries offered ample visible evidence of pollution and poor working conditions: in high technology the evidence was simply less visible. In fact, there was already serious chemical pollution in the Mecca of high technology, Silicon Valley. [16] There were also most of the problems traditionally associated with smoke-stack industries—overcrowding, traffic congestion, smog, poverty, and even hunger. [17] It is quite wrong to imagine that thriving high-technology is kind to the environment and gentle with humanity. [18]

THE COLD LIGHT OF THE NEW DAWN

The benefits most prominently claimed by policymakers for high technology were not to eventuate. Some were quite impossible, and none was as instant as the promises which proclaimed them. Of all that high technology was supposed to bring, its contribution to the restructuring of developed economies was by far the most important. But this was always going to take time, patience, and more insight than was evident among policymakers into the nature of the structural changes that were taking place. The diffusion of information technology is only an indicator—and a very rough one at that—of an information revolution; the force of the revolution—if that is what it is—is information itself. But in proportion to its importance as the major form of wealth in a developed economy, and as a prerequisite for the production of all other wealth, little is known about information. Government policy now seems to have returned to regarding the manufacturing sector as the only possible engine of growth, to recognizing wealth only in tangible form, and to valuing information as just another input to the production of 'real' wealth. It is no coincidence that policy interest in the service sector achieved something of a peak during the high-technology decade, but it was a prominence which could not be sustained against the argument that manufacturing really does matter without a thorough understanding of why information also matters. High-technology policy never showed much sign of this understanding. High-technology industries use information resources that many other industries have either neglected or used inefficiently. [19] Other parts of the economy—perhaps all other parts—must acquire the same facility, and must undergo the reassessment and reorganization resulting from the new utilization of a major resource. High-technology industries, by their example, by their own growth, and by the diffusion of their products throughout the economy, have an essential leadership role to play in what is proving to be a protracted and painful restructuring process.

It is not that the role of high technology as leading sector was unappreciated by policymakers; they made much of its importance, but other sectors were expected to follow its example as instantly as the employment and other benefits were to be realized. When even these did not eventuate in quite the profusion anticipated, the remaining wisps of the patience required to reap long-term benefits evaporated. The structural benefits of high technology would also be immediate. And because there was precious little appreciation among policymakers of the importance of information to high-technology industries, they could put hand on heart and declare that all manner of unlikely spots would be ideal for the location of new biotechnology, micro-electronics, and information technology industries. These places might lack the resources and infrastructure required for other sorts of economic activity, but high technology did not seem to depend on these. [20] That high technology might need something else altogether, and that this resource had its own distinctive characteristics, escaped the attention of most policymakers.

Although some governments occasionally offered vast sums to entice established firms to move to their own regions, the incentives available to new firms were generally much more modest. Even so, there were major costs. The most severe of these were probably opportunity costs associated with reliance on high technology to bring benefits that would have been brought more effectively by other means. Because high-technology policy had to be seen as special and discrete, it was seldom integrated with other policy and there was often conflict. [21] Indeed, emphasis on location brought conflict even among high-technology policies themselves as region vied with region to attract the most appropriate firms. [22] In places, a legacy of high-technology policy is highly protected high-technology firms, unable to survive unaided by governments unwilling to admit that policy has failed. Elsewhere there has been some success, but always accompanied by doubt about how much is attributable to government involvement.

INFORMATION AND HIGH-TECHNOLOGY INDUSTRIES

The assembly of various bits of information into a new pattern is the essence of innovation. In many mature industries, the marginal information content of a new product or process over its predecessor may be small, and the information pattern may be little changed. Large firms within such industries may already possess much of the information required for this modified pattern. They may find, however, that their own complex and rigid organizational systems tend to inhibit the assembly of new information patterns. Indeed, large firms, especially in established industries, are often castigated for their lack of innovative zeal, although this is usually attributed to lack of incentive to innovate rather than to their inability to exploit information resources.

High-technology industries are markedly different, as might be surmised from the proportion of small, new firms they contain, and the importance attributed to such firms. It is not that a high-technology firm necessarily requires more information than other firms in order to innovate, but it does require more information relative to other inputs. Its activities are information-intensive; so much so that it cannot possibly rely on internal sources for all the information required. The high-technology firm must actively seek information outside, and is dependent on its information channels—and those of its employees—to the world beyond. Though the high-technology firm will exploit formal means of information acquisition as much as any firm, its formidable information requirements inevitably force it to resort to informal means of acquiring information as well. Silicon Valley in California provides the archetypal example of this behaviour. Policymakers may have shown little interest in the information behaviour of high-technology firms, but they were utterly fascinated by Silicon Valley. It has been the universal aim of high-technology policy just about everywhere to replicate Silicon Valley. [23]

The high technology of Silicon Valley is heavily reliant on personal, informal channels for its information requirements. Key employees have their own networks of individuals who readily supply information which is not obviously proprietary in exchange for other information. Personnel mobility has long been high in the industry as these employees take advantage of the information they possess and carry it with them to new jobs. [24] A mixture of technical and commercial information seems to be valued most. Certainly the headhunters, increasingly employed now that high-technology industries in the area have grown far too large to be embraced by a single informal network, hunt for heads which contain just this blend. [25] Very often the information that is most valued is apparently insignificant, more related to practical experience and inspiration than to the sort of information acquired on a university course.

The way in which information travels in Californian high technology is partly cause and partly consequence of its frantic pace of technological change. Because information can flow fully and rapidly when there are personal and informal channels, change is swift. Because change is swift, there is a need for information to flow fully and rapidly. The one begets the other. High-technology firms must change continually; even the semiconductor industry —now more than forty years old—has refused to adopt the characteristics of a stolid, mature industry. [26] High-technology industries in other countries have often had great trouble keeping pace, most notably the large established firms of Europe, the great white hopes of their governments for technological supremacy, and the recipients of so much of their largesse before policy discovered high technology. [27] At least part of the problem faced by these firms lay in organizational systems which neither appreciated nor accommodated information flow along personal and informal channels. The Japanese, with equally large firms but rather different information channels, have managed somewhat better.

THE FAILURE OF HIGH-TECHNOLOGY POLICY

With no real understanding of what it was that would produce the benefits they craved, much less how it might do this, policymakers sought inspiration, guidance, and perhaps a degree of reassurance from an area of the world renowned for its high technology. They focused on Silicon Valley, determined to see high technology for themselves. What had Silicon Valley got that was so conducive to high-technology industries? Delegations of politicians and bureaucrats descended on Silicon Valley to judge for themselves what Silicon Valley had that was so special. They left thoroughly satisfied with what they had seen. Certainly the place had a pleasant enough climate, local universities, and lots of venture capital, but these existed elsewhere and at least two of them—perhaps even three—could be created with appropriate policy. The disadvantages of the place cheered them greatly: they could easily offer high-technology firms lower housing costs, cheaper labour, and a reliable electricity supply. [28] Clearly

FIG. 8.1 German towns queuing to be Silicon Valleys

there was nothing particularly special about Silicon Valley, at least nothing that could not be duplicated or avoided elsewhere. The conclusion was that just about anywhere could offer conditions as suitable for high technology, and policy set forth to create new Silicon Valleys just about anywhere. Fig. 8.1 is one academic's impression of the enthusiasm of German towns to be Silicon Valleys. Indeed, as high technology was obviously so undemanding in its locational requirements, and so outstanding in the benefits it offered, there was considerable pressure on policy to put high technology in places which needed it most rather than places which suited it best.

To establish new technology-based companies a country must have a well educated population, a sound industrial base, a stable economy and an adequate pool of capital. Within Australia we have all these qualities . . . [29]

In England, the location near Cambridge of a handful of high-technology firms was discussed in terms of a new Silicon Valley. [30] Bradford, in Yorkshire, presented itself as the perfect site for microelectronics firms because its workers were 'dextrous, skilled, hard-working, cheerful and friendly'. [31] In Scotland, Silicon Glen ran between Glasgow and Edinburgh, where a few small Scottish firms had established a working relationship with the multinationals in electronics. [32] Perfect conditions for the Northern Irish Silicon Valley were discovered somewhere between Derry and Belfast. [33] Japan was to have a whole Silicon Island, built on the advantages of Kyushu, namely lots of clean water, lots of airports, and lots of women. [34] An unpolluted environment often figured among the qualifications of places to be new Silicon Valleys, the reasoning being that semi-conductor processing requires cleanliness. Thus, Tasmania was said to offer perfect conditions for the semiconductor industry because it has clean air. [35]

Most of the Australian states declared themselves ideal spots for new Silicon Valleys. Queensland's Gold Coast was claimed to be almost identical to the original, [36] and the area between Newcastle and Wollongong in New South Wales was also thought remarkably similar because it had lots of universities, lots of people, and some electronics firms. [37] Local universities were seen as a key feature in many places, [38] certainly in South Australia, where Technology Park Adelaide was referred to as 'the first Australian answer to America's Silicone [*sic*] Valley', [39] and in Western Australia, where the role of Stanford was to be played by the Western Australia Institute of Technology. [40] Canberra was to become Silicon City, based on the presence of the Australian National University and the incentives offered to National Semiconductor to locate a plant there. [41] The latter, according to the responsible minister, would lead 'to the establishment . . . without any shadow of a doubt, of an applications industry with a capacity to employ in excess of 100,000 people at the end of the decade'. [42] The fervour to emulate Silicon Valley was not restricted to policy-makers outside the United States. Within the country there were some 4,500 economic development agencies vying to be recognized as ideal locations for high-technology industry. [43] Silicon Gulch in Austin and Silicon Bayou in Louisiana were but two.

What was missed in all this enthusiasm of policy for high technology was that high technology was not like this at all. Even Silicon Valley was not as the policymakers perceived. It was, of course, possible to mimic the obvious characteristics of Silicon Valley elsewhere, to construct what were often no more than Hollywood film sets of Silicon Valley. But there was no understanding at all of what makes its industry tick. Even at the most practical level, comprehension was missing. For example, many high-technology processes certainly require cleanliness, but of such an order that it must be created artificially; the natural quality of the water and air is really quite irrelevant. ·Or again, the seminal role attributed to Stanford University was quite misleading; the University probably owes more to Silicon Valley than ever Silicon Valley owes to the University. Policymakers saw in Silicon Valley and in high technology not so much what they wanted to see as what they were prepared to see. What they missed were the intricate networks of surging information channels which supply high-technology firms with their basic requirement. Without these, Silicon Valley would be nothing special, and without these this is just what most of the myriads of pseudo-Silicon Valleys have become.

Looking back on the high-technology decade, it is hard not to conclude that means were confused with ends. So certain were the benefits from high technology taken to be, and so uncertain was understanding of high technology itself, that the means by which the benefits were to be achieved were allowed to substitute for the benefits themselves. The creation of Silicon Valley look-alikes came to be accepted as the primary goal. Other means —stimulation of local venture capital markets, establishing innovation centres and high-technology advisory units, and incentives to entice existing high-technology firms from elsewhere— were seen as leading to this goal. In these circumstances, one means seemed so appropriate that it achieved an extraordinary prominence in high-technology policy. The technology park, a mini-Silicon Valley, typically on a campus and receiving the

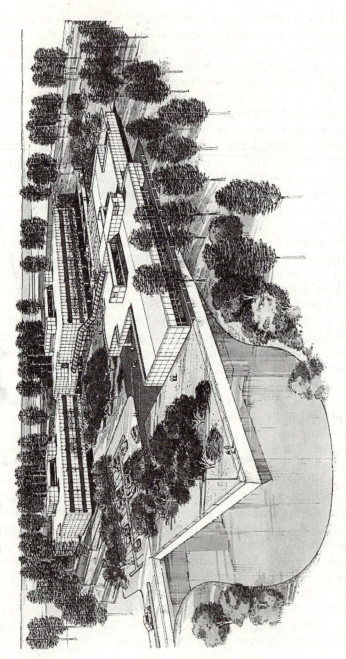

FIG. 8.2 Core buildings, Western Australian technology park

research input from the university, was a fascinating amalgam of greenfield research site, the linear notion of R&D, and Silicon Valley myth. [44]

Just as there is no agreed definition of high technology, there is no definitive understanding of what a technology park may be. Whatever the meaning of the term, it is widely used synonymously with science park, research park, science centre, research centre, innovation centre, and with various combinations of these. [45] Technology parks are quite fascinating: they are high technology as perceived by politicians and bureaucrats, translated into physical form by planners and architects. Fig. 8.2 gives some idea of the sort of plans they produced. They generally offer a pretty landscape, space-age buildings, potential agglomeration of firms, insulation from nasty industrial activity, a regulated environment, and—above all—proximity to a university. From the university, specifically from its science and engineering departments, the information required by high-technology firms is to flow. So overwhelming was the enthusiasm of policymakers for technology parks that the private sector often sought to cash in on the boom. Industrial estates were rechristened, refurbished factories renamed; [46] even the notion of a high-technology warehouse did not seem too outlandish (Fig. 8.3). The plans for a technology park at Homebush Bay in Sydney (Fig. 8.4) were somewhat out of the ordinary, not so much because they were based on the design of another technology park—in this case, that intended for Dundee, for no better reason than that a sketch was to hand [47]—as because of the triumph of the pragmatic over the aesthetic. An internal government report noted then that 'the description of the area as a potential "advanced technology park" goes against all conventional wisdom on technology parks', an observation prompted only in part by the noxious fumes from the local abattoir. [48]

The university was always seen as the core of the technology park, and those lacking some sort of educational institution were never considered to be in the same high-technology league. The argument is that there lies within the university information that will provide adjacent high-technology firms with competitive

FIG. 8.3   Advertisement for high-technology property

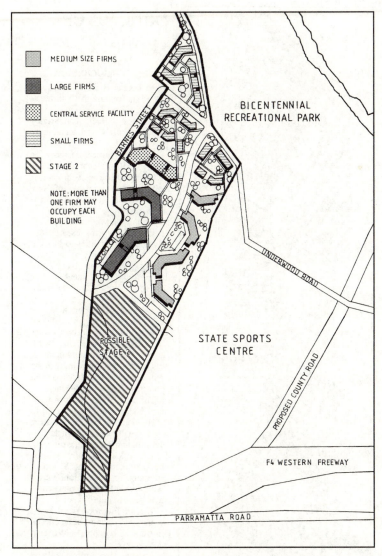

FIG. 8.4 Sydney advanced technology park at Homebush Bay, Stage I

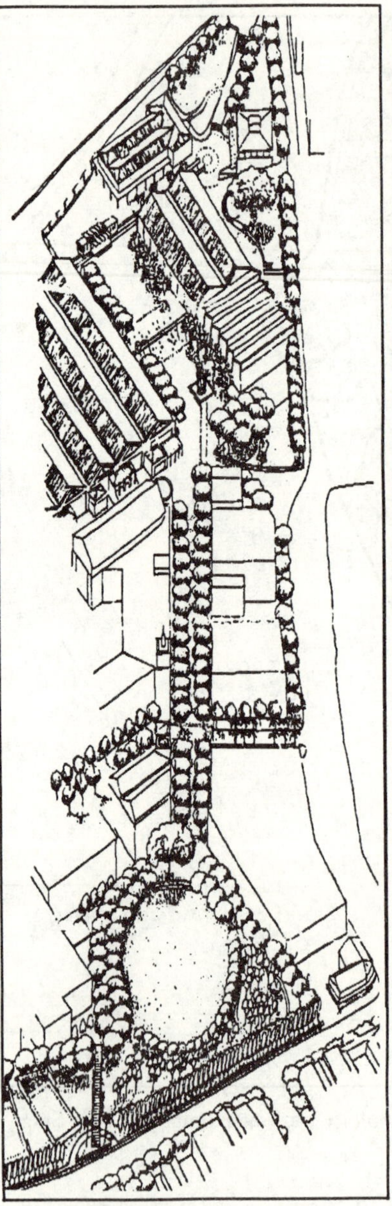

Technology park takes shape

By CHRIS JOHNSTON

TOM Forgan is the driving force behind the venture that will transform the former Everleigh Railway Workshops at Redfern in Sydney into Australia's first technology park.

He is the project designer for the Australian Technology Park (ATP), an infrastructure project involving the universities of New South Wales, Sydney and Technology, Sydney.

Its mission was to provide international-standard research and development facilities to link the resources and skills of the three institutions with the objectives of business and government .

"The technology will die in the universities — all we are doing is accelerating the opportunities for development," Forgan explained during a media briefing on Tuesday.

The 13.8 hectare site, worth around \$A37 million unimproved, was chosen for its proximity to the central business district, airport and three main Sydney universities.

The New South Wales government had provided funding of up to \$22 million over the next five years, and \$26 million came from the federal Building Better Cities program.

The park's first tenant will be the Australian Graduate School of Engineering Innovation, which will move into the former works manager's building in April.

The briefing took place in the expansive former new engine shop that will become the National Innovation Centre.

Another two storeys will be added to the building, providing an environment where start-up and spin-off companies could operate.

"I believe our technology park will be the premier technology park in the Asia-Pacific," Forgan said.

The ATP will be officially launched in March.

ATP planning . . . opportunities

FIG. 8.5 *The Australian Technology Park*

Source: *Wollongong Campus Review*, 26 January–1 February 1995, p. 5.

advantage, even that this information lode is a prerequisite to the functioning of such firms. Technology parks are the supreme example of acknowledgement that information is the key to high technology—and the supreme example of how inadequate is acknowledgement without understanding. The technology park phenomenon shows how desperately an information perspective was required, as well as the consequences of its absence.

Many universities and technical colleges find themselves with spare capacity and the need to spread their costs. Those with a curriculum of advanced sciences may contemplate setting up a science park. [49]

Proximity was thought to be the key to information flow from university to high-technology firms, especially important when the information was embodied in academic personnel. All other justification for technology parks was dependent on either this fundamental assumption or the locational consequences arising from it. Being near a university, high-technology firms could benefit from ready access to university equipment and services, and academics desperate to become risk-taking entrepreneurs could perform their metamorphosis in the technology park with minimum inconvenience. Concentration of high-technology firms on a technology park permitted the agglomeration economies of the Silicon Valley model, and it allowed the provision of buildings, organization, and management considered appropriate to the very specific requirements of such firms. In particular, a parklike environment could be provided, compatible with neat and clean industrial activity, and considered conducive to the success of high-technology firms. Once established, the technology park was supposed to become a regional core, a local focal point for high-technology activity, with all the psychological and promotional advantages that more dispersed activity would lack. [50] Fig. 8.5 is typical of such reasoning, and remarkable in that, even after all these years of experience, it is still acceptable, though perhaps only in Australia.

TECHNOLOGY PARKS IN PRACTICE

There were only three technology parks in Britain at the beginning of the eighties. By 1985, a further ten had been established, seven more were under construction, and another eight were in advanced stages of planning. [51] There are now very many more. By 1985, over £36 million had been spent in the previous three years on buildings and infrastructure for technology parks. Of this, about a third had come from private developers and from park tenants. [52] The remaining two-thirds had come from the public purse, mainly from government agencies, local authorities, and universities themselves. [53] In Europe, three-quarters of funding was estimated to have come from the public sector. [54] University support for these ventures cannot be explained simply in terms of their enthusiasm for high technology. Universities were being hard-pressed by government to demonstrate that they had forsaken their ivory towers and were in close contact with the market. [55] Beyond pleasing the major source of university funding, technology parks seemed to hold prospects of yielding some sort of financial return. The extent of the transition in university attitude can be gauged by the refusal of Cambridge University a decade earlier to accommodate the European research headquarters of IBM on the grounds that such enterprise was not compatible with university activities. [56] Universities had become desperate to demonstrate their market credentials, and the occasional observation that links between high-technology firms and universities could not be established overnight was never likely to dampen their determination.

I fear that many of the recent crop of science parks will fail to produce substantial and mutually beneficial interactions between universities and industry and will only serve to reinforce the worst prejudices of both sides and much of this will be attributable to half-hearted management on the part of universities who have failed to appreciate that good relationships with industry do not just happen by chance. [57]

In charge of each British technology park was a board comprising representatives of the sponsors, enthusiasts fired with ideas of high technology which they expected park managers and individual tenants to implement. The technology park was to be filled immediately with high-technology tenants, but only those which satisfied the board's current definition of high technology. Prospective tenants had to have existing links with the university to be accepted on some parks; on others, intending tenants had to establish links no matter how little they wanted them. Technology parks were to be landscaped to look like the board's perception of high technology, and their buildings were to look appropriately futuristic, no matter how unenthusiastic the tenants.

The pace and purpose of board members accustomed to the ways of council and university committees were always likely to be incompatible with those of high-technology firms. While the firm wanted to make money quickly, boards were much more concerned with the basic principles of technology parks. This became all too evident on a tour of British technology parks in 1985 which involved meeting many of those responsible for establishing them. [58] One board member was able to talk for an hour about the importance of his university's technology park, but then had considerable difficulty finding it. In another case, a fountain played at the vice-chancellor's insistence; in yet another, £40,000 was spent each year on cutting grass, and saving a single decaying tree had already cost £10,000. While all board members saw links with the university as absolutely fundamental, a check with one university library revealed that no tenant had ever borrowed a book from it. High technology was seen as inseparable from high security. Communal social facilities, as opposed to working facilities, were meagre—tenants were often expected to take business guests to meals in the university canteen—and the general atmosphere was often as convivial as that in the library. The tenants' links were to be with the university, not with each other. The assumption that high-technology entrepreneurs are miserable, teetotal automata, conditioned to work furiously when within the aura of a university and surrounded by greenery, is without foundation, and yet just this assumption pervaded the thinking of many of those responsible for technology parks.

Probably of much more importance than anything else a university location can offer a high-technology firm is credibility. For new firms supplying novel goods and services to markets yet to be created, credibility is vital. That is why a prestigious university has something of value to bestow, information which young firms can certainly sell, but which has nothing to do with science or engineering. A less august institution has much, much less to offer. One fascinating survey asked firms whether they would prefer to be located on the technology park at Brunel, a technological university and probably full of information relevant to high technology, or on the technology park at Cambridge: the firms were quite unequivocal in their response. [59]

The instigators of British technology parks were unaware of the importance of credibility. In their visits to Silicon Valley —visits which underwrote their own credibility—they had overlooked the intangible information infrastructure which is the strength of high technology there. Consequently, they were poorly equipped to understand the significance of even the high-technology trappings the Valley sports. The manicured and irrigated grass surrounding a Silicon Valley firm is intended to express status and confidence, not to be trodden on: the grass on a British technology park provides somewhere to eat lunchtime sandwiches, somewhere for a quick knock-around with a football. Again, a Californian 'trim trail' allows overweight executives to exercise in subtle seclusion: one British equivalent—ignored by executives—is the park's dominant feature, painted in bright primary colours like the equipment in a children's playground. The same developer had planted 230,000 shrubs, 'to create the right environment', according to the landscape architect. The right environment for technology parks was seen to be a facile prettiness of winding paths, bushes, ponds, and fountains; this for firms which, above all else, desperately needed evidence that they were to be taken seriously.

WHAT WENT WRONG?

The fundamental premiss of technology parks is flawed. High-technology firms are supposed to gain competitive advantage through the access to information that location alongside a university provides. The notion emerged from the Silicon Valley model, and particularly from the belief that the Silicon Valley complex had grown out of Stanford Industrial Park, itself a product of Stanford University. While the University certainly did establish the Park, it did so primarily because industrial growth in the region had increased the value of Leland Stanford's bequest, and consequently the property taxes it incurred, so much so that the University could no longer afford its retention as farmland. [60] Unable to sell the land, the University was forced to make it pay for itself. Stanford Industrial Park is very much the product of Silicon Valley's industrial prosperity, rather than vice versa. Yet, Silicon Valley and Route 128 around Boston, both quite unplanned high-technology concentrations and nothing to do with technology parks, [61] were commonly used to justify technology park development elsewhere. [62] Meanwhile, the very chequered performance of many genuine technology parks in the United States was conveniently overlooked. By one estimation, 'well over 50 per cent of science and high technology parks have failed'. [63]

While they are certainly dependent on information, high-technology firms are not dependent on the sort of information available from university science and engineering departments. Even if they were, it would be unrealistic to expect any more than a tiny fraction of this information to be contained within the departments of a single university. The blend of commercial and technical information has always been of more use to high-technology firms than the purely technical. Blending comes through personal experience and results in a package of tacit and uncodified information. Because this is hard to acquire, firms value highly the means by which it is obtained. In contrast, technical information is often conveniently screened by educational and academic systems, and the means of its acquisition taken for granted. The linear supposition that high-technology firms are engaged in an industrial extension of basic research, that all their endeavours are dependent on science, is naïve and makes little sense to those who work in high-technology firms. In their anxiety to eschew undirected enquiry, they are decidedly non-scientific in their approach; theirs is a black-box strategy: they urgently seek to make the box work in the market, and to avoid ever having to open it. In that primary endeavour, they can be as antagonistic towards scientific curiosity as academics were once said to be towards the pragmatism of those who toil in industry.

If the fundamental premiss that vital information flows readily from the university to firms on the technology park is flawed, then doubt must be cast on advantages claimed to arise from this assumed flow and from the location by which it is thought to be facilitated. It is apparent that usage of university information is not a function of contiguity. One survey concluded that 'the majority of knowledge-based companies do not require close proximity to academic institutions', [64] and another that 'very close proximity is not a necessary condition for establishing research links between [high-technology] industry and the University'. [65] Indeed; and in that technology parks are often battlegrounds for conflicting values and interests, there is much to be said for keeping the campus clear of high-technology firms.

[T]he chief appeal of a university-based science park should lie in . . . industrial-academic collaboration. But it was also widely observed that fruitful interaction between universities, academics and business tenants was almost universally absent from British science parks. [66]

As for the technology park tempting academics to become high-technology entrepreneurs, there may have been too many of them doing just that. Good academics do not necessarily make good entrepreneurs, any more than good entrepreneurs make good academics. Academics have founded new firms with the greatest of ease, and have managed any subsequent growth with the greatest of difficulty, so much so that some venture capitalists came to insist on the removal from management of all academics as a condition of further funding. [67] Nor was it ever quite clear why those academics with appropriate high-technology skills and information should be attracted to their local technology parks. If their skills and information are of value, then they are of value internationally. It is not obvious that local boy should make good in local high technology. Even in Silicon Valley, where there has long been every incentive for Stanford graduates with high-technology ambitions to linger, of the 243 high-technology firms started in the 1960s only six had full-time founders who came direct from Stanford University. [68]

The take up of land on the technology parks has been slow. It has been noted that a concentration of information technology and software firms has grown up around the inner Brisbane suburb of Milton. It is interesting that such concentrations can sometimes arise from the normal operation of the property market without any government planning or intervention. [69]

In contrast to the agglomeration advantages offered by major concentrations of high-technology firms, the most important of which is probably access to the information networks of many individuals, technology park agglomeration offered only a formal, miniature network, destined to remain tiny as long as firms and individuals elsewhere perceived the technology park as a barrier to contact. Contact was further constrained by the notion that single universities embrace all the technical information required by high-technology firms. Only weak universities can pretend to be self-contained: the strong realize that they are but nodes of academic information networks to which high-technology firms may seek access.

Although technology parks were justified on the grounds that they offered conditions conducive to high-technology firms, little effort was made to determine what these conditions really are. High-technology firms are as various as their technologies and their demands tended to be for flexible, multi-purpose buildings rather than for structures which expressed an architect's vision of the industrial future. [70] And while generously verdant landscaping and regulations prohibiting all but respectable high-technology activity on technology parks seemed instinctively appropriate, appeared to fit the Silicon Valley model, and provided planners with a creative challenge, there was no evidence of any link between such factors and the prosperity of firms. In the United States, high-technology growth was actually greatest in urban areas with high pollution and without cultural amenities. [71] In the harsh world of high technology, it is hard to believe that a critical influence is exerted by nice neighbours and the company of ducks.

One reason that a high technology project is so successful is that the location is quite attractive, has a campus setting, and represents a very nice place to work. . . . Colors: Should be mostly earth tones to merge with the environment; colors to be avoided are those that clash or are simply too bright such as blues, reds and yellows. [72]

THE LESSON

Policy portrayed high technology as something magical: apply public money with the right incantation and wondrous things would happen. When they failed to happen, there was no incentive for policymakers to explain what had gone wrong. The good performer hides his embarrassment and quickly moves on to the next trick. The audience will never be told why the high-technology miracle never happened. But behind the scenes, there is the opportunity for policymakers and their political masters to learn from what went wrong. The lesson is remarkably simple: it is that there is nothing at all magical about high technology.

Consequently, high-technology policy, no matter how appropriate and successful, will never delight and amaze.

There is, though, something special about high technology. This is its ability to deal with information. Other firms have much to learn from this ability, but then so do policymakers if they still wish to reap the benefits that high technology has to offer. The lesson should be the easier for a decade of experience of what went wrong. But policymakers and politicians are not renowned for even acknowledging failure, much less for learning from it. So, instead of making a valuable contribution to learning, the experience of the high-technology decade will mean that the lesson takes a little longer to learn.

REFERENCES

1. See Doreen Massey, Paul Quintas, and David Wield, *High Tech Fantasies: Science Parks in Society, Science and Space* (Routledge, London, 1992).
2. Department of Science and Technology, *Creating High Technology Enterprises* (Australian Government Publishing Service, Canberra, 1981), 3. See also Lynn Bollinger, Katherine Hope, and James Utterback, 'A review of literature and hypotheses on new technology-based firms', *Research Policy*, 12 (1983), 1–14.
3. E. Carlson, 'Listing top high-tech States depends a lot on definition', *Wall Street Journal*, 3 Jan. 1984.
4. Stuart Macdonald, 'Technology beyond machines', in S. Macdonald, D. Lamberton, and T. Mandeville, *The Trouble with Technology* (Frances Pinter, London, 1983), 26–36.
5. C. Armington, C. Harris, and M. Odle, *Formation and Growth in High Technology Businesses: A Regional Assessment* (Brookings Institution, Washington, DC, Sept. 1983), appendix A.
6. R. Premus, *Location of High Technology Firms and Regional Economic Development*, Joint Economic Committee, US Congress (US Government Printing Office, Washington, DC, 1983), 56.
7. Tsuruhiko Nambu, *The Role of Government in the High Technology Industries* (Australia–Japan Research Centre, Australian National University, Canberra, 1986), 18.
8. J. Wild, 'High technology—is it the answer?', *Australian Director*, June/July 1984, 47–8.

9. R. Rumberger and H. Levin, *Forecasting the Impact of New Technologies on the Future Job Market*, Project Report 84-A4, School of Education, Stanford University, Feb. 1984; R. Riche, D. Hecker, and J. Burgan, 'High technology today and tomorrow: a small slice of the employment pie', *Monthly Labor Review*, 106:11 (1983), 50–8.

10. 'Commentary: the science education stampede . . . A dissenting view on computer "revolution" ', *Science and Government Report*, 1 Oct. 1983, 6–7; K. Windschuttle, 'High tech and jobs', *Australian Society*, 3:5 (1984), 11–13.

11. D. Tomaskovic-Devey and S. Miller, 'Can high-tech provide the jobs?', *Challenge*, 26:2 (1983), 57–62.

12. Tom Mandeville and Stuart Macdonald, 'Information technology and employment levels', in Macdonald *et al.* (eds.), *The Trouble with Technology*, 169–77.

13. See A. Markusen, *High Tech Jobs, Markets and Economic Development Prospects*, Working Paper 403, Institute of Urban and Regional Development, University of California, Berkeley, Apr. 1983.

14. Mike Ahern, Queensland Minister for Industry, Small Business and Technology, 'Technology and politics—a necessary partnership for economic growth in Queensland', paper presented to National Party symposium, Brisbane, Apr. 1985, 1.

15. Barry Jones, Australian Minister for Science and Technology, 'Keynote address', Management Technology Education Conference on Sunrise Industries, Sydney, 31 May 1983, 7.

16. J. LaDou, 'The not-so-clean business of making chips', *Technology Review*, May/June 1984, 23–8; S. Begley and J. Carey, 'Toxic trouble in Silicon Valley', *Newsweek*, 7 May 1984, 85; B. Soiffer, 'Toxic suits pile up in Silicon Valley', *San Francisco Chronicle*, 18 June 1984, 2.

17. D. Kutzmann, 'Valley's congestion chases job-seekers away', *San Jose Mercury*, 18 Mar. 1984; M. Dianda, 'The Silicon Valley being reshaped by Silicon sprawl', *Peninsula Times Tribune*, 22 Apr. 1984, A1-A8; R. Rudy, 'Hunger on Peninsula a concern, experts say', *Peninsula Times Tribune*, 28 Jan. 1984, A1-A8.

18. Everett Rogers and Judith Larsen, *Silicon Valley Fever* (Basic Books, New York, 1984).

19. Don Lamberton, Stuart Macdonald, and Tom Mandeville, 'Productivity and technological change: towards an alternative to the Myers' hypothesis', *Canberra Bulletin of Public Administration*, 9:2 (1982), 23–30.

20. See A. Gregerman, 'Competitive advantage—framing a strategy to support high-growth firms', in *Commentary of the National Council for Urban Economic Development*, Washington, DC, Summer 1984, 18–23.

21. 'How to cut unemployment', *The Economist*, 28 May 1983, 15; Office of Technology Assessment, *Technology, Innovation and Regional Economic Development* (US Congress, Washington, DC, July 1984).

22. I. Feller, 'Political and administrative aspects of state high technology programs', *Policy Studies Review*, 3:3/4 (1984), 460–6.

23. Stuart Macdonald, 'High technology policy and the Silicon Valley model', *Prometheus*, 1:2 (1983), 330–49.

24. See M. Baram, 'Trade secrets: what price loyalty?', *Harvard Business Review*, 46:6 (1968), 66–74.

25. Stuart Macdonald, 'Headhunting in high technology', *Technovation*, 4 (1986), 33–45.

26. Ernest Braun and Stuart Macdonald, *Revolution in Miniature: The History and Impact of Semiconductor Electronics* (Cambridge University Press, Cambridge, 1982).

27. 'Europe's technology gap', *The Economist*, 24 Nov. 1984, 99–110.

28. M. Chase, 'Electronics companies move out of "Silicon Valley"', *Australian Financial Review*, 25 Mar. 1980, 28; 'Sand in the works for Silicon Valley planners', *Australian Financial Review*, 16 Apr. 1980, 20; 'Delicate bonds: the global semiconductor industry', *Pacific Research*, 11:1 (1980), 6.

29. David Thomson, 'Official opening', in Department of Science and Technology, *Finance for Technology Ventures* (AGPS, Canberra, 1983), 4.

30. 'Silicon Valley comes to Britain', *The Economist*, 11 July 1981, 83–4.

31. *Punch*, 5 May 1982, 3.

32. 'Scots on the move—into the microchip age', *The Economist*, 15 Aug. 1981, 19–20.

33. *The Economist*, 22 Aug. 1981, 11.

34. 'Silicon Island—tomorrow's world leader?', *Japan Quarterly*, 29:4 (1982), 445–7.

35. M. Townley, *Hansard*, Australian House of Representatives, 25 Mar. 1981, 716.

36. R. McKilliam, 'Opening of new ERA', *Brisbane Courier-Mail*, 15 Sept. 1981, 22.

37. V. Gledhill, 'High technology industry in New South Wales', *Australian Computer Bulletin*, Sept. 1981, 22–7.

38. William Henkin, 'Silicon Valley: incubator of high technology', *Economic Impact*, 41 (1983), 43–9.

39. *Australian Stock Exchange Journal*, June 1981, 230.

40. J. Poprzerzny, 'Institute plans "Silicon Valley" industrial park', *Australian*, 12 Aug. 1981, 11.

41. B. Buchanan, ' "Silicon City" plan for developing Canberra', *Brisbane Telegraph*, 9 June 1981, 30.

42. M. Hodgman, *Hansard*, Australian House of Representatives, 26 Mar. 1981, 951.

43. e.g. 'The Maryland high-tech phenomenon', *High Technology*, Sept./Oct. 1981, special advertising section. See also 'America rushes to high tech for growth', *Business Week*, 28 Mar. 1983, 50–6.

44. Richard Joseph, 'Silicon Valley myth and the origins of technology parks in Australia', *Science and Public Policy*, 16:6 (1989), 353–65; Richard Joseph, 'The Silicon Valley factor: Australia's technology parks', in Pam Scott (ed.), *A Herd of White Elephants* (Hale and Iremonger, Sydney, 1992), 75–89.

45. For limited elucidation, see *Electronics Location File*, 7 (Oct. 1983), 53.•

46. See UK Department of Industry and Shell UK Ltd., *Helping Small Firms Start Up and Grow: Common Services and Technological Support* (HMSO, London, 1982), 41–2.

47. Scottish Development Agency, *Dundee: The High Technology Future* (Glasgow, 1984).

48. Ross James, *Homebush Bay Advanced Technology Park: An Assessment* (NSW Department of Industry Development, Sydney, Jan. 1985), 7.

49. Herring Son and Daw, *Property and Technology—the Needs of Modern Industry* (London, 1984), 3.

50. See Jacqueline Senker, 'Small high-technology firms: some regional implications', *Technovation*, 3 (1985), 243–62.

51. Jean Currie, *Science Parks in Britain: Their Role for the Late 1980's* (CSP Economic Publications, Cardiff, 1985), 8–9.

52. Ibid. 32.

53. The issue was rated sufficiently important for the ruling political party to make 'the encouragement of science parks' an election issue. See *Conservative Manifesto 1983* (Conservative Central Office, London, 1983), 20.

54. Peter Marsh, 'Commerce takes an interest in expanding world of science parks', *Financial Times*, 3 June 1986.

55. Anthony Moreton, 'Science parks', *Financial Times*, 1 Oct. 1984, 21–2; Pearce Wright, 'Pioneers of the white-hot revolution', *The Times*, 17 Apr. 1985, 17–18.

56. David Dickson, 'Britain's ivory tower goes high tech', *Science*, 227 (29 Mar. 1985), 1560–2.

57. John Ashworth, 'Industry/university co-operation in the future', paper delivered to the Confederation of British Industry, 27 June 1984, 18–19.

58. For details, see Stuart Macdonald, 'British science parks: reflections on the politics of high technology', *R&D Management*, 17:1 (1987), 25–37.

59. Elaine Willey and Alun Jones, *Science Parks: The Vision and the Reality. Report on a Study of the Science Park at Cambridge and the Proposed Parks at Brunel and Surrey Universities*, Technical Change Centre, London, Sept. 1982, mimeo.

60. Board of Trustees, *Stanford University Land Use Policies*, Stanford University, 12 Mar. 1974.
61. N. Dorfman, 'Route 128: the development of a regional high technology economy', *Research Policy*, 12 (1983), 299–316.
62. e.g. Hugh Cannings, 'The role of science parks', *Chemistry and Industry*, 4 Sept. 1982, 641–3; Louise Kehoe, 'Silicon Valley grew out of Stanford campus', *Financial Times*, 21 Jan. 1983, sect. IV, p. 11.
63. Charles Minshall, *An Overview of Trends in Science and High Technology Parks*, Economics and Policy Analysis Occasional Paper 37, Battelle Memorial Institute, Columbus, Oh., Oct. 1983, 18. See also Office of Technology Assessment, *Technology, Innovation and Regional Economic Development* (US Congress, Washington, DC, July 1984); 'The high-technology park: ingredients for success', *Economic Impact*, 3:51 (1985), 7.
64. Debenham Tewson and Chinnocks, *High-Tech: Myths and Realities* (London, July 1983), 50.
65. B. Moore and R. Spiers, 'The experience of the Cambridge Science Park', paper presented to Research Technology and Regional Policy Workshop, OECD, Paris, Oct. 1983, 29.
66. J. Turney, 'Science and industry mix put to the test', *Times Higher Education Supplement*, 3 Dec. 1982, 11, cited in Senker, 'Small high technology firms'.
67. Macdonald, 'Headhunting in high technology'.
68. A. C. Cooper, 'Technical entrepreneurship: what do we know?', *R&D Management*, 3:2 (1973), 59–64.
69. Department of Industry, Technology and Commerce/Australian Science and Technology Council, *Technology Parks in Australia: A Review of State Experiences* (DITAC, Canberra, 1989), 13, cited in Joseph, 'The Silicon Valley factor: Australia's technology parks'.
70. Debenham Tewson and Chinnocks, *High-Tech: Myths and Realities*.
71. Amy Glasmeier, Peter Hall, and Ann Markusen, *Recent Evidence on High-Technology Industries' Spatial Tendencies: A Preliminary Investigation*, Working Paper 417, Institute of Urban and Regional Development, University of California, Berkeley, 1984, 63.
72. Minshall, *An Overview of Trends in Science and High Technology Parks*, 12.

9

Transfer without Transaction:
Policy for Information Acquisition

TAPPING THE LEAKS

The linear view of innovation sees science and technology information as seminal. As research and development are perceived to create this sort of information, it seems to follow that the more R&D performed by firms, the more of this information will be produced, and the more innovation will result. As innovation benefits the economy, it behoves governments to encourage the performance of R&D. But government exhortation to firms is not enough. Because this precious information tends to leak from the organization despite the efforts of government and firms alike to secure it, [1] governments are often expected to compensate firms for their loss. Without this compensation, it is argued, firms will perform less R&D than they should. [2]

A twist to this argument, one that has made its contribution to government policy in recent years, is that science and technology (S&T) information must surely leak from foreign firms as well, and must therefore be out there somewhere, waiting to be acquired. Rough calculations suggest that this leakage of R&D information from foreign firms must be huge: after all, no matter how much R&D is performed by an individual firm, or by a single country, it is dwarfed by all that the rest of the world performs. Consequently, government programmes to tap this lake of lost information, and to supply national firms— especially small firms, which are considered to be unable to search the world on their own account—would seem to offer attractive returns.

Many governments run such information acquisition programmes, though they take a huge variety of forms and are not usually recognized, or organized, as information programmes, much less as part of information policy. When they are, as they were in the Soviet Union in its attempts to secure technological information from the West, or as they have been for many years in Japan, [3] other governments are not wholly approving. In the United Kingdom, the Department of Trade and Industry (DTI) had four such schemes in the late eighties which it was considering incorporating into a single Inward Technology Transfer programme. This required investigation of how the schemes were performing, an investigation which revealed just how pressing was the need for an information perspective. [4]

The schemes were all run on the supposition that there were only two parts to Inward Technology Transfer: the collection of S&T information overseas, and its distribution to UK firms. Because there was obviously masses of information out there, collecting some of it was not seen to be a problem and the emphasis of the schemes was firmly on the transfer of the information collected. An information perspective indicates that the transfer of information cannot easily be separated from its acquisition, and that the acquisition of information requires some concern for information transactions. Supplying information to UK firms made little sense if the firms could not use the information, if there was no link between demand and supply. An information perspective indicates that this link might have been facilitated through information exchange, through UK firms supplying information to foreign firms in exchange for the information received from them. This was not a transaction which the government was willing to contemplate. The whole point of these schemes was to take from foreigners something of value to UK firms. To return something of equal value rendered the schemes pointless. Competitive advantage for UK firms was seen to lie in having something the opposition did not have. Moreover, the schemes had to be seen to be bringing foreign information to UK firms; this visibility would be obscured if firms and individual employees resorted to their own information transactions rather than the formal mechanisms installed by government. The schemes were never seen as providing the basis on which UK firms could continue to acquire foreign S&T information for themselves. There were other problems, mostly caused either directly or indirectly by trying to deal with information when the importance of its characteristics was less than fully appreciated, but the core problem was the mercantilistic approach to information demanded in the justification of the schemes. Information was reckoned to be valuable and taking it from foreign firms to give to UK firms would obviously make UK firms much better off.

Of the four schemes, two sent employees of UK firms overseas to pick up information, and two supplied UK firms with foreign S&T publications. None was generously funded and none was a central plank of any government policy. The DTI ran all four schemes, but had never made much attempt to coordinate them. The task, then, was to see if a single cohesive programme could be shaped from the four schemes, and for this an information perspective seemed appropriate.

THE VISITING ENGINEERS SCHEME (VES)

The theory behind VES was that young engineers from UK industry should spend a year working in Japanese firms. They would then bring back to their own employers, and to other firms in the UK, information they had picked up in these Japanese firms (Fig. 9.1). In information terms, this makes sense: people are excellent containers of information and a year participating in Japanese innovation would provide the opportunity to absorb the sort of information that could not easily be transferred by other means. Better, of course, than sending an empty container in the hope that it will be filled is to import one already full, but this would have been seen as inviting enemy spies into British organizations, allowing them to steal from storehouses of British information. It is interesting that this attitude did not seem to be an obstacle to British engineers gaining access to Japanese organizations.

Although ministers were particularly fond of drawing public attention to VES, the scheme hardly existed in practice. Started in 1982, it had dispatched only 13 young engineers to Japan by 1988. This compares with 65 young Irish engineers sent to Japan by their government in 1988 alone. In fact, the Japanese themselves were more active in bringing British engineers to Japan: the Japanese Science and Technology Agency arranged six visits that year, and the Japanese Society for the Promotion of Science

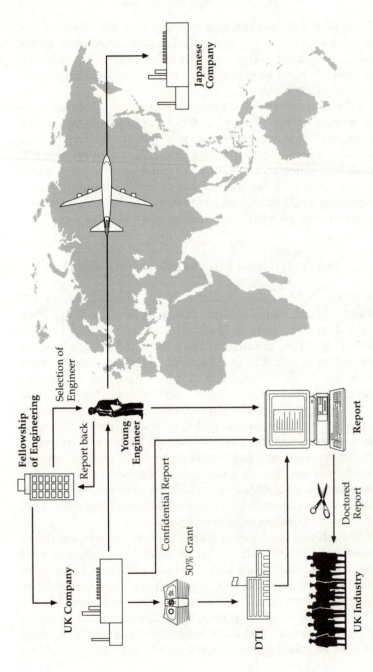

FIG. 9.1 The Visiting Engineers Scheme

sponsored ten. Even individual Japanese companies had larger schemes than that of the DTI. Moreover, with the single exception of a 'young' engineer aged 54 from a research association, all the British engineers worked for large British companies which already had links with Japanese companies. Many of these companies had planned to send their candidates to Japan anyway. One young engineer was first interviewed for the scheme in his garden on a Sunday afternoon, only hours before his flight to Japan.

The scheme was administered on behalf of the DTI by the Fellowship of Engineering, a prestigious group with an invited membership of one thousand senior engineers. But the Fellowship was never paid much and lacked resources to advertise the scheme widely or to interview large numbers of candidates. Consequently, Fellows tended to recommend worthy young engineers from their own firms, arguing—with some justification— that only such large firms could afford to spare a promising engineer for a year. The Fellowship tended to see the scheme as educational rather than informational. This familiar perspective of information acquisition and dissemination as education had filtered back to the DTI and came to be incorporated in its own publications.

DTI suggests that production, technical or personnel directors should regard VES as a step in the training and future development of a young engineer, to be undertaken at a suitable time in his career. [5]

On his return, each VES engineer was expected to write a report on his experiences and to give a public seminar, which normally took place about a year after the young engineer's return. Such means of dissemination to the rest of UK industry may have been inadequate. Reports were first submitted to employers, who, perhaps because they had to match the government grant for the trip, regarded the information as their own. Some firms had already bound their young engineers by non-disclosure agreements.

The trainee shall not during the term of the Program and for (3) years thereafter, without the prior written consent of Toshiba disclose to any third party excluding Rolls-Royce any technical, management or other information whatsoever concerning the business or affairs of Toshiba or any associated company until such information is in the public

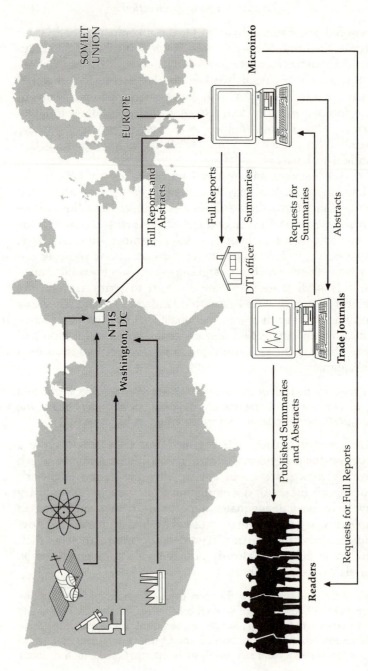

FIG. 9.2 The TechAlert Scheme

domain. Rolls-Royce shall have the responsibility to keep such information within Rolls-Royce and not to disclose to any third party. [6]

What engineers tended to do was produce one report for
their UK employer, and another, stripped of any information
they thought might be of value to other UK firms, for public
consumption. One public seminar was attended by the young
engineer's boss, who insisted he was there not to learn, but to
make sure that the young engineer said nothing of importance.
Of the 478 attendees at seven seminars held between 1983 and
1989, precisely 12 were from small firms. Just 23 organizations
accounted for 60 per cent of all attendees.

TECHALERT

TechAlert was a scheme which arranged for the publication
in UK journals of abstracts of overseas science and technology
publications. Readers could then order complete reports. The
scheme started in 1979 and was run by the DTI until 1986, when
it was contracted out to Microinfo, a private firm in Hampshire
(Fig. 9.2). Some 70 per cent of reports used by TechAlert came
from the National Technical Information Service (NTIS) in Washington, the world's largest repository of science and technology
reports. NTIS supplied Microinfo with abstracts of all its reports,
from which Microinfo selected those it judged most appropriate
to each of the journals it served. Microinfo then wrote new
abstracts. These it dispatched for the consideration of journal
editors, who then either asked Microinfo for fuller summaries
or simply printed the abstracts they had received. Fuller summaries were arranged by Microinfo and written by a public
servant working from home, once he had obtained the relevant
full reports from NTIS via Microinfo. Journal readers wanting
full reports ordered them from Microinfo.

There were several problems with these arrangements. The
most obvious was that their complexity meant that everything
took an awfully long time, an important matter when the value of
information is related to its timeliness. What with re-abstracting,
summarizing, negotiations with editors, and the lead times of
journals, it was quite normal for six months to pass between
receipt of an abstract by Microinfo and the publication of a

revised version or a summary in a journal. The scheme was also expensive. Microinfo claimed a European monopoly on NTIS material—a position reinforced by the DTI scheme, though disputed by the British Library, and, indeed, by NTIS itself—and insisted that full reports be bought only through the company. To this end, abstracts and summaries did not contain sufficient bibliographic information for readers to procure the reports from other sources. A typical NTIS report of between 51 and 100 pages cost £24 in hard copy from Microinfo, £9 direct from NTIS, and just £6 from the Document Supply Centre at the British Library. TechAlert did not inform readers that the same reports were available from the British Library at a fraction of the cost. The DTI itself, in common with large UK firms, had made arrangements to acquire reports for its own needs direct from NTIS, a case of the information-rich managing to obtain yet more information quickly and cheaply, while the information-poor—including the small firms which TechAlert was supposed to help—obtained their information slowly and expensively.

Of the 857 abstracts sent to 21 journals between October 1987 and June 1988, only 266 were published. By the end of the contract year in September, journals had published 403 abstracts. The contract specified 400. While the success of the scheme's information dissemination was measured in terms of the number of abstracts published multiplied by the combined circulation of all the journals publishing them, this was slightly misleading. In 1988, Microinfo supplied requests for 955 copies of reports in hard copy and microfiche. This compares with about 10,000 NTIS reports supplied by the British Library. Average cost to Microinfo customers was about £16 per report. Average cost to the DTI, which subsidized Microinfo heavily for its services, was about £75 per report.

Microinfo was faced with the basic problem of deciding which of so many NTIS abstracts were most suited to the readerships of each of more than 20 UK journals, and then, without specialist technical knowledge, of converting the abstracts supplied to NTIS by research scientists and engineers into abstracts appropriate for the practitioner audience of each journal. Responsibility seems to have been delegated to a single employee, whose chief criteria for choice were the brevity and intelligibility of the original NTIS abstract.

Most editors were very happy indeed to receive copy from Microinfo to help fill their pages. Their objections were that the abstracts they were sent often seemed inappropriate to the interests of their readers, and that the DTI insisted on printing all abstracts in blocks, headed by the DTI and TechAlert logos. Editors protested that interest in the reports was much greater when the information they contained was integrated in features, an observation confirmed by Microinfo's sales statistics. The observation had no influence on the government's insistence on acknowledgement of its role in bringing information to UK industry.

THE OVERSEAS TECHNICAL INFORMATION SERVICE (OTIS)

Half a dozen or so British embassies include science counsellors among their complements, part of whose responsibilities it is to send science and technology information back to the UK. [7] Essentially, this information is for the use of government departments, but it had been apparent to the DTI for some time that the information might also be of use to UK industry. As the information was being sent back anyway, UK industry could have it at marginal cost (Fig. 9.3).

In fact, the task of determining which firms wanted which information was a major one, and the costs of attempting this considerable. The size of both was largely hidden until August 1985, when the operation was contracted out to the Production Engineering Research Association (PERA) at Melton Mowbray. After an initial sifting by DTI to remove esoteric and classified material, the task of distributing the information to UK firms was left entirely to PERA.

PERA is unusual among research associations in that it has demonstrably changed from serving only the core research needs of its members to serving the information needs of a much wider community; it has become an extremely information-intensive operation, anxious to extend its information functions. Its first task on receipt of the reports the science counsellors had sent DTI was detailed classification of the material and preparation of a summary for each piece, a task to which it devoted

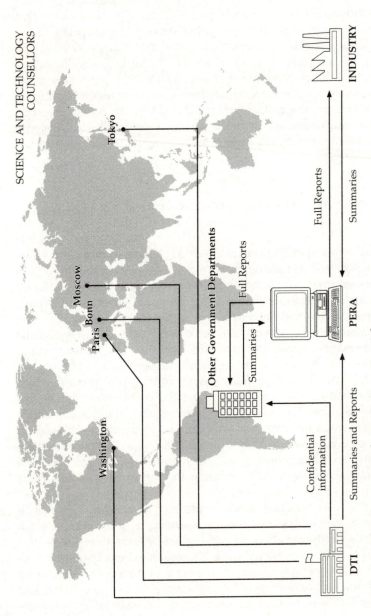

FIG. 9.3 The Overseas Technical Information Scheme

considerable resources. Customers for the Overseas Technical Information Service (OTIS) had already registered the subject areas of interest to them and were sent batches of appropriate summaries at regular intervals. From these, they selected which full reports they wanted to receive and requested copies either from PERA or direct from the author. Unlike Microinfo, PERA provided full bibliographic details of each report. In 1988, PERA made about 1,000 summaries, dispatched over 100,000 copies of these, and sent out about 3,000 copies of full reports, most as photocopies (PERA charged customers only the actual costs of photocopying), but nearly a third as loans.

Parts of the system worked well, but not the whole. One problem was that OTIS did not benefit from the economies of scale that information services allow. There were only 335 non-government customers in April 1987, 311 in January 1988, 292 in March, and by December that year, just 262. There were also about 200 government customers of PERA, who did not pay directly for the service. Surveys suggest that both sets of customers were well pleased with the service and the material they received through OTIS, which satisfied government evaluation criteria. The problem lay, though, not with what customers received, but with what they did not receive—something much harder to measure.

Tables 9.1 and 9.2 relate demand, as expressed by categories of technology about which customers had asked to be sent summaries, to OTIS supply, as measured by the categories of the documents they received. Table 9.1 looks at government customers; Table 9.2 at non-government customers. Quite clearly, the two groups had no interests in common. The idea that information for government departments could be supplied at marginal cost to UK firms ignored the problem of matching supply of information to demand. But this fundamental information problem had hardly been tackled even for government customers in as much as science counsellors received no feedback from OTIS or anyone else about what use was being made of the information they supplied. Science counsellors were left to guess what information civil servants back home might want, and seem to have concluded that only information on science and technology policy was certain to be of interest. The only way that civil servants could influence this supply

TABLE 9.1 Government Customers of OTIS

	% of customers expressing interest*	% of total incoming reports
Science and technology policy	35	34
Air pollution and control	30	4
Computers	28	4
Production planning and control	27	1
Semiconductors	26	6
Water pollution and control	26	3
Computer software	25	5
Artificial intelligence	25	2
Public administration	25	0
Solid wastes pollution and control	24	3

* Customers could select as many categories of technology as they wished.

TABLE 9.2 Non-Government Customers of OTIS

	% of customers expressing interest*	% of total incoming reports
Ceramics	26	3
Composites	22	2
Optoelectronics	22	2
Adhesives and sealants	21	0
Production planning and control	21	1
Biotechnology	20	9
Materials processing	19	2
Plastics	18	1
Finishes	17	0
Robotics	17	2

* Customers could select as many categories of technology as they wished.

was through personal approaches direct to individual science counsellors.

Although the science counsellors supplied almost all the information available through OTIS and were consequently central to it, OTIS was less essential to the science counsellors. They had other duties, all of which their primary master, the Foreign and Commonwealth Office, tended to rate more highly. OTIS work was slipped in when there was nothing more important to be done. So, for example, the science counsellor in Paris dispatched 39 reports to London in August 1987. Paris closes down in August. During the spring and the rest of that summer (peak season for UK visitors to the embassy in Paris), the science counsellor sent only 17 reports. The Science and Technology section there had also assumed CoCom responsibility for controlling the export and use of high technology. Consequently, the whole section had been rendered secure to prevent information leaving it, an arrangement hardly conducive to the ready supply of information to OTIS. In fact, supply of material to OTIS varied markedly from post to post, with the Washington counsellor dispatching 547 reports in 1987, the counsellor in Tokyo 257, those in Bonn and Paris 68 and 96 respectively, and our man in Moscow just one. Such variation was largely a function of individual perceptions of the task and of its importance, but UK firms might have been forgiven if they had been left with the impression that their government considered S&T information from the United States vastly more important than information from anywhere else, and that information from the Soviet Union was of no consequence at all.

There were also funding difficulties occasioned by a confusion of constraints on the budgets of different departments. Thus, though the DTI paid for briefing visits to bring science counsellors and British staff to the UK, staff who had been recruited locally, staff who were least familiar with the information needs of UK firms, did not qualify. Those who already had some familiarity with the information needs of UK firms could make themselves more familiar. Similarly, the DTI budget for the purchase of publications could not be spent overseas. Thus, the counsellor in Tokyo bought Japanese material in London which was sent to Tokyo to provide him with information for OTIS in the UK.

Shortly after my arrival here in August, I asked for a subscription to Nikkei to be placed by the Embassy, but found that there were simply no funds available. It would make sense if the Embassy received a copy here first, then sent it (as is usual with all publications received) straight

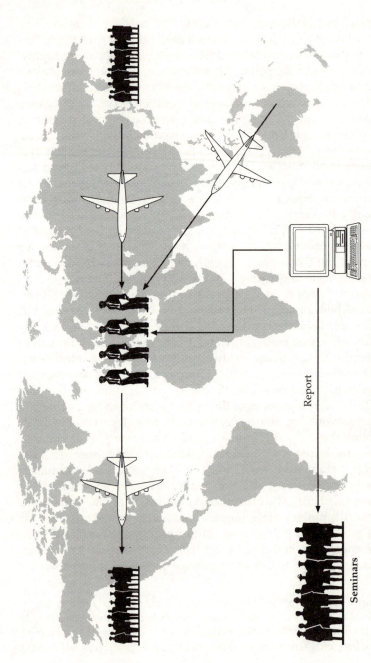

FIG. 9.4   The Outward Science and Technology Expert Mission Scheme

Report

Seminars

on to DTI for further dissemination. However, in the current circumstances, I should be grateful if you could arrange for a copy of each Nikkei High Tech Report to be sent by air mail from London to Tokyo as soon as it is received. [8]

There was also a translation problem. PERA had no translation facilities in-house and those of the DTI were in demand for other purposes. Consequently, the onus was on the science counsellors and their small staffs to translate. Not surprisingly, this introduced yet another filter in that documents which needed little or no translation were much more likely to be made available to UK firms than those which required extensive translation. And yet, of course, it was the material which required translation which was least accessible to UK firms.

THE OUTWARD SCIENCE AND TECHNOLOGY EXPERT MISSION SCHEME (OSTEMS)

OSTEMS started in 1986, justified, as was VES, by the belief that personal experience is an excellent means of acquiring information. In this case, though, the experience was that gained by UK businessmen undertaking a fortnight's foreign tour of firms in their industries. By the end of 1987, some 42 such missions had taken place, each comprising about half a dozen businessmen. Organization of the missions was delegated to research associations and professional institutions, which would select the technology to be investigated, the itinerary, and the mission members for approval by the DTI (Fig. 9.4).

Most of the missions went to Japan, and most of the remainder to the United States. Inviting individuals to join the mission was the responsibility of the sponsors, who found, as had VES, that those who worked for small firms could seldom be spared. So, the missions came to be dominated by employees of large firms, firms which often sent these managers overseas anyway. Moreover, these were senior managers—more than a third were directors of firms—sufficiently important to insist that the scheme upgrade from the original economy-class travel to business class. Also changed during the course of the scheme was the composition of the parties in that an academic came to be added to each mission. The purpose was to increase the coherence of the party, but the main advantage of the academic seems to have been in assisting the dissemination of information after the party's return.

Dissemination turned out to be by far the weakest part of the OSTEMS scheme. Mission members were obliged to contribute to a collective report for presentation at a public seminar and distribution afterwards. Part of the justification for their business-class travel was that this would make writing easier on the return journey. Organization of the seminars was the responsibility of the sponsors, as was dissemination of the reports. In general, there was little enthusiasm for dissemination; as the costs of both mission members and sponsors had been only partly covered by the DTI, both felt they had some property rights in the information gathered. Moreover, DTI policy was that seminars and reports should be priced to cover costs, a policy which made no allowance for the unusual price elasticity in the demand for information. One research association, which had managed to sell only a handful of reports at £10 each, gave the rights to a consultancy in Scotland. The consultancy charged £500 for the report and sold many hundreds of copies. Consultants, because of their contacts, were often chosen by sponsors to organize the missions and to accompany them. Their participation was nearly always rejected by the DTI on the grounds that they would try to make money out of information that was supposed to be freely available to UK industry. The DTI was even more insistent that the reports were not to be sent overseas or made available to foreigners or employees of foreign companies. Enforcement of this information mercantilism was quite impractical, but it did prevent the information that had been gathered overseas from being sent back to the very firms which had provided it. As a courtesy, providing these firms with the report to which they had contributed was elementary, but as a means of propagating the information networks which might have led to the flow of more information from these overseas sources, it was absolutely essential.

INFORMATION AND POLICY

This raft of schemes never did make a single information programme. The schemes were modestly funded and always inadequate to the ambitious task of bringing overseas science and technology information to UK firms. They are of interest here in that such schemes are an acknowledgement that information programmes are a legitimate responsibility of government, and in that these particular examples demonstrate their inevitable inadequacy in the absence of an information perspective.

Without this information perspective, it is hard for governments to be quite sure what it is that information schemes are trying to do, and are achieving. Information mercantilism pervaded all the schemes: the objective was to take information from foreigners in order to make UK industry as a whole more competitive. This attitude was replicated in participants: having paid some of the costs of acquiring the information, they were reluctant to let other UK firms acquire it. Small firms, those least able to procure overseas information by themselves and least able to participate in the schemes, were particularly disadvantaged by this dissemination failure. In general, the schemes illustrate how those who already exploit their own sources and channels to acquire information are able to exploit others to gain yet more.

Information schemes are hard to monitor and evaluate in any meaningful way. What can be counted most readily is not necessarily what is of most value. The large number of bits of information handled by the schemes allowed ministers and officials to trumpet their impact on innovation, which discouraged any investigation of what use was made of the information, and of the degree to which the schemes would assist firms to acquire information for themselves. The schemes made very little use of information technology and it is interesting to consider what difference this might have made. Certainly the indicators of performance would have been even more impressive, and probably the information problems inherent in the schemes would have been better masked, but the problems themselves would still have existed. IT would not have been a solution.

It is difficult not to feel that these schemes would have been more effective and efficient had they been dealing with anything other than information. Because perceptions of information are so nebulous, there was always a tendency, evident in government and participants alike, to adapt the schemes so that they achieved a more recognizable objective. The schemes arose from a variety of initiatives, and each seemed like a good idea at the time. Only when they were assessed collectively in terms of the information they were supposed to be providing UK industry did their inadequacies become apparent. But even had each of these schemes been functioning precisely as intended, there would still have been questions to which responsible policy-makers should have required answers. What, for example, is the impact of such schemes on firms' own information activities? What market distortions arise from the government's involvement in information provision? What are the consequences of the private sector selling government information? [9] Answers to such questions were never required because the questions were never asked. In the absence of an information perspective, they tend not to be asked, and schemes which pretend to bestow all manner of information benefits tend to proliferate.

REFERENCES

1. Edwin Mansfield, 'How rapidly does new industrial technology leak out?', *Journal of Industrial Economics*, 34 (1985), 217–23.
2. Stuart Macdonald, 'Theoretically sound: practically useless? Government grants for industrial R&D in Australia', *Research Policy*, 15 (1986), 269–83.
3. For an interesting account of the development of the Japanese government's methods of securing technical information from overseas see Kaoru Sugihara, 'The development of an informational infrastructure in Meiji Japan', in Lisa Bud-Frierman (ed.), *Information Acumen: The Understanding and Use of Knowledge in Modern Business* (Routledge, London, 1994), 75–97.
4. A full account of this investigation is contained in Stuart Macdonald and David Reams, *Inward Technology Transfer* (DTI, London, Mar. 1989).
5. Department of Trade and Industry, Visiting Engineers Scheme leaflet, 1988.
6. Agreement between Toshiba and Rolls-Royce, 27 Oct. 1987.
7. For an account of the Belgian scheme see Wim Van den Panhuyzen, 'Technology transfer through technological attachés: the Belgian experience', *Technovation*, 3:1 (1985), 69–72.
8. British Science Counsellor, Tokyo to DTI, Dec. 1988.

9. See Tom Mandeville, Don Lamberton, and Stuart Macdonald, 'Marketing public sector information: some issues', *Computer Law and Security Report*, 10:5 (1994), 234–7; Diane Smith, 'The commercialization and privatization of government information', *Government Publications Review*, 12 (1985), 49; Calvin Kent, 'The privatizing of government information: economic considerations', *Government Publications Review*, 16:2 (1989), 113–32; Jean Smith, 'Information: public or private?', *Special Libraries*, 75:4 (1984), 275–82.

10

Hidden Information Flow:
Innovation in Eighteenth-Century Agriculture

SYSTEMATIC CHANGE

Agriculture, never mind eighteenth-century agriculture, may seem an unpromising focus for the information perspective. The contribution of agriculture to the economy may be critical, but it is generally small in the developed world, and so is agricultural employment. Yet, it is not so very long since the agricultural sector—much like the 'information sector' now—accounted for much more growth and employment than all other sectors. Moreover, the future being unknown and the present but a fleeting moment, it is through study and understanding of the past that we learn about ourselves. If an information perspective has no part to play in this, it has no part to play at all.

Here the information perspective is focused on the improvements in agriculture which took place in Britain in the late eighteenth century and on into the early nineteenth century, and which were collectively of such magnitude that their adoption is considered an 'agricultural revolution'. For the same reasons that schooldays have often left the impression that the industrial revolution was all caused by the spinning jenny, there are many who understand the agricultural revolution in terms of Jethro Tull's plough, or Coke of Norfolk's four-course rotation. Greater knowledge of the subject may enhance ability to expound, but it does not necessarily alter initial perspective. If the turnip is admitted to have been of crucial importance in eighteenth-century agriculture, and the context is its part in a Norfolk rotation, it is almost inevitable that Coke too acquires a prominence.

Contemporary observers tried valiantly to make sense of the agricultural change that was taking place around them. With the benefit of hindsight and without the distortion of proximity, political economists and then agricultural historians have used these observations to aid their own understanding of what was going on. Unwittingly but perhaps inevitably, they have depended most on those contemporary observations compatible with a perception of change that is systematic. An orderly process is always easier to describe and understand than one that is erratic and scarcely a process at all. Indeed, for many, it is only when events, past or present, can be understood as process that they are truly worthy of study.

There is surprisingly—suspiciously—little discrepancy between the view of British agricultural innovation prevailing in the late eighteenth century and many of the views that have prevailed since. There may have been political tumult elsewhere, but large parts of British agriculture knew nothing but growth and prosperity. God was in His heaven, and all beneath Him strove for earthly approximation. By the middle of the next century, it was to become clear that God was actually British—probably English —and that everyone had an allotted place in His scheme. A century later, it had come to to be functions rather than people which had their places. There were ways of doing things, and if things were to change, there were ways by which this would happen. With no real revolutions in Britain, the British have some trouble seeing change as anything other than a peaceful process devoid of blood and chaos, an organizational process in which the individual contributes by playing the part he is assigned. Even eccentricity is institutionalized as a national characteristic. Consequently, there is a striking similarity in views of innovation among, say, public servants, professional scientists, and industrial leaders, views which, in principle at least, would not have shocked an Anglican clergyman of the mid-nineteenth century, nor an agricultural writer of the late eighteenth. There is an alternative perspective.

THE IMPROVING LANDLORD

It has long been common wisdom that the information required for technological change in late eighteenth-century agriculture emanated from a few progressive landlords, who advised—instructed, more like—their tenants what to do. [1] Thus, Coke of Norfolk has been portrayed (albeit by another large landlord) as a revolutionary, leading the way to a new agricultural order by example and persuasion, [2] a portrayal at some variance with Coke's own, more modest, assessment of his role. [3] Despite Coke's own assertion that no tenant copied his growing of wheat for 9 years, or his use of the drill for 16 years, and that his improvements did not spread at the rate of even a mile a year, it has still been concluded that 'by the timely impetus which he gave to agriculture, he raised the whole standard of cultivation throughout the kingdom, so that, before Bonaparte became all powerful, England became self-supporting'. [4]

The simplicity of the heroic is always seductive in the study of change, and nowhere more than in agriculture, where so much activity is otherwise anonymous. [5] Moreover, estate records have left a profusion of evidence about the activities of landlords; there are few surviving farm records. [6] Consequently, much is known about landlords and how they saw agricultural innovation; much less about the rest of the agricultural community. Certainly the landlord was generally better educated than his tenants and had both a social responsibility and an economic incentive to enlighten them. And certainly landlords exerted a powerful influence on the course of agricultural improvement through their control of the agricultural infrastructure—the terms and conditions of leases, for example. [7] The opinion of the day was firmly that an infrastructure of long leases, large farms, substantial tenants, and convertible-alternate husbandry was conducive to agricultural innovation, and these matters were largely in the hands of landlords. And yet, landlords probably played a lesser role in agricultural innovation than they claimed, and than has since been claimed on their behalf. An information perspective helps to put them in their proper place.

Of course landlords knew things about farming their tenants did not, and no doubt landlords were often keen to make this information available to tenants, but this does not mean that the landlord's information was necessarily used. [8] As a source of new ideas, the landlord was deficient in that his information was often limited to what he could pick up from his own contacts, generally other landlords, the least trained of all the agricultural classes. [9] Yet, these contacts, together with the resources to explore the information they provided, were seen as advantages which the landlord possessed over the farmer, said to be

the least likely of all men to pursue . . . experiments to an impartial and accurate conclusion. His practice is founded upon the custom of his vicinity and his own observation and experience, but he is . . . too often prejudiced against any innovation. [10]

The landlord's means of transferring information were inhibited by a major transaction problem: tenants were not always convinced by what their landlords told them. Information from those whose profits produced their innovations did not impress those whose innovations had to produce their profits.

The example of one who is a good farmer, must have a much more beneficial effect in his neighbourhood, than that of a great landholder, however successful his practice may be. . . . To such a man occasional failures are of little importance, though they might be serious to ordinary farmers, who, on this account, are seldom very forward in venturing out of their usual routine. [11]

Progressive experiments on the home farm were all very well, but the home farm was not usually expected to make money. A home farm in profit was so exceptional that it was well worth writing a book on the subject. [12] Those who did write such books were sometimes slow to appreciate why many farmers were sometimes reluctant to share their enthusiasm for agricultural improvement.

I never converse with farmers without a fever; I would as soon argue with a methodist, and deem a horse in a mill a superior character. [13]

THE INNOVATING FARMER

Evidence from working farmers is scant, but what survives is revealing. It suggests a burning interest in innovation among at least some of them, but always innovation that was likely to increase profits. A burning resentment was felt towards those whose interest in innovation was driven only by curiosity and noble ideals. Consider the following diatribe from George Boswell, a Dorset farmer with some expertise in the local practice of watering meadows, to George Culley, a farmer in the north of England.

> I've just had a letter from Sir John Sinclair acquainting me with the establishment of a Board of Agriculture, and with Desiring me to Attend it in London as they wished to try an experiment of watering Hyde Park & Saint James Park. I have not yet answered it—He is quite ignorant of my situation in Life—it will not suit my inclinations nor pocket to go two hundred miles as [*sic*] my expense to gratify the idle curiosity of every person that chuse to ask it—I have had one or two of these excursions already—*pro bono publico*, won't always do. I very much doubt of the utility of these things in the hands of Lords and Dukes. Plain Country Farmers are not *at home* when they are with such sort of Folks. My hand, heart & Table such as it is are allways at the command of my Friends and nothing give me greater pleasure than to exchange mutual knowledge; but to dance attendance upon great Folk, & to answer such Questions as they may deign to ask you & then with an ungracious Nod be told you are done with—will not suit the stomach of your sincere Friend. [14]

The attitude of farmers towards progressive landlords is interesting for the alternative perspective it provides, and important because it was the farmer, not the landlord, who had to implement innovation. While the landlord could afford to be an idealist, the working farmer, as Boswell makes quite plain, could not. George Culley, Boswell's correspondent, was not a 'good' farmer in the textbook sense: he was fined for breaching the agricultural conditions of his lease, he broke rotation to take consecutive grain crops when prices were sufficiently tempting, he resorted to the primitive practice of paring and burning as a preparation for turnips, he would forestall in his grain dealings, and he was guilty of selling mediocre cattle and rotten sheep for a quick profit. [15] Such a farmer could relate to other farmers.

FORMAL INFORMATION ACQUISITION

If landlords were limited in the contribution they could make to agricultural innovation, there were other sources of information for the farmer, and other means by which information might be transferred. An information perspective suggests that these were not very effective either, though they were often accorded an influence sufficient to cross the social and economic divide between landlords and at least leading farmers.

Much valuable information has been diffused by the establishment of private model farms, agricultural societies, books, farmers' clubs, implement depots, museums, etc. The chief benefit, however, arising from these institutions, has been conferred upon the landowners, and on the best educated and best informed farmers. The great body of farmers, who rarely read a book, or travel beyond their market-town, have received comparatively little benefit from them. [16]

There was a thriving agricultural press from the late eighteenth century, which published not only accounts of new methods on the home farm, but also the county surveys organized by the Board of Agriculture, agricultural monographs on all manner of innovations, farming journals, the proceedings of local agricultural society meetings, and agricultural contributions to newspapers. Much of this encountered a cynical response from working farmers, not least because these sources of information were heavily influenced by landlord opinion. Culley, whose own book, *Observations on Livestock*, had been attacked for not dealing with the sort of scientific experimentation 'which in this enlightened age of natural philosophy is universally expected', [17] paid lip-service to the utility of experimental farms, but when efforts were made to organize one locally, would have nothing to do with it. He had little involvement in agricultural shows and, though he was punctilious in identifying the sources of his agricultural information, only once does he mention using an idea from a printed source. He had been inspired by the *Farmer's Magazine* to try a crop of yellow turnip in 1807: it failed miserably and was not attempted again. [18] In public, he praised Arthur Young, sometime Secretary to the Board of Agriculture and a prolific scribbler on matters agricultural, and once even requested some of his chicory seed: his private correspondence indicates that he regarded Young the farmer as an incompetent, though an expert on chicory. [19] Just occasionally, such views were openly expressed. One farmer wrote to his local newspaper to complain of

such men as Lord Brougham, who, at the different meetings, makes a boast of his ignorance, and who, in his dotage, pours out such ravings as would not be allowed for a moment from any poor farmer. [20]

The editor was quick to dissociate himself from the observation, asserting that the farmer must have written 'in the sourest and most cynical of moods'. [21] In private correspondence, the editor of the *Farmer's Magazine* was more forthright.

I am under the Necessity sometimes of inserting Communications that are not altogether to my Mind, merely because that better cannot be got and also from a desire to keep well with people, who though imperfectly qualified to write are yet good friends to the Magazine. [22]

Newspapers certainly reached many farmers: an interesting piece of market research from 1841 indicated that farmers accounted for a quarter of one paper's circulation and that each copy bought by a farmer was read by an average of six people. [23] Farmers might have read the paper for information on agricultural innovation, though not for information they were likely to take seriously. Newspapers provided information on agricultural innovation more to stimulate the imagination than to assist critical appraisal and emulation. For example, caterpillars could be eradicated from turnip fields if ducks were sent in to devour them, [24] mice from haystacks with the aid of a few sprigs of mint, [25] and great things were expected of a plough designed to work by wind power. [26] Once a £200 subscription had been filled (a common enough way to secure the disclosure of agricultural inventions), it was revealed that the problem of turnip fly could be overcome by planting radishes with the turnips, the fly apparently preferring the taste of radish to that of turnip. [27] Another subscription, this time of 2,000 guineas, was raised by one Henry Vagg, who promised an even better remedy for the same problem. The subscription filled, Mr Vagg announced that the real enemy was not the fly at all, but slugs, and these could best be destroyed at night by flattening them with a roller. [28] Newspapers also carried advertisements for new sorts of implements and for the services of agricultural machinery builders. These farmers could, and did, take seriously, though they provided scant information and nothing to guide the implementation of innovation. As a source of this sort of information, the sort most valued by innovating farmers, newspapers failed dismally. Much of the advice appearing in the agricultural periodicals was no more profound; for example, the best way to avoid breeding black sheep was to ensure that ewes looked upon nothing black while mating. [29] It mattered little:

the *Annals of Agriculture,* edited by Arthur Young, was one of the most prominent of farming publications and its circulation averaged only four copies per county in 1788. [30]

Much was made at the time, and a good deal has been made since, of the role of agricultural societies in providing farmers with information about innovations. These societies held regular meetings at which papers were delivered and new ideas discussed. Often they published proceedings and some boasted libraries and even museums. They certainly proliferated; some 30 were founded in north-east England before 1850, [31] though none of these ever received coverage in the local press to rival that given to the Society for the Improvement of the English Marigold. Not that these agricultural societies were socially disreputable: of the 101 members of the Tweedside Agricultural Society in 1812, just 22 were mere farmers, [32] and membership of the Durham Agricultural Society in 1803 was restricted to an exclusive 21, with no visitors allowed. [33]

The agricultural societies also held shows, which might have encouraged innovation through competition and emulation. However, only one society in the North-East sponsored a competition in agricultural implements—an area of major interest to farmers as adopters, but of far less interest to landlords, who tended not to tinker with machinery. Wherever there was competition, there were prizes, but it does seem that the same few contestants won most of these. In the sheep category of the Tyneside Agricultural Society shows, 47 prizes went to 21 winners between 1805 and 1821. One winner took a quarter of all these prizes, the top four took over half, and a quarter of all the winners went by the name of Bates. [34] Far from encouraging new blood, the agricultural societies confirmed innovation as the legitimate preserve of old blood. More local and plebeian, and less formal, were the farmers' clubs, which began to displace the societies from the 1830s. [35] They may have played a more important role in innovation: their meetings debated strictly practical subjects and their membership was one of social and occupational equals. At least they abandoned prizes for the servant who had been with his master longest, and the servant who had raised most children without resorting to the parish.

Experimental farms were mooted in the late eighteenth century as a means of reducing theory to practice. Few got off the ground: run by farmers they were socially unacceptable, and run

Fig. 10.1 The Royal Dairy

by landlords they were of little agricultural value. [36] Coke held his famous annual sheep-shearing in Norfolk from 1790 until 1820, a sort of week-long garden party with sheep, and Arthur Young showed off his techniques on his farm at Bradfield in Suffolk to the amusement of visiting farmers.

At Mr Young's I did not see much worth attention, indeed there my disappointment was great—in reading his Annals he immediately discovers the smallest fault in any other person's management, from that I imagined to find an example of the old Arcadian Agriculture—instead of that I met with a hodgepodge of everything without arrangement or system—Chicory the chief production. [37]

The model farm did not come into its own until much later, basically not until the Victorian era of high farming between about 1840 and 1870. High input in order to get high output was the nub of high farming, and the model farm—not unlike the technology park in high technology—demonstrated just how much input the really determined could put into farming. The Prince Consort was probably the most notorious model farmer, his cows in the Royal Dairy at Frogmore enjoying particular luxury (Fig. 10.1). The exterior was Renaissance; inside, the floor was designed to resemble a Turkish carpet, the walls were white and green with mauve stars, there were bas-reliefs on agricultural themes and medallions supported by sea-horses and dolphins. There were fountains, one with a nymph pouring water from a jar, and another 'a fountain of majolica ware, designed by the late Mr Thomas, rising from a shell supported by a heron and bulrushes'. [38] And there were cows.

But rivalling in renown even Albert's agricultural follies was the model farm of John Joseph Mechi at Tiptree in Essex. Mechi was an enthusiast, an entrepreneur who had made his fortune by inventing and selling Mechi's Magic Razor Strops. When the fashions of the Crimean War decimated demand for shaving equipment, Mechi turned his attention to gas lamps. He patented a device for removing the noxious fumes and made a second fortune. But it was his first fortune that allowed Mechi to indulge his agricultural fancy at Tiptree from 1840. He spent all his money on the place and toured the country addressing meetings to explain how this feat had been achieved.

I do not hold up my farm as an example for the ordinary class of land-lords and farmers, for it is quite clear that their general capital is totally inadequate to similar proceedings. [39]

Indeed, so was even his own. Mechi died in penury in 1880.

I believe I was the first who attempted to send out all the manure in this way [by pipe to the fields]. Last year I had 20 dead horses and some dead cows, besides the puddings [dung] in my tank; I had 30 feet of solid stuff.... Luckily it dropped into my head to apply the air-pump ... All those dead horses, except the large bones, have gone through a hole the size of my finger. [40]

FARMERS AND INFORMATION

It may be that farmers did receive the information they required to innovate from a combination of landlord, experimental farm, agricultural society and show, and the agricultural press, but an information perspective suggests that this is unlikely. Farmers were not passive recipients of innovation any more than are modern firms. They wished to try for themselves whatever was likely to use resources more efficiently than existing methods, which in practice meant whatever was likely to make more money. And then, just as the modern firm does, they adapted what they had adopted to suit their individual circumstances. There might appear to be two steps here: the first equivalent to the technology transfer central to studies of the diffusion of innovation, [41] and the second the addition of the farmer's own information to the information package he has received from elsewhere. In fact, there is but one step and that an information transaction.

The farmer was more likely to receive information about innovation if he was able to give information about innovation in return. Where information exchange took place, the farmer had some assurance that he would be able to use, and to adapt, the information package he received. The nature of information ensures that this transaction is always easiest among equals, which would suggest that a peer group emerged at the van-guard of agricultural innovation, a group exchanging informa-tion by means of informal, personal networks. This is precisely what did happen. Leading farmers made pilgrimages to the farms of other leading farmers, they toured extensively to keep contact with their peers and to view their practices at first hand, they corresponded avidly with their equals on agricultural matters, and they even turned their farms into training camps for the sons of leading farmers from other districts.

While the late eighteenth-century mail was fast, [42] at least over short distances, it was expensive and its regular use by farmers confined to the more prosperous. Use it they did though: when in 1800 Culley abetted in hiding a Lincolnshire farmer from his creditors, he felt it necessary to send the poor man even further north, into Scotland, because his neighbours were in such regular correspondence with Lincolnshire farmers that there was no hope of keeping his presence a secret from them. [43] The correspondence that survives takes agricultural improvement seriously; pleasantries are cut to a minimum and there is little discussion of social or religious matters, and definitely no politics. In 1794, Culley was approached by a would-be correspondent from whom he had not heard in thirty years with the suggestion that correspondence be resumed.

[A]s many agreeable changes in that most valuable Science have happened during so long a Period of time, if it be agreeable to you, I have no Objection to have a little Conversation with you by Letter relative to such Improv'ments as are already made in Agriculture. [44]

Culley, whose habit was to pencil draft replies on letters received, expressed a very brief and very clear intention not to oblige.

The information about innovations contained in letters could never be full and specific enough to satisfy the requirements of a potential adopter. There was no real alternative to travel for acquiring information about practices elsewhere. As it happens, this may have been no disadvantage: personal experience allows the acquisition of tacit information, particularly necessary for the application of agricultural innovation; it makes easier the information transaction necessary to obtain such information; and it establishes and reaffirms the personal relationships upon which these transactions are based. Robert Peel was undoubtedly correct in his observation that the greatest obstacle to the diffusion of agricultural innovation was the 'general unwillingness on the part of ordinary farmers to travel beyond the bounds of their own parish'. [45] Most farmers did 'not get far from home, and they have little opportunity of improving; consequently they go on with the same kind of implements and the same patterns as used by their forefathers'. [46] But some farmers—leading farmers—certainly did travel. Take George Hughes, who farmed some 2,000 acres in Northumberland and about whom little would now be known had not his diary survived. [47] This lists his travels between July 1789 and October 1800. Hughes made many a journey to market in those eleven years, mainly to his local market town, but occasionally to others within a radius of about fifty miles. But he also made a single trip of several weeks to Scotland, a tour of farms whose practices he wished to inspect. As the nobility saw Europe on the Grand Tour, so the wealthier farmers of Britain toured in their own country. [48] Oblivious to cathedrals, stately homes, and scenic wonders, they journeyed from farm to farm, scrutinizing everything agricultural. This was business, unquestionably tax-deductible. Typically they travelled in groups of three or four, having made contact with a few farmers on the proposed route before setting out. Further recommendations came along the way in true network fashion as farmers encountered practices of particular interest.

George Culley, probably the best known of Northumberland farmers of the period, and an inveterate traveller, listed those areas of Britain he had not toured as 'Shropshire, Sussex, Devonshire, Cornwall, and a great part of Wales'. [49] His papers refer frequently to the neighbours being away from home on tour. One of their regular destinations seems to have been the Dorset farm of George Boswell, whence he wrote to Culley in 1793.

Pray Sir, What kind of Folks are left behind in the North? Are we to judge by the samples you've sent us? Upon my word and credit we make a very ridiculous appearance, accepting [sic] one or two of my acquaintance, ... they all stand and look like stuck piggs, with their mouths open. I have only to request, you will continue me on your list of acquaintances and let me often hear from You, and let me see as many of your Country men as you can spare to travel this way. What I have seen charm me, Tho' they are not Bakewell's [sic] and crusty, They are *Ready enough* and friendly, which I much more value. [50]

Another means of affording farmers practical experience of unfamiliar techniques was the system of agricultural apprenticeship.

Farmers' sons would often be sent from home to spend a year or so with a renowned farmer in a more progressive area, [51] during which time the young man would be expected to work on his host's farm. [52] Culley frequently housed half a dozen students at a time and it is clear that his neighbours were engaged in the same business. [53] With fees of between £60 and £100 a year for board and instruction (at a time when an agricultural labourer's annual wage might be £30), this was a major information business.

When so much of an innovation can be encapsulated only in the experience of individuals, successful adoption often becomes dependent on the transfer of people. This is why the transfer of individuals is so often required to transfer the know-how that accompanies a patent licence, and why there is such high mobility of key personnel in high technology. It also explains the eighteenth-century demand for those familiar with the practices of advanced agricultural districts. Estates in more backward areas frequently advertised for tenants from progressive regions in the hope that their skills would rub off on the local tenantry. It was Scotland and the North which supplied the rest of the country with enlightened foremen, bailiffs, and tenants. [54] Even the 'half crazy, half cunning, Scotchman, Gourlay', who crossed swords with William Cobbett in Winchester, had, according to Cobbett, come 'to teach the moon-rakers "hoo to farm, mon"'. [55]

LABOURERS AND INNOVATION

This insistence on personal experience of innovation is interesting. In information terms, it is confirmation that much information is best transferred in people, and that the user of innovation contributes his own information to the information he receives. But the real users of innovation were perhaps no more the prosperous farmers than they were the dilettante landlords. The real users of innovation were probably the agricultural labourers. What evidence is there that these individuals had a role of any importance to play? Quite a bit, as it happens, though they were often seen at the time—as workers have often been seen since— as immovable opponents of change.

I am sure that anyone who has had anything to do with the introduction of a new implement will bear me out, that we have the greatest difficulty in getting our men to use even common judgement in its use. They hate—with a dreadful hatred—any innovation . . . [56]

When Sir John Delaval was seized with a desire in 1783 to improve his northern estates, he sent from London a succession of implements for evaluation. They encountered what was interpreted as the intransigence of the farm labourers, but what was actually resistance to the means by which innovation was being imposed rather than to innovation itself.

The two ploughs was received some time ago and has been tried. Matthew [the ploughman] says they will nether of them answer well for this strong Land—they can't get the smaller one to answer at all, he imagines the Beam has been made of Green wood, or otherwise has been twisted since it was made and stands quite from the Land. The larger one goes much better and I do not hear of any fault only its not effactually turning the furrows. [57]

A double plough arrived next, which did 'not meet with Matthew's approbation', [58] followed by a drill rake which Lady Delaval had ordered to be built from instructions in Harte's *Essays on Husbandry*. That was sabotaged by strapping the machine to an untrained horse which was followed by a procession of a dozen women and children to obliterate the drills. [59] A scythe dispatched later that year was evaluated on the stoniest of fields, specially selected by a labourer skilled in the use of the sickle: the scythe was found to be wanting. [60]

There is a considerable literature on the plight of the oppressed agricultural labourer, which was certainly real enough in the South, where wages were inadequate, employment uncertain, and literacy uncommon. [61] Here there was little incentive for labourers to learn new ways which would undermine existing expertise. William Lester put it nicely in 1811 when he noted that new skills 'will set them back in life, even on a par with the youth that is just entering on business, without his incitements to persevere'. [62] This logical reluctance was often perceived as sheer indolence; in 1808, Andrew Grey referred to

the unwillingness (by no means unnatural) of the labouring servants, to take the trouble, by a fair trial, of acquiring the same facility in managing the improved instruments, as that which they had attained in managing those to which they had been so long accustomed. [63]

Without education, the labourer's expertise could be based only on years of his own accumulated experience. According to Jesse Collins, this could be of considerable value: even the southern labourer

had a shrewd common sense, while his knowledge and powers of observation with regard to crops, weather, seasons, and all other things that came within the narrow range of his hard and dismal life, were marked and hereditary. [64]

But without education, the labourer had no means of placing this experience in context, and of passing it on to others. In short, the South wasted a major agricultural resource. As one observer reported in 1882

from my intercourse with the labourers in country villages for the last forty years I can say it confidently, that many keen intellects have been wasted from want of cultivation; many more than those who class all rustics as bumpkins, chawbacons, louts, have any idea of. [65]

If the southern labourer did chance to become educated above his station, he was not slow to leave it for an urban existence. [66]

The image of the farm labourer as a miserable, ignorant wretch, implacably opposed to anything new, fitted well with a notion of innovation controlled by social systems. It was, however, at odds with the opinions of those on the ground. Farmers' sons spending their educational year on progressive farms were advised to leave their horses behind and to mix with the labourers as much as possible as this was the only way to learn. This, though, was in the North, where there was not only no shortage of innovations to observe, but also labourers aplenty able to pass on the expertise they had acquired in applying them. In the north of England and throughout Scotland, literacy among farm labourers was just about universal.

It is said there are very few servants or labourers in the agricultural districts of Scotland, who are not able, from their education, to take a bailiff's place! To the superior education of the Scotch may, in part, be attributed their successful agriculture; for it cannot be expected that the land will be properly cultivated by an ignorant peasantry. [67]

Education provided the means by which the labourer could transfer information, but more fundamentally, it provided the labourer with an appreciation that he participated in innovation not to enhance the glory of British agriculture, but to enhance his own welfare. Aware that the information he carried had some real value to himself and to others, the labourer was able to become an active participant not simply in information transfer, but in information transactions.

Where there is evidence of labourers mastering a technology in one area and then being used to transfer the technology to other areas, it may be assumed that these labourers possessed information that was not conveniently embodied in machinery or as readily available from landlords, diagrams, newspapers, societies, experimental farms, or the voluminous agricultural literature. In coming to terms with innovation, labourers made adaptations to suit their own requirements; they made user modifications which determined the ultimate success of the innovation. It was George Boswell, the farmer, who provided the new type of drill for his Dorset farm in 1789, but his labourers determined how thickly the seed was to be sown. [68] William Dawson, newly returned to Scotland from an agricultural apprenticeship in England, supposedly introduced drill husbandry to the Borders, but it was from his labourer, James MacDougal, that the region learned the associated skill of ploughing with two horses abreast. [69]

When labourers took technological change with them from one region to another, they carried not just the information they themselves had received, but also that which they had added to make the innovation successful. Thus, Berwickshire reapers in 1790 refused to exchange their sickles for the scythe-hooks provided by farmers, but rapidly accepted the new implement when imported labourers demonstrated just how it could be used to obtain superior performance. [70] Changes in hand-tool technology tend to have been neglected by students of innovation in favour of changes associated with agricultural engineering (much as radical innovation has overshadowed the contribution of incremental innovation), yet the former probably made a much greater contribution to growth in productivity. [71] The successful adoption of new implements was especially dependent on the knowledge of labourers. There was really little point in introducing a new implement without also acquiring a labourer familiar with how the implement worked.

Boulton and Watt, selling their steam engines overseas, were constantly faced with demands from customers to send an engineer to work the machine, and to remain with the machine to ensure that it kept working. [72] Such individuals, suddenly thrust into an environment where they were the only source of essential information, had some trouble adapting to the dissolute lifestyle the value of their information permitted. [73] They took to drink or women, or both. Less dramatically, the Duke of Northumberland's interest in more wire fencing in 1852 required the return from Scotland of one Charles Duff, the 'first rate labourer' who had assisted in the Duke's first fencing venture. [74] When George Culley sought to introduce the water-meadow system to Northumberland, he was advised by Robert Bakewell, yet another improving farmer, to import a labourer from George Boswell in Dorset. [75] Boswell was uneasy with this strategy.

[B]y his self consequence, and *acquired* importance . . . [he] might withhold much useful instruction. The method I shall submit to you is; to fix upon a healthy, robust Man, who has been *used to labour* . . . it is absolutely necessary for him *to be a Labourer* and to be both willing and able to go through the manual part of the work in all weather, as the Watermen do here. [76]

This was precisely what happened; Culley's labourer spent three months in Dorset and returned to construct the first water-meadows in Northumberland. Culley himself was constantly pestered by correspondents from all over the country wishing to be sent skilled labourers for a year or so until their skills had been learnt by local workers.

If it happens that you know of a sturdy good Ploughman unmarried, and who has been accustomed to work oxen . . . [77]

if any steady young Man who has merely been accustomed to go with Draughts etc is willing to come to this country . . . [78]

Lord K wishes much to have a good Plowman from you—and one that will be steady and not led foolishly away by the men of the Country. [79]

Northern newspapers regularly carried advertisements to entice labourers with specific skills to go south—a knowledge of drill management, or the ability to mow with an Aberdeen corn scythe, for example. [80] But frequently it was credential enough simply for the labourer to come from an advanced agricultural region.

Wanted immediately, as a steward and Hind, to take the management of a Farm in Berkshire, which will be entered on the 29th of this Month,—an experienced Husbandman, who is well acquainted with the modern improvements in Agriculture, particularly those practiced in Northumberland. [81]

For such an individual, landlords and farmers were willing to pay handsomely and to go to some trouble. One labourer, imported in 1801 because he was 'said to understand a Mill well', engaged his new employer in months of negotiation. Eventually the farmer promised to buy all the household goods the labourer could not sell to neighbours, to guarantee a good house, pay £1 to cover any breakages, a further £5 for conveyance, and to appease the labourer's wife, described as a 'whinging, peevish, fretfull body'. [82] For this amount of bother, there must have been anticipation of considerable return.

PERSPECTIVES OF THE JOURNEY TO MECCA

George Culley hailed from the Glendale region of north-west Northumberland, famous in his time as 'the Mecca of agricultural pilgrimage'. [83] The adulation is strangely reminiscent of that afforded another valley very much later: Silicon Valley, the Mecca of high technology, has also seen more than its share of pilgrims searching for the secret of innovation. [84] Few visitors to either valley seem to have found the Kaaba. Given the conflict between the practice of innovation and the perception of innovation prevailing in the eighteenth century, and just as dominant now, this is hardly surprising. Both see change as something arranged by those who know best and implemented by those who know their place.

The view of agricultural change as inspired and directed by the landlord, and fuelled by formal information systems, is not so very different from an impression of change that is determined by the policymaker and executed through government programmes, or of change that is ordered by the chief executive and implemented under the control of the organization. These are views of change as part of a system, subservient to that system—change as subsystem, change as process.

It is no part of the argument here to insist that this perception is wrong. But any single perspective is inevitably restricted. An information perspective allows innovation in eighteenth-century agriculture to be seen in another light, one that reveals information transactions among people whose role in innovation would not otherwise be apparent; in fact, whose role is hidden by their insignificant place in systems. This information perspective is no more correct than any other, but it is no less correct either. What it reveals is agricultural innovation to have been very much the product of those who worked most closely with the innovations themselves, farmers and labourers. This may seem hardly the most startling of revelations, yet it is quite at odds with a prevailing view of innovation as a process within a system, a process controlled from above and implemented below, a process which can be learnt, a process which excludes the uncertainty of the external, which does not threaten systems because it is part of those same systems. Faith in this orthodoxy is so strong that it could be argued that change actually does occur in this way simply because there is so much belief that it should—a case of faith moving mountains. Alternative views are, therefore, redundant. Maybe, but they are at least refreshing.

REFERENCES

1. e.g. Lord Ernle, *English Farming Past and Present*, 4th edn. (Longmans Green, London, 1932), 207.
2. Earl Spencer, 'On the improvements which have taken place in West Norfolk', *Journal of the Royal Agricultural Society*, 3 (1842), 9.
3. R. A. C. Parker, 'Coke of Norfolk and the Agricultural Revolution', *Economic History Review*, 8 (1955), 155–66 and *Coke of Norfolk: A Financial and Agricultural Study* (Oxford University Press, Oxford, 1975), 199.
4. A. M. W. Stirling, *Coke of Norfolk and his Friends* (John Lane, London, 1912), 174–5, 190. See also Naomi Riches, *The Agricultural Revolution in Norfolk* (University of North Carolina Press, Chapel Hill, NC, 1937).
5. See Stuart Macdonald, 'The role of the individual in agricultural change: the example of George Culley of Fenton, Northumberland', in H. S. A. Fox and R. A. Butlin (eds.), *Change in the Countryside* (Institute of British Geographers, London, 1979), 5–21.

6. E. L. Jones and E. J. T. Collins, 'The collection and analysis of farm record books', *Journal of the Society of Archivists*, 3 (1963), 86–9.
7. Stuart Macdonald, 'The lease in agricultural improvement', *Journal of the Royal Agricultural Society of England*, 137 (1976), 19–26.
8. G. E. Mingay, *English Landed Society in the Eighteenth Century* (Routledge and Kegan Paul, London, 1963), 166.
9. James Caird, *English Agriculture in 1850–51* (Longman, London, 1852), 493.
10. John Grey, *Account of Experiments with Manures* (1843), Northumberland County Record Office (NCRO)/ZHE/34/16.
11. *Farmer's Magazine*, 21 (1820), 480.
12. F. M. L. Thompson, 'English great estates in the nineteenth century', in *Communications of the First International Conference of Economic History* (Stockholm, 1960), 392.
13. *Annals of Agriculture*, 4 (1785), 37.
14. George Boswell to George Culley, 1793, NCRO/ZCU/18.
15. Macdonald, 'The role of the individual in agricultural change'.
16. *Newcastle Courant*, 4 Feb. 1848.
17. *Annals of Agriculture*, 4 (1786), 414–15.
18. George Culley to Alexander Hamilton, 3 June 1807, NCRO/ZCU/31.
19. Macdonald, 'The role of the individual in agricultural change'.
20. *Westmorland Gazette*, 20 Oct. 1849. Quoted in Elizabeth Edwards, 'The Agricultural Societies of the Upper Eden Valley, 1840–1900', (University MA thesis, 1974), facing p. 45.
21. Ibid.
22. Editor of the *Farmer's Magazine* to George Culley, 17 Mar. 1803, NCRO/ZCU/25.
23. *Newcastle Courant*, 1 Jan. 1841.
24. *Newcastle Courant*, 5 Aug. 1780, 26 July 1783, 30 July 1836.
25. *Newcastle Courant*, 26 Oct. 1793.
26. *Newcastle Courant*, 13 Apr. 1811.
27. *Newcastle Courant*, 3 July 1802.
28. *Newcastle Courant*, 26 Apr., 14 June, 5 July 1788, 8 Aug. 1789.
29. Robert Wallace, *Farm Livestock of Great Britain* (1885), 16.
30. *Annals of Agriculture*, 10 (1788), 593.
31. Stuart Macdonald, 'The Development of Agriculture and the Diffusion of Agricultural Innovation in Northumberland, 1750–1850', (University of Newcastle Ph.D. thesis, 1974).
32. *Newcastle Courant*, 25 Apr. 1812.
33. *Farmer's Magazine*, 4 (1803), 283–6.
34. Stuart Macdonald, 'The diffusion of knowledge among Northumberland farmers, 1780–1815', *Agricultural History Review*, 27 (1979), 30–9.

35. Nicholas Goddard, 'Kentish farmers' clubs in the mid nineteenth century', *Cantium*, 6:4 (1974), 80–3.

36. Stuart Macdonald, 'The model farm', in G. E. Mingay (ed.), *The Victorian Countryside* (Routledge and Kegan Paul, London, 1981), vol. 1, pp. 214–26.

37. William Mure to George Culley, 31 Mar. 1783, NCRO/ZCU/18. See also G. E. Mingay, *Arthur Young and his Times* (Macmillan, London, 1975), 9–11.

38. J. C. Morton, *The Prince Consort's Farms* (London, 1863), 108.

39. J. J. Mechi, *How to Farm Profitably: Or the Sayings and Doings of Mr Alderman Mechi* (London, 1859), 183.

40. Ibid. 153–4.

41. See Everett Rogers, *Bibliography on the Diffusion of Innovations*, Diffusion of Innovations Research Report 6, Department of Communication, Michigan State University, 1967. Succeeding work turned the user from passive recipient of diffusion to active participant in innovation. See Dorothy Leonard-Barton and Everett Rogers, *Horizontal Diffusion of Innovations: An Alternative Paradigm to the Classical Diffusion Model*, Working Paper 1214, Sloan School of Management, MIT, Cambridge, Mass., 1981.

42. George Culley corresponded regularly with the manager of his family farm in south Durham. The weekly letter, posted at Darlington late on Monday afternoon, travelled well over 100 miles and was generally in Culley's hands by the Tuesday afternoon, or the Wednesday morning at the very latest. Correspondence in both directions cost Culley about £5 a year.

43. George Culley to Mr Foreman, 22 Mar. 1800, NCRO/ZCU/31.

44. T. Carlisle to George Culley, 24 Apr. 1794, NCRO/ZCU/18.

45. Quoted in Caird, *English Agriculture in 1850–51*, p. viii.

46. Joseph Laycock to Newcastle Farmers' Club, 8 Oct. 1847, Newcastle Literary and Philosophical Society, Bolbec N630.6/1.

47. NCRO/ZSI/46.

48. John Bailey, *General View of the Agriculture of Durham* (London, 1810), 67.

49. George Culley, *Observations on Livestock*, 3rd edn. (Robinson, London, 1801), pp. vii–viii. See also D. J. Rowe's introduction to John Bailey and George Culley, *General View of the Agriculture of Northumberland, Cumberland and Westmorland* (1805; repr. Newcastle 1972), pp. i–xxiv; D. J. Rowe, 'The Culleys, Northumberland farmers, 1767–1813', *Agricultural History Review*, 19:2 (1971), 156–74; Stuart Macdonald, 'The role of George Culley of Fenton in the development of Northumberland agriculture', *Archaeologia Aeliana*, 3 (1975), 131–41.

50. George Boswell to George Culley, 25 July 1793, NCRO/ZCU/30. Bakewell farmed in Leicestershire and was renowned both for the

improvements he made to Leicester sheep and longhorn cattle and for his reluctance to divulge any information that might damage the market for his improved stock.

51. *Farmer's Magazine*, 7 (1806), 153–6.

52. For an account of such a year, see Stuart Macdonald, 'The diary of an agricultural apprentice in Northumberland, 1842', *Local Historian*, 12:3/4 (1976), 139–45.

53. Joseph Oxley to Sir John Delaval, 14 Dec. 1782, NCRO/2DE/4/14/42; George Culley to Matthew Culley, Oct. 1784, NCRO/ZCU/9; George Culley to Thomas Wakefield, 17 Aug. 1796, NCRO/ZCU/21; George Culley to ?, 13 July 1806, NCRO/ZCU/32.

54. G. E. Mingay, *Rural Life in Victorian England* (Heinemann, London, 1977), 70–1; G. E. Fussell, 'The "foreign" invasion of Essex', *Essex Farmers' Journal*, 30:5 (1951), 41–3; Leonce de Lavergne, *The Rural Economy of England, Scotland and Ireland* (Edinburgh, 1855), 286; Cuthbert Headlam, *The Three Northern Counties of England* (Northumberland Press, Gateshead, 1939), 129.

55. William Cobbett, *Rural Rides* (Macdonald, London, 1958), 328–9.

56. R. M. Weeks, 'On grubbers, cultivators and autumn cleaning', paper read to Newcastle Farmers' Club, 1 July 1854, Newcastle Literary and Philosophical Society, Bolbec N630.6/3.

57. John Bryers to Sir John Delaval, 14 Feb. 1783, NCRO/2DE/4/20/35.

58. Joseph Oxley to Sir John Delaval, 22 Feb. 1783, NCRO/2DE/4/15/3.

59. John Bryers to Sir John Delaval, 14 Mar., 4 Apr. 1783, NCRO/2DE/4/20/39, 42.

60. John Bryers to Sir John Delaval, 28 Sept. 1783, NCRO/2DE/4/20/66.

61. e.g. W. Hasbach, *A History of the English Agricultural Labourer* (Frank Cass, London, 1966); J. L. Hammond and B. Hammond, *The Village Labourer* (Longman Green, London, 1913).

62. William Lester, *A History of British Implements and Machinery Applicable to Agriculture* (Longman, London, 1811), 205–6.

63. Andrew Grey, *The Plough-Wright's Assistant* (1808), p. xi.

64. Jesse Collings, *Land Reform* (Longmans, London, 1906), 24.

65. Treasurer Hawker, 'The Devonshire farm-labourer now and eighty years ago', *Reports and Transactions of the Devonshire Association*, 14 (1882), 332.

66. Rowland Prothero, *The Pioneers and Progress of English Farming* (Longmans, London, 1888), 224; Collings, *Land Reform*, 23; William Coles Finch, *Life in Rural England* (Daniel, London, 1928), 114.

67. Jonathon Binns, *Notes on the Agriculture of Lancashire with Suggestions for its Improvement* (Preston, 1851), 95.

68. George Boswell to George Culley, 6 Apr. 1789, NCRO/ZCU/14.
69. *Farmer's Magazine*, 4 (1803), 316–17.
70. *Farmer's Magazine*, 23 (1822), 235–6.
71. E. J. T. Collins, 'Harvest technology and labour supply in Britain, 1790–1870', *Economic History Review*, 22:3 (1969), 453–73.
72. Jennifer Tann, 'Marketing methods in the international steam engine market: the case of Boulton and Watt', *Journal of Economic History*, 38:2 (1978), 363–89.
73. Jennifer Tann and M. J. Breckin, 'The international diffusion of the Watt Engine, 1775–1825', *Economic History Review* 31:4 (1978), 541–64; see also Kristine Bruland, *British Technology and European Industrialization* (Cambridge University Press, Cambridge, 1989).
74. ? to Mr Burnett, 1852, NCRO/ZHE/34/9.
75. Robert Bakewell to George Culley, 8 Feb. 1787, in H. C. Pawson, *Robert Bakewell* (Crosby Lockwood, London, 1957), 107.
76. George Boswell to George Culley, 25 Mar. 1787, NCRO/ZCU/12.
77. Martin Dalrymple to George Culley, 16 Oct. 1806, NCRO/ZCU/28.
78. George Laing to George Culley, 19 Apr. 1803, NCRO/ZCU/25.
79. William Mure to George Culley, 31 Mar. 1793, NCRO/ZCU/18.
80. *Newcastle Courant*, 5 Mar. 1808, 5 Sept. 1845.
81. *Newcastle Courant*, 8 Sept. 1804.
82. Matthew Culley to John Welch, 26 Mar. 1801, NCRO/ZCU/6.
83. Richard Welford, *Men of Mark 'Twixt Tyne and Tweed* (W. Scott, London, 1895), vol. 1, p. 673.
84. Stuart Macdonald, 'High technology policy and the Silicon Valley model: an Australian perspective', *Prometheus*, 1:2 (1983), 330–49.

11

The Illusion of Order:
Innovation and the Patent System

INFORMATION AS PROPERTY

The essence of intellectual property rights (IPR) is the application of ownership to information by means of such devices as copyright, trademarks, and patents. In one sense, this acknowledges the peculiar characteristics of information, in that very specialized legislation is applied. In a more fundamental sense, these peculiar characteristics are set aside in the attempt to make information fit conventional notions of property. Information does not fit easily.

An information perspective struggles to make sense of the intellectual property system, the primary aim of which is to allow information to be treated like any other good, any other property. Only when the characteristics of information are totally uncompromising are concessions made. So, for example, ownership is bestowed not on information itself, but on the right to use information. Were it otherwise, were information itself owned, the information of another could be used without depriving him of his property. But such concessions are avoided where at all possible by the pragmatic assumption that information is a good like any other, by rejecting an information perspective.

While the pretence may be sufficiently robust to bear the immediate arguments it supports, its fundamental weaknesses tend to become evident when subsequent and consequent arguments are heaped on top. The logic behind copyright shows obvious signs of strain when it is stretched from literature to computer software. Similarly, extending patent protection from mechanical contrivances to plants and genetic material turns flaws in the logic into gaping cracks. This being so, a valid observation might then be that an information perspective is redundant;

the strengths and weaknesses of IPR are already evident from existing perspectives. It might then be concluded—indeed, it has been—that the strengths and weaknesses of IPR tend to cancel each other out so that the social and economic importance of what remains is really neither here nor there. Certainly there is some discrepancy between empirical observation and the claims made for the intellectual property system as universal regulator of the world's innovation.

But this does not mean that the intellectual property system is not influential in some circumstances, nor that its influence is necessarily direct and obvious. It will be argued here that the major impact on innovation of IPR arises from the compatibility between that system and how innovation is widely perceived. A view of innovation as the outcome of process, as something contained within, and controlled by, the organization, readily finds room for that part of the intellectual property system which is concerned with the ownership and control of information. It is much less compatible with that part of the intellectual property system intended to encourage the dissemination of information. The theory of intellectual property reflects the attempts of legal logic to grapple with information, and an information perspective reveals only the problems in trying to do this, problems already evident enough from many other perspectives. In practice, the intellectual property system reflects, and is reinforced by, a perception of innovation which ignores the characteristics of information. This is not evident from other perspectives, and here an information perspective has a useful role to play.

THE PATENT SYSTEM

The patent is the instrument of the intellectual property system best known and most closely associated with innovation. The patent is the outcome of a bargain between an inventor and society by which society grants the inventor certain rights to his invention in return for the inventor's disclosure of whatever it is he has invented. [1] Without these rights, it is argued, the inventor would be unable to reveal his invention for fear that others would steal it. Consequently, the inventor would have

little incentive to invent and society would forgo the invention
and its benefits. Thus, the patent system neatly allows the inventor to exploit his invention, and provides society with an invention it would not otherwise have had. Nothing could be more
straightforward.

Actually, the patent system does not work like this at all. [2]
It is assumed to work this way because the assumption suits the
purposes of diverse interests. Like the linear model of technological change, which reinforces the patent system, which in
turn supports the model, the patent system is something in
which belief is convenient and, from some perspectives, necessary.
Belief in the value of the patent system is very much entrenched
in other beliefs and values. Without these, faith in the patent
system would crumble.

If we did not have a patent system, it would be irresponsible, on the
basis of our present knowledge of its economic consequences, to recommend instituting one. But since we have had a patent system for a long
time, it would be irresponsible, on the basis of our present knowledge,
to recommend abolishing it. [3]

It is no part of the current endeavour to recommend replace-
ments for, or even improvements to, the patent system. Rather,
the purpose is to demonstrate how distorted views of what the
patent system does are a product of a failure to apply an information perspective. Perennial recommendations for the improvement of the system—for it is difficult not to notice the gap
between patent theory and patent practice, and tempting to
speculate on the benefits that changes would produce—tend to
reinforce these views in that any analysis demands that what is
analysed be taken seriously. [4] In the great scheme of things,
the patent system itself is neither here nor there. What is important about the patent system, and what an information perspective reveals, is that it fosters certain impressions of innovation
and allows them to flourish. But even this limited analysis suggests a potency which the patent system does not really possess:
these notions of innovation are already deeply entrenched in
society and the economy and are simply justified by the patent
system. The patent system is effect rather than cause, and much
of what is done with, and in the name of, the patent system,
and intellectual property systems generally, is more compatible

with innovation as we wish to imagine it than with innovation as it really is.

PATENTS AND INNOVATION

Although it is evident that neither inventor nor society can reap much benefit from invention itself, that whatever rewards there are will come from innovation, [5] the patent system scarcely concerns itself with innovation. Invention is what it protects, either on the grounds that invention is of value in itself, or on the linear grounds that invention leads to innovation and is its core component. The observation that the early patent system was more concerned with innovation and less with invention has encouraged a conviction that one road to improvement leads back to this primitive state, [6] an optimism which blithely disregards the intensity of vested interests in the system's current emphasis. [7] Vested interests are hardly new; centuries ago the patent system was being exploited to reward royal favourites through the granting of monopolies. The patent system is still sufficiently flexible to accommodate a range of applications, an accommodation which only endears its users further to the model of innovation that it represents. It is, of course, quite fanciful to imagine that the independent inventor and the gigantic pharmaceutical firm, who together probably account for the majority of the world's patents, use the patent system in the same way. The patent system obliges both, allowing them to imagine innovation and the means by which it comes about in ways with which each is comfortable, ways that fit. But first, a couple of examples of the patent system in practice. They, too, are wildly different, but each presents a situation in which innovation can be perceived tidily in terms of the patent system, and in which it is quite misleading to do this.

THE THRESHING MACHINE

The mechanization of British agriculture in the late eighteenth and early nineteenth centuries put new resources at the disposal of British farmers, allowing them to produce more to support a growing, and increasingly urban, population. There had always been some degree of mechanization in agriculture—the plough, after all, is a machine. There had always been innovation, but the pace of innovation accelerated to such an extent during this period that the term 'Agricultural Revolution' is commonly deployed to indicate a comparability with the slightly later Industrial Revolution. In the vanguard of these new battalions of farming machinery was the threshing machine, a device for separating grain from straw. This most fundamental of agricultural tasks had previously been accomplished by hand-flailing, beating mounds of reaped corn with heavy hinged sticks, an exhausting, lengthy, and—given the dust it raised—unhealthy task.

The threshing machine changed all this, at least in the north of the country, where labour was expensive and scarce, and farms were large. What is remarkable about the threshing machine is less that it was the precursor of so much other innovation in farm machinery than that it was such a radical innovation. This was not some spindly Heath Robinson device cranked by hand; this was a substantial machine, rapidly developed into a behemoth occupying two floors of the barn and requiring its own external power source. Eight horses were common, though there were horse-mills turned by a dozen or even sixteen, and a few of the largest threshing machines had their own water- or windmills. This power was needed by the threshing machine for only a few weeks of the year and its availability for the remainder did much to stimulate the development of machinery to carry out other agricultural tasks, especially when coal-fired boilers and steam engines came to be applied to threshing. In southern England, where tenancies were small and labour both plentiful and cheap, adoption of such monstrous machines was always exceptional, so much so that they were sufficiently notorious to be a convenient focus for the Captain Swing disturbances in the early 1830s. [8] (The swingle was the leather hinge linking the wooden handle of the flail to the heavy wooden stave which hit the corn.) In the North, though, threshing machines soon came to be universal on farms of any size, and even on farms where little grain was grown, so enabling was their power source. [9]

The threshing machine was a major agricultural innovation which spread, if not to southern England, then to many of the

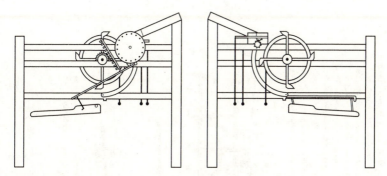

FIG. 11.1   Meikle's threshing machine of 1786

larger farms of northern Europe. It was an innovation which understandably attracted considerable attention at the time, particularly that of the most prominent enthusiasts for agricultural improvement. This was an age in which agricultural innovation was not only fashionable, but also patriotic; even George III, under the *nom de plume* of Robinson, contributed his ideas to agricultural journals. Actually, in its passion to apply science for the benefit of humanity, the fervour for agricultural improvement transcended mere patriotism; George Washington was writing to leading British farmers on agricultural matters throughout the American War of Independence. The great and good chose to see themselves, and to be seen, as the leaders of agricultural improvement, an impression which has left its mark on the attitude of some historians towards the agricultural innovation of the period. In such a scenario, there was no major role for the tenant farmer or the agricultural labourer, except as followers, ready and willing to learn from their betters. [10] There was, though, in such a neat and tidy view of innovation, a role for the patent. For such a major innovation as the threshing machine, patents must have been important. The machine might separate the grain from the straw, but an ordered view of innovation required that a patent separate the wheat from the chaff.

One Andrew Meikle of East Lothian in Scotland applied for a patent on the threshing machine in 1786. [11] Meikle's threshing machine was some way from perfection and of dubious originality, but the patent was granted nevertheless (Fig. 11.1). Certainly Meikle's patent was quite irrelevant to the extraordinarily rapid

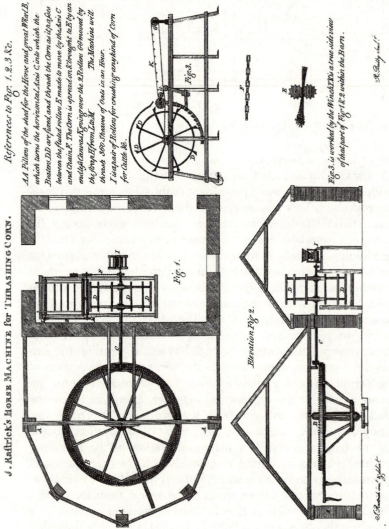

FIG. 11.2 Raistrick's threshing machine

diffusion of the threshing machine in southern Scotland and northern England, and Meikle himself played only the tiniest of parts. [12] Threshing machines were adopted by farmers made aware of their merits through personal experience of adoption by other farmers. The machines themselves were constructed by small builders, of which Meikle was but one of many. It was this virulent diffusion which, years later, prompted Meikle to claim his patent rights.

Sir, I have the orders of Mr Meikle the Proprietor of the Patent for Threshing Machines to require you to send me without delay a list of every Threshing Machine you have made and Erected . . . you are Also required to write down . . . the names of every Millwright, Joiner or others that you know of who have Erected Threshing Machines. [13]

Meikle proposed that all those farmers who had adopted the innovation should pay him a licence fee. To their rescue came one John Raistrick, civil engineer, inventor, and crank, who had been building threshing machines for years and asserted that the invention was his (Fig. 11.2). [14] The dispute went to law in 1799, which resolved nothing and cost Meikle £2,000. Raistrick crowed that he had saved farmers thousands of pounds in licence fees, and was rewarded with a few hundred from public subscriptions. Meikle, being altogether a more respectable sort of person, received his reward from landlords through a subscription organized by the Highland and Agricultural Society.

Here we have the patent system performing none of the functions for which it is supposedly intended. It did not encourage threshing machine inventors to invent, it did not protect the owner of the threshing machine patent, and it played no part at all in disseminating information about the invention. No doubt Meikle and Raistrick and a good many other agricultural machine builders made their own amendments to basic threshing principles, but these principles were always fairly obvious and were being implemented years before Meikle applied for his patent. The secret of a good threshing machine lay in the combination of function, strength, and power; it had to be a device with sufficient force to thresh effectively without self-destructing. These were not attributes embodied in the invention; they had to be built into each machine during its construction on the farm. The major contribution to the innovation came from the individuals who erected them. Their skills were in making a series of principles practical and functional, and their success in applying these skills was a dominant factor in the wide and rapid diffusion of the threshing machine. The patent denied this reality, and in doing so helped perpetuate a very different notion of innovation.

Castings, iron and brass complete, for this machine (or even the wood patterns) may be had at Mr Parker's foundry, Stourport ... but I do not know of any particular workman who now professes making and erecting them. [15]

[In 1802] a Mr Prentiss, from Edinburgh, erected in Pennsylvania, New Jersey and Delaware, six or seven machines upon the Scotch principle, which were found to answer well. But on account of the extreme care required in feeding them and the inability of common workmen to keep them in repair, the builder being engaged in another business at a distance, prevented their general adoption. [16]

THE EARLY SEMICONDUCTOR INDUSTRY

As the name tries to imply, a semiconductor is one of a group of elements (of which silicon is the best known) which will sometimes conduct electricity and sometimes insulate. The application of this property provided an alternative to vacuum tubes, the transistor, invented and patented in 1947 by Bell Laboratories in the United States. Though the invention can easily lay claim to being the most significant of the century, Bell made its patented information, and much other information, freely available to the whole electrical industry, arguing that so much development was needed before a telecommunications organization (such as AT&T, Bell's parent) could hope to reap benefit from the invention that the resources of the entire industry would be required. In fact, the resources of an entirely new industry were brought to bear, and collective resources are still brought to bear now in the competitive collaboration that is a dominant feature of the microelectronics industry. The discrete transistor has long since been superseded by the integrated circuit and the microchip in a protracted orgy of innovation. The pace of innovation continues unabated despite years of prognoses of deceleration—a triumph of Moore's Law over patent law. [17]

The semiconductor industry is the original, and probably still the classic, high-technology industry, spending large sums on R&D and with a tradition of rapid technological change, much of it emanating from small firms. [18] The patent system should have much to offer such an industry: in practice, its value is not quite what is often imagined. Firms in the industry do patent, but patents are traditionally taken out neither to reward the inventor—at least not directly—nor to disseminate information. Patents are a form of currency in the industry in that they are exchanged for other patents. The right to use information is bought with the right to use other information, but after rather than before the information has been used. Patent licences are no more than formal acknowledgement that one firm has been infringing another's patent rights, and are granted to legitimate access to another firm's technology rather than for royalties. The information itself travels by other means altogether, propelled by exchange transactions which help ensure that information received is also information which can be used. [19] Only after all this has taken place do patents play their part as a sort of unit of account in the book-keeping exercise of determining what information has gone where.

Considering how much use semiconductor firms make of information that has been patented by other firms, litigation is rare, generally resorted to only when an offending firm's profits become unexpectedly large, or when a firm seems more willing to take information than to give. This is understandable when customers expect all component suppliers to ensure that second and even third sources are available for the components they sell, and when the market for many new products must first be created by the dissemination of those products. The semiconductor industry has never really been able to associate patent rights with innovation and commercial success. In 1956, 80 per cent of semiconductor patents in the United States were held by nine large electrical corporations; the following year, 64 per cent of the market was in the hands of new firms. [20]

So, the semiconductor industry uses the patent system in a way which pays very little regard to patent theory. Were it to use patents as theory says they should be used, there would be much slower, and much less, innovation in the semiconductor industry. This adaptation has not prevented some of those who seek to understand the industry's innovation from looking for enlightenment in its use of the patent system, sometimes even counting patents to get a measure of its innovation. Of course, it can be argued that high-technology industries are not like other industries, and are quite atypical in their approach to the patent system. The counter-argument is that there are now an awful lot of high-technology industries, their products are essential to all other industries, and other industries can no longer allow their own innovation to be incompatible with that in high technology. This does not mean that all industry will come to use the patent system as the semiconductor industry uses the patent system, but it does suggest that other industries may find a patent-dominated view of innovation increasingly inappropriate.

No one doubts that the patent system, and intellectual property law generally, are less than perfect. In both these examples, the system was inappropriate to the circumstances of innovation. In both cases, innovation was very much the responsibility of those who were in a position to acquire and apply the information of others, information that did not emanate from the patent system. From an information perspective, the itinerant builder of threshing machines has much in common with the mobile semiconductor expert. Patents were, however, appropriate to the view of innovation held by landowners in the case of the threshing machine, and by the established electrical firms in the case of semiconductors. Landowners would have found it profoundly disturbing to acknowledge that innovation was dependent on the efforts of individual builders, and the established firms in the electrical industry—or any other for that matter—that innovation is the product of continual immersion in an information maelstrom. The patent system encourages an odd perception of innovation, but one with which institutions and organizations—and those who control them—are as comfortable as can be expected.

PATENTS AND PATENT THEORY

It is difficult to decide just where to enter the maze of theory that has sought to make sense of a system built on only the most rudimentary of theoretical foundations. An obvious way in is through the notion that inventions benefit society and so society, through its legal system, should do what it can to encourage them. Inventors incur costs in producing inventions (and, to digress, in patenting them too), and should be reimbursed for these costs. The inventor should receive for his invention his costs plus whatever is the minimum amount necessary to induce him to incur these costs. If he is paid less, he will presumably cease inventing; if more, then society is being profligate with its resources, and would perhaps be encouraging inventing rather than inventions. From this perspective, the only problem is calculating the level of inducement required to persuade an inventor to invent, a level which presumably varies from inventor to inventor.

There is a problem which this exploration fails to reveal. The actual value to society of an invention would appear to be irrelevant, with society providing as much inducement to inventors to produce a better mousetrap as a cure for cancer. Nor does this reasonably direct route through the maze pay attention to how much invention the system should encourage; just one invention would appear to be enough to justify the system, and innumerable inventions would seem to be equally acceptable. [21]

If the system accounts for a net increase in inventions having a value to society exceeding the costs society pays for them, the patent system is justifiable in economic terms. [22]

Arrow has observed that only in an ideal socialist economy can the reward for invention be completely separated from any charge to the users of information. [23] Given the provenance of the patent term in the time taken to produce skilled labour for society (seven years to train an apprentice and a further seven to provide sufficient return to his master), and given that an essential part of the basic bargain between society and the inventor is that the inventor's information be made available to society as a whole, it could be argued that the patent system is fundamentally socialist. Certainly it functioned quite adequately under communist regimes, though their rewards to inventors appear trivial, even comical, to societies which have adjusted to a market-driven patent system. In anything at all like a market economy, inventors will feel stronger pressure to invent some things than to invent others, simply because the market will offer a higher price for some inventions than for others, which preference may well influence the direction of inventive activity. Here, of course, the market is hopelessly imperfect: all the market demand in the world will not necessarily supply the invention required. Resources poured into research do not necessarily produce even more invention, never mind the right sort of invention. They do not necessarily produce even more patents.

Emphasis on the role of the market in the patent system alters the nature of the bargain between the inventor and society. No longer is protection given in exchange for the release of information: monopoly power is granted in exchange for what the market really wants, which is innovation. Society attempts to mask the fact that it is reneging on the deal by pretending that market pressures are not brought to bear until after the patent is granted, when the value of the inventor's monopoly can be negotiated in the market. The attitude is explicit in the insistence of many firms that an independent inventor have a patent before they will begin to enter into negotiations. Certainly it is easier to bid for an invention than to bid for the prospects of an invention, but even a patented invention, in isolation from the other contributions required for innovation, is of uncertain value. Nevertheless, in a market economy, the incentive the patent system gives to invent is the prospect of successful negotiations with the market. What we have, then, is a system with strong socialist undertones, a system capable of providing the minimum level of reward necessary to produce public goods, adapted to produce private goods in a market. It is an uneasy conversion. Consider, for example, Macaulay's nice observation on the incentive that copyright monopoly would have given Dr Johnson.

Would it have stimulated his exertions? Would it have once drawn him out of his bed before noon? Would it have once cheered him under a fit of the spleen? Would it have induced him to give us one more allegory, one more life of a poet, one more imitation of Juvenal? [24]

The monopoly granted to the inventor that he may reap his reward in the market place is a restriction on society's use of the invention, not that society could make much use of an invention anyway. It is innovation that can be of use. While patent theory presents the duration of the patent in terms of the time required by the inventor to reap sufficient reward from his invention, the market sees the patent term as the time required to create an innovation and then to reap reward appropriate to the resources necessary to do this. The arguments of the pharmaceutical industry for extensions of the patent term make this perception particularly vivid.

Since, today, it takes an average ten years and over $100 million to develop a new drug, only seven or eight years are left for the product to recover its entire investment before manufacturers who made no R&D investment at all are free to copy and compete with it. In the United States, the 1984 Patent Restoration Act has added up to five years of life to a pharmaceutical patent to make up for some of the time lost in the governmental approval process.... If the United States is to avoid further erosion of its competitive position, a new framework for growth must be envisioned... in which intellectual property rights are protected and in which investment and innovation are encouraged. [25]

This view certainly encompasses the reality that the resources required for innovation generally far exceed those required for invention, but it also reveals an awkward confusion between society's responsibilities and those of the market. Society is expected to underwrite innovation as if it were merely invention. Yet, an inventor who fails to invent is simply not granted a patent and costs society nothing, except the loss of his individual time and effort. An innovator who fails to innovate may cost society a great deal because his monopoly rights prevent all others using his information for their own innovation. [26] In riposte, it is argued that others would be unwilling to put their resources into the development of an innovation unless they too had the security that a monopoly provides. The argument is sound enough, but it does imply that the value of the patent system lies less in the encouragement it gives to innovators to contribute resources than in the discouragement that it gives to others. This would seem to be a clumsy way to encourage innovation.

INNOVATION AND INFORMATION

Innovation can be seen as a process occurring largely within the confines of the organization; it commonly is seen this way.

This is an exceptionally restricted view, but one with which the notion of a market-led patent system is in perfect harmony. Another view of innovation depicts it as a social process, with the firm's innovation as dependent as much on what happens outside the organization as on what happens within. [27] Innovation is seen to be particularly dependent on the flow of information among firms, a flow which allows the gathering of bits of information from various sources and their assembly in new patterns within the firm. [28] In fact, most of the information required for innovation is gathered rather than created, no matter how strong the firm's R&D. And most of the information required for innovation is to be found outside the firm rather than within.

Technology builds on technology in a cumulative manner, reflecting two characteristics of information. Information cannot be exhausted, it cannot be destroyed, but its quality can be enhanced by adding new information to existing stock. And since the cost of production of information is independent of the scale of information use, it pays an industry as a whole to share information as widely as possible. Silicon Valley is outstanding in that the participants in its high-technology industries have acknowledged, at least tacitly, that external information is fundamental to their innovation, and have accommodated mechanisms appropriate to its flow. [29] These include informal networks, highly mobile experts, and second sourcing. They do not include the patent system, though it has been accommodated for other purposes.

Though the pace of innovation is less furious in other industries, innovation in even the largest and most self-contained of firms in the most sedate of industries is still dependent on information from beyond the firm's own purlieu. [30] The nature of information dictates that informal mechanisms are often more efficient in acquiring this information than formal. Among the least effective of formal means would seem to be the patent system. This is ironic in that a fundamental part of patent theory is that the inventor is granted rights to information only on condition that this information is released to society at large. Even where the patent system does effect the dissemination of information, it is information relevant to invention, not information relevant to innovation. The latter, beyond whatever contribution is made by invention, has no patent protection and the patent system has no responsibility to disseminate it. This is of little moment for those who are happy in the belief that only the information from invention contributes to innovation, and that one innovation has little influence on the creation of another.

While there certainly are some dead-weight losses associated with restrictions on the use of particular techniques, and some waste involved in the race to be first to come up with an invention or to invent around somebody else's patent, I suspect these costs are small compared with social costs that would be involved if the background knowledge to facilitate the next round of R&D effort was kept largely proprietary. [31]

In fact, the next round of R&D is as likely to be based on information from innovation, information which the patent system suggests must be kept secret, as on information from invention. This may help explain why there is such toleration of the poor dissemination of patent information. The patent specification is primarily a legal document, not a source of information. One respondent to a survey of professional engineers who had taken out patents encapsulated the situation nicely: 'I could barely recognise my own inventions in legalese'. [32]

I also feel that it is difficult to gain any information from filed patents as they are written in legal terms rather than engineering terms and therefore extremely hard to understand for people with engineering education. [33]

Despite the concern of patent theory with dissemination, the patent system is seen as a means of controlling information. Dissemination is equated with loss of control and is imagined to be in conflict with the basic aim of the system. Of the screeds that have been written about the application of the patent system, the vast bulk is concerned with the rights of the inventor over his information; very little is concerned with the rights of society to this information. True, patent information is published, but only in the sense that a newspaper may publish an announcement that Fred Higgins is no longer responsible for the debts of Florence Higgins. Presumably such an advertisement does not immediately galvanize the community into being on the alert for Florence Higgins; it is a formality, a legal nicety. So is the publication of patent specifications. Basically, the information contained in patent specifications is available only to those who consult them directly, or who pay others more adept at arcane classifications and the language of lawyers to do so. [34] There also tends to be a delay of a year or two between the filing of an application and the publication of a specification, a delay far greater than the pace of change in some industries. Moreover, the criteria by which patents are granted pay no heed at all to the contribution the patent information might make to innovation. Details of inventions which can make no conceivable contribution are frequently published, as are those of patents designed to mislead or obstruct. [35] There is no public benefit from such publication.

From an information perspective, the publication and dissemination of information should be an essential function of the patent system. [36] It is also apparent why they are not: formal systems of information handling—be they directed towards invention or towards innovation—are often not well suited to the information requirements of the economy. The more information-intensive the economy, the more inappropriate are mechanisms intended to make information an exclusive private good. For example, it has proved somewhat awkward to extend the patent system beyond mechanical inventions to those that are more information-intensive, to plants and genes. [37] The application to software, whose value is transitory, of copyright protection for fifty years—and possibly seventy years in Europe—is less than appropriate. A useful parallel may be drawn with the export control system, also originally intended to prevent the acquisition by others of the latest machines, and also extended to protect the know-how surrounding them. [38] The system never could deal with information, at least not with more than was embodied in tangible goods. But this very failure became justification for extending the scope of export control regulations so that they might cope better with information. Similar arguments are employed for the extension of the patent system.

There is no need here to emphasize that the collection of the information required for innovation is assisted and accelerated by the ready flow of that information, itself encouraged by information exchange. The monopoly powers bestowed on an innovator inhibit this exchange and hence slow down the pace of innovation. Society as a whole, and more particularly certain elements within it, has reason to welcome a degree of retardation.

Rampant innovation is disruptive; it raises the level of uncertainty. For organizations with capital sunk in existing ways of doing things, rapid and unpredictable change is not welcomed wholeheartedly, especially when it is forced on them by the innovation of competitors. The very nature of organization, social or economic, is antagonistic to rapid and unpredictable innovation. Consider a world in which rapid and unpredictable change was normal, a high-technology world extended to all other activities. Such a world would be extremely disconcerting for most people and for all organizations. The patent system may actually slow down the pace of innovation, but much more important is that it gives the impression that there is some control over the rate and direction of innovation. Without this impression, our attitude towards innovation would be even more timorous than it already is.

THE WHOLE AND THE PARTS

Those who seek reassurance in the patent system find themselves allies of those who take the patent seriously because it is in their interests to do so. This is an uneasy alliance, entwining those who find value in the general impression of order left by the whole system with those for whom value lies in the specific exploitation of the parts. The latter group seems to gain more than the former. Its exploitation of the parts is rendered acceptable by the inclination of the former towards the belief that the patent system as a whole produces social and economic benefits. Yet, this exploitation diminishes what social and economic benefits there are. Amongst the most ardent supporters of the patent system, on the grounds that it is essential for innovation, are patent attorneys, not a group renowned for innovatory zeal in any other context. Their enthusiasm tends not to be matched by that of inventors for patent attorneys, or indeed, for the patent system itself. Nor is it an enthusiasm always shared by those who administer the system. Patent officials see nothing of innovation; they are predominantly concerned with assessing novelty and are often hard put to repress the cynicism engendered by the apparent pointlessness of much of the novelty they find. Nor are economists, keen though they be to wallow in the morass that intellectual property theory affords, equally keen on the system itself. Their conclusions on the overall value of the patent system tend to be less than conclusive.

It would not be in order to conclude that patent protection is not justified, but only that the arguments pro and con are more complex than had previously been realized. [39]

Policymakers are almost as enamoured of the patent system as patent attorneys, and for reasons almost as obvious. Policies and programmes to encourage innovation are virtually universal, the unaided market being reluctant to replace the old and familiar with the new and uncertain. Innovation programmes require specific aims and objectives, means of monitoring, and evaluation. Above all, they require justification. It is important to believe not only that the public resources devoted to innovation actually produce innovation, but also that they give value for money. There is no room for doubt, much less failure, when public money and political reputations are at stake. The policymaker is instinctively and pragmatically in tune with the patent system, with the notion that resources go in and innovation comes out, that the process is contained, that public institutions and the market should work together to produce innovation.

These same policymakers are especially eager to measure the innovation that arises from their programmes. This is no mean task, and they must generally resort to measuring what goes into innovation rather than what comes out. Worse still, they must content themselves with measuring what goes into research—typically money and, to a lesser extent, manpower—rather than into innovation. Patents are a godsend because, inadequate though they may be, they are one of the few output measures of research available. Even universities, the vast bulk of whose research is quite unpatentable, are happy to use patents as one measure of their research activity. Patents are also used as an output measure by some independent inventors, and by some employee inventors. The US patent system is especially conducive to individuals patenting in their own name and immediately assigning the patent to an employer. This allows such individuals to list their patents in résumés, much like their publications, to show what they have achieved in life.

In partial contrast, commercial organizations often attach less significance to the existence of patents. Patenting practice varies from firm to firm even within the same industry and poor patenting performance is as likely to be a function of a miserly patenting budget as of the amount or success of a firm's research. Among industries, patenting practice is even more variable; most of the service industries simply do not produce anything patentable. For those who count patents in order to compare the research output of one industry or one firm with another, these differences in propensity to patent pose something of a problem, typically ignored, or acknowledged with a rider to the effect that no better data are available. [40] The use of patent statistics to trace innovation through invention says much more about the perceptions of the users than the statistics say about innovation. [41] Beyond the most obvious inadequacies of the data, their use to measure innovation tends to suggest that innovation is to be found wherever there are patents, and, implicitly, that there should be patents wherever there is innovation. The use of patent statistics to measure innovation inevitably emphasizes the role of the private sector. When R&D statistics are used, a quite different impression emerges, emphasizing the dominant role of the public sector. In Australia, 80 per cent of all research in 1980 was performed by the public sector, and 73 per cent of applied research, [42] a situation presented graphically in Fig. 11.3. The distortion was intended to suggest the need to expand the industrial R&D body: of course, it was much easier for the government to adjust the proportions by shrinking the science head. The perception was not that the body was too small, but that the head was too big. How innovation is perceived is not unrelated to how innovation is measured. When patents are used as a measure of innovation, much more is implied than is ever revealed.

No one would argue that all patented inventions make an identical contribution to innovation, a basic objection to mindlessly counting the things. But it is possible to argue that patents which are also taken out in foreign countries are likely to be making a greater contribution to innovation than those taken out only domestically. [43] Foreigners who seek patent protection in the United States can be assumed to be on their way to producing an innovation full of commercial promise. With this

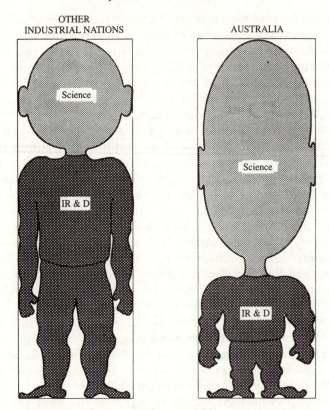

FIG. 11.3   R&D proportions for innovation

Source: ICI Australian Ltd. submission to Senate Standing Committee on
       Science and the Environment, *Industrial Research and Development in
       Australia* (AGPS, Canberra, 1979), p. 300.

explanation (and the computer disks on which US patent statistics are now available), it can be shown how much more
innovation, or how much less innovation, comes out of, say, the
German electronics industry than the British. [44] Extending the
logic, the same comparison can be made between individual
firms—at least for those which choose to patent, and to patent
in the US, and whose patented inventions make roughly the
same contribution to innovation as those of other firms which
choose to patent in the US. [45] Whether such analysis does
show this, or anything at all, is not the point at issue here. Much
more important is that the analysis itself reveals a desperate

desire to see innovation as a process sufficiently contained that it can be represented in terms of patents. Even the protestations of patent officials, those who compile the figures, that patent statistics should not be used in this way are not allowed to thwart this desire.

The pharmaceutical industry also likes to see innovation as it is portrayed in the patent process. The reasons are obvious enough: regulation prevents rapid innovation of pharmaceutical products, demanding extensive and expensive testing as part of their development. The protection the industry feels it needs during these years of development is thoroughly compatible with the notion of the patent system protecting innovation. Moreover, the pharmaceutical invention tends to be a formula, codified information easily transferred to those who have not performed the research. Similarly, the results of pharmaceutical testing are much more valuable than details of standard testing procedures, and these too can be readily conveyed. The patent system suits very nicely the innovation practices of the pharmaceutical industry, and the industry is anxious to preserve the system; better still to strengthen the features of the system most appropriate to its innovation practice. Understandably then, much of the pressure for extension of the patent term comes from the pharmaceutical industry, arguing that if society imposes such hefty development costs and such lengthy development periods, it must also allow the developer of the innovation sufficient time to recoup these costs. For many years, the industry insisted that its special circumstances required extra patent protection for specific pharmaceutical innovations, an argument which inevitably implied that the patent system did not accord with the reality of innovation. In recent years, the pharmaceutical industry has changed tack, arguing instead that the patent term should be extended universally to give greater protection for all innovations. The pharmaceutical lobby is a potent force in the patent system, and this is precisely what has happened. Its power has been a decisive factor in the lengthening of the general patent term in recent years, not just the term of specific pharmaceutical patents.

We are most interested in a strengthening rather than weakening of the Australian patent law, especially for pharmaceuticals. Substantial weakening might prompt us to drastically shortcut investments in Australia. [46]

The real strength of the industry's argument lies not in logic, but in the match between its innovation practice and the view of innovation encouraged by the patent system. It is the predominance of this view, rather than the weight of the pharmaceutical industry's arguments, that has produced both a general extension of the patent term and the expectation that innovation in all industries will benefit as much as innovation in the pharmaceutical industry.

Other industries have certainly not rushed to protest over the lengthening of the patent term. Those that do not patent are assumed not to innovate and have little say in the matter. Those that do patent are generally quite content to retain their monopoly power for longer. It seems to them that retention of control over the right to use information has every advantage over loss of control. In fact, the patentee's control over information is quite illusory; for example, the patentee has no control at all over the indirect use of patented information, as when a competitor decides to alter its R&D in response to the granting of a patent. Despite all attempts to see the patent system as rendering information a private good, information retains much of the essential characteristics of a public good.

TOLERANCE AND ACCEPTANCE

The longevity of the patent system is usually attributed to a persistent inability to devise anything better. But the resilience of the institution is also attributable to its accommodation of perceptions of innovation that are readily acceptable to society and the economy. Radical change in the patent system would demand radical change in these perceptions of innovation. Consequently, only minor changes in the patent system are welcomed, and these—the lengthening of the patent term, rewards for employee inventors, and so on—are just the sort of changes the patent system has undergone in recent years. [47]

This tinkering demands that the demonstrable failings of the patent system be overlooked. For example, those who should benefit most from the protection the patent system provides—independent inventors and small firms, because they must involve others in their innovation—tend to benefit least. The patent affords protection only when the patentee can afford to enforce his rights, which may mean that he has no protection at all. [48] As the journal *Nature* noted long ago:

the consideration for which patent rights may be enjoyed is nowadays not so much the introduction of a new invention as the possession of exceptional wealth. [49]

Or again, many patents—there are no means of telling how many —are likely to be defensive patents, taken out not to be worked, but to prevent others from working. The block-patenting by pharmaceutical companies of dozens of formulae akin to those they are likely to exploit is defensive patenting.

The patent system provides a model that helps innovation seem part of social and economic process. This way of thinking makes the new seem less threatening, less out of control. Innovation is being regulated and monitored by society's institution, by professionals. Innovation generally, not just that of the pharmaceutical industry, can be seen as benign and beneficial. Yet, innovation is not like this at all. It is irregular and disruptive, [50] certain to bring uncertainty and not necessarily even improvement over what has gone before. To deny this reality in favour of a neater model may bring comfort, but it will not bring an understanding of innovation.

The complexity of patent theory, and of the patent system itself, are such that it is all too easy to be distracted by detail, to lose a sense of proportion. It has been calculated that patent information is worth about three-quarters of one per cent of firms' R&D expenditure, and so an even tinier proportion of total innovation costs. [51] Precisely how well patents play their part in generating innovation is much less important than the realization that this part is actually a very small one. In the staging of the intricate drama of innovation, the patent is unlikely to have more than a walk-on, one-line part somewhere in Act II. Just occasionally, the whole plot may depend on that part, though not often. But our perception of the play is altered entirely when our own child has the one-line part. The whole play is dominated by her performance. The patent system, too, is our own creation, and viewing innovation in terms of this system, and in terms of intellectual property generally, gives an equally distorted view. In the real world of messy, uncertain, protracted, and reluctant innovation, the patent system itself is of little significance, but in sustaining the comforting delusion that innovation is other than it is, the perspective the patent provides is very significant indeed.

REFERENCES

1. See C. T. Taylor and Z. A. Silberston, *The Economic Impact of the Patent System* (Cambridge University Press, Cambridge, 1973).
2. T. D. Mandeville, D. M. Lamberton, and E. J. Bishop, *Economic Effects of the Australian Patent System* (Australian Government Publishing Service, Canberra, 1982).
3. Fritz Machlup, *An Economic Review of the Patent System*, Studies of the US Patent System No. 15, US Senate Subcommittee on Patents, Trademarks and Copyrights (US Government Printing Office, Washington, DC, 1958), 80.
4. Michael Polanyi, 'Patent reform', *Review of Economic Studies*, 11:1 (1943), 61–76.
5. See, for example, F. M. Sherer, *Industrial Market Structure and Economic Performance* (Rand McNally, Chicago, 1971), 350; 'Planning for technological innovation. Part 1: Investment in technology', *Long Range Planning*, 10 Dec. 1977, 40–4; Sven Malmstrom, 'Innovation and the economic crisis', *Scandinaviska Enskilda Banken Quarterly Review*, 3:4 (1978), 85–97.
6. William Kingston (ed.), *Direct Protection of Innovation* (Kluwer Academic, Dordrecht, 1987) and 'Innovation warrants: a lifeline to industry?', *Creativity and Innovation Network*, 10:1 (1984), 13–18.
7. Tom Mandeville and Stuart Macdonald, 'Innovation protection viewed from an information perspective', in Kingston (ed.), *Direct Protection of Innovation*, 157–70. Some of this chapter is drawn from this account.
8. Eric Hobsbawm and George Rude, *Captain Swing* (Lawrence and Wishart, London, 1969).
9. *cf.* J. A. Hellen, 'Agricultural innovation and detectable landscape margins: the case of wheelhouses in Northumberland', *Agricultural History Review*, 20:2 (1972), 140–54.
10. Stuart Macdonald, 'The diffusion of knowledge among Northumberland farmers, 1780–1815', *Agricultural History Review*, 27:1 (1979), 30–9.

11. Stuart Macdonald, 'The early threshing machine in Northumberland', *Tools and Tillage*, 3:3 (1978), 168–84.

12. Stuart Macdonald, 'The progress of the early threshing machine', *Agricultural History Review*, 23:1 (1975), 63–77 and 'Further progress with the early threshing machine', *Agricultural History Review*, 26:1 (1978), 29–32.

13. Letter from one of the agents appointed by Meikle, John Whinfield of Pipewellgate Foundry, Gateshead, to Thomas Walker, millwright of Newcastle, written sometime before 1803, Northumberland County Record Office/2DE/44/10.

14. Stuart Macdonald, 'John Raistrick, civil engineer of Morpeth', *Durham University Journal*, 64:1 (1976), 67–75.

15. Letter from J. B. Turner, 26 Dec. 1807, *Agricultural Magazine*, 9 (1808), 161–7.

16. *US Census Preliminary Report*, (Washington, DC, 1860), 96.

17. Moore's Law states that the speed of computer chips doubles every eighteen months. 'Hang on', *The Economist*, 19 Oct. 1996, 28.

18. Ernest Braun and Stuart Macdonald, *Revolution in Miniature: The History and Impact of Semiconductor Electronics* (Cambridge University Press, Cambridge, 1982).

19. Stuart Macdonald, 'The need to succeed', *Journal of General Management*, 4:3 (1979), 36–47.

20. Braun and Macdonald, *Revolution in Miniature*, 68.

21. J. Hirshleifer and J. Riley, 'The analytics of uncertainty and information—an expository survey', *Journal of Economic Literature*, 17 (1979), 1375–1421.

22. Jesse Markham, 'Inventive activity: government controls and the legal environment', in National Bureau of Economic Research, *The Rate and Direction of Inventive Activity* (Princeton University Press, Princeton, 1962), 587–608.

23. Kenneth Arrow, 'Economic welfare and the allocation of resources for invention', in ibid. 609–26. See also Z. A. Silberston, 'The patent system', *Lloyd's Bank Review*, 84 (1967), 32–44.

24. 'Macaulay on copyright', *Journal of Political Economy*, 86:5 (Oct. 1978), back cover.

25. William Miller, 'Productivity and competition: a look at the pharmaceutical industry', *Columbia Journal of World Business*, Fall 1988, 85–8 (88).

26. See Fritz Machlup and Edith Penrose, 'The patent controversy in the nineteenth century', *Journal of Economic History*, 10:1 (May 1950), 1–24; Harry Johnston, 'Aspects of patents and business as stimuli to innovation', *Portfolio—International Economic Perspectives*, 5:2 (1977).

27. See Nathan Rosenberg, *Perspectives on Technology* (Cambridge University Press, Cambridge, 1976).
28. See T. J. Allen, M. L. Tushman, and D. M. Lee, 'Technology transfer as a function of position in the spectrum from research through development to technical services', *Academy of Management Journal,* 21:4 (1979), 694–708.
29. Everett Rogers, 'Information exchange and technological information', in Devendra Sahal (ed.), *The Transfer and Utilization of Technical Knowledge* (Lexington Books, Lexington, Mass., 1982), 105–23; Everett Rogers and Judith Larson, *Silicon Valley Fever* (Basic Books, New York, 1984).
30. Eric von Hippel, *The Sources of Innovation* (Oxford University Press, New York, 1988).
31. Richard Nelson, 'The role of knowledge in R&D efficiency', *Quarterly Journal of Economics,* 97:3 (Aug. 1982).
32. Tom Mandeville, 'Engineers and the patent system: results of a survey of members of the Institution of Engineers', in *Supporting Papers for Economic Effects of the Australian Patent System* (Australian Government Publishing Service, Canberra, 1982), 12.
33. Ibid.
34. Felix Liebesny, 'Patents as sources of information', in F. Liebesny (ed.), *Mainly on Patents* (Butterworth, London, 1972), 117–19.
35. Jacob Schmookler, 'Inventors past and present', *Review of Economics and Statistics,* 39 (1957), 321–33.
36. Tom Mandeville, 'Australian use of patent information', *World Patent Information,* 5:2 (1983), 79–82.
37. Salomon Wald, 'Biotechnology: how to improve patent protection', *OECD Observer,* 136 (Sept. 1985), 15–17.
38. Stuart Macdonald, *Technology and the Tyranny of Export Controls: Whisper Who Dares* (Macmillan, London, 1990).
39. Hirshleifer and Riley, 'The analytics of uncertainty and information', 1406.
40. On growth in the use of patents as indicators see Keith Pavitt, 'Patent statistics as indicators of innovative activities: possibilities and problems', *Scientometrics,* 7:1 (1985), 77–99.
41. It might be argued that heavy reliance on patent statistics has damaged Schmookler's reputation. See Nathan Rosenberg, 'Science, invention and economic growth', *Economic Journal,* 84 (1974), 90–108. For a diehard defence of Schmookler and his use of patent statistics see G. J. Wyatt, *The Determinants of Inventive Activity Reconsidered,* Working Paper No.2, Department of Economics, Heriot-Watt University, 1977–8.
42. Department of Science and the Environment, *Project Score* (Australian Government Publishing Service, Canberra, 1980), 22–5.

43. Luc Soete and Sally Wyatt, 'The use of foreign patenting as an internationally comparable science and technology output indicator', *Scientometrics*, 5:1 (1983), 31–54.

44. e.g. John Cantwell, 'The globalisation of technology: what remains of the product life cycle model?', *Cambridge Journal of Economics*, 19 (1995), 155–74.

45. e.g. Pari Patel and Keith Pavitt, 'Large firms in the production of the world's technology: an important case of "non-globalisation"', *Journal of International Business Studies*, 22 (1991), 1–21 and 'Patterns of technological activity: their measurement and interpretation', in Paul Stoneman (ed.), *Handbook of the Economics of Innovation and Technological Change* (Blackwell, Oxford, 1995), 14–51.

46. Survey response of a large US pharmaceutical company in Tom Mandeville and Jean Bishop, 'Economic effects of the patent system: results of a survey of patent attorneys', in *Supporting Papers for Economic Effects of the Australian Patent System*, 16.

47. D. A. Littler and A. W. Pearson, 'The employee inventor and the new Patents Act', *Planned Innovation*, 2:10 (1979), 335–8; Neal Orkin, 'Rewarding employee invention: time for change', *Harvard Business Review*, 62:1 (1984), 56–7.

48. See E. Mansfield, M. Schwartz, and S. Wagner, 'Imitation costs and patents: an empirical study', *Economic Journal*, 91 (1981), 907–18.

49. 'The grant of invalid patents', *Nature*, 9 Nov. 1929, 713.

50. Alan Kantrow, 'The strategy-technology connection', *Harvard Business Review*, 58:4 (1980), 6–21.

51. Taylor and Silberston, *The Economic Impact of the Patent System*, 212.

12

Information and Control:
Strategic Change in the Organization

STRUCTURE AND STRATEGY

The organization requires information to do whatever it exists to do. This is information contained within its boundaries. The organization also requires information to change. This new information must be sought outside the organization. Internal information flows along organizational channels, and its transfer from one part of the organization to another requires few transactions. This is the advantage of organization. External information has no organizational channels along which to flow and transactions are necessary if it is to be found, acquired, and transferred to the organization. From an organizational perspective, which is the perspective normally adopted in studies of the organization, change is seen in terms of the organization's capacity to learn and adapt, and these as internal processes involving only the organization's own resources. [1] From an information perspective, the fundamental resource required for change appears to be external information, a resource beyond the control of the organization.

The empirical evidence presented here comes from a range of large international companies based in the UK. Senior managers in these companies were interviewed intensively over several years to discover how they learnt to change the company's strategy, to match organizational resources to the conditions of the environment in which the company operates. [2] Their own words are used to illustrate the arguments. Particular attention is given to two large engineering concerns in order to demonstrate some of the difficulties of relying on organizational systems for the information required for strategic change; and to a large telecommunications company, which, given its business, might be

expected to have some expertise in the information requirements of such change. A basic requirement is that information
from the environment cross the organizational boundary and
find its way to senior management, those responsible for the
formulation of strategy. It seems that organizational information systems are not particularly effective in satisfying this
requirement; indeed, that the requirement may be in conflict
with the very structure of the organization.

It should be possible to communicate without screwing up the structure. . . . One should seek opportunities from time to time to gain information from elsewhere. . . . [As Chairman] I have this in spades now.

Of the many problems facing the most senior management in
large organizations, simply not knowing what is going on must
rank among the most fundamental. To tackle the problem, one
chief executive pays business leaders around the world to report
directly to him on how his company is faring in these regions.
He finds it essential to circumvent all the company's official
channels of communication in order to know what is really
going on. This is not a practice which his managers accept with
equanimity.

It pisses off the operating managers terribly. Of course it does. It would
piss me off if I was running an operation. You automatically assume
that the chairman has got somebody running round in your territory,
going to see you, and immediately phoning him up and telling him
about everything.

There is nothing more embarrassing incidentally than being at the international level in a business and the Chairman, for instance, will say at
a meeting, 'What's happening in this particular place? I hear so and
so,' because he has got it via another source.

That those at the helm can feel they must take extraordinary measures to find out what is really happening would seem
to be an indictment of the way the large organization gathers
and manages its information. In as much as these individuals
are charged with the responsibility of formulating corporate
strategy, it might be expected that a primary function of the
organization would be to supply its leadership with just such
information. [3] Why, then, does the organization so often seem
incapable of arranging this supply? Presumably there is no
specific intention to deprive the leadership of basic information

essential to the formulation of strategy. [4] It may be simply that formal information flow—that which is arranged by the organization—is unable to provide all the information required for the formulation of strategy, [5] and that informal information —information not provided by the organization—is needed to compensate. Yet, there is at least a *prima facie* case that the organization is antagonistic to informal information flow, [6] that such flow is regarded as at best disruptive, and at worst a threat to power and control. [7]

One of the problems with engineers is that they take great delight in solving problems, and the more complex the problem, the greater the delight an engineer normally has in giving away the solution. Now we think a little different; I'd like to be paid for what I know as well as for what I deliver.

Senior management wishes to exploit informal information flow while maintaining a formal flow compatible with organizational structure and operational requirements. Senior management wants it both ways.

There is an interesting—and certainly relevant—body of writing on the means by which the organization finds information to support its strategic activities. These corporate scanning studies can be less than completely satisfying: they commonly acknowledge the critical importance to decision-making of information procured by informal means, [8] and then, regarding this situation as quite unsatisfactory, recommend rectification in terms of improved organizational information systems. [9] The discovery that informal mechanisms are important has rarely led to further investigation of these mechanisms, but rather to greater interest in how institutional information systems might be improved. This is perverse, perhaps explained by the Pavlovian alacrity with which those who study organizations seize an organizational perspective.

INFORMATION FOR STRATEGY

It is hardly practical to examine all information flow in a group of large firms. Here the focus is on an area which is likely to present difficulties for all such firms—information flow to and from the corporate centre and the periphery. It is with information that the centre directs and controls what goes on at the periphery, and it is with information that the periphery accounts to the centre for its activities. But the centre requires more from the periphery than just accountability; the formulation of strategy requires a vast range of information about operating circumstances and the business environment. Here a basic problem emerges. The information the periphery sends the centre to satisfy accountability requirements tends to be highly codified financial information, delivered in a form that can be instantly understood and directly used by the centre.

There is no doubt that the financial information is the most structured information that comes through to head office. I think, in common with most companies I have worked with, that the financial people get into a routine of having deadlines and meeting them. So, I think there is little doubt that the structured information, the financial stuff, is definitely at the forefront. No doubt about it at all.

Of all the information acquired by the large firm, financial information is valued the most. In firms with highly devolved responsibility, and obviously in holding companies, most of the centre's strategic decisions are likely to be based on financial information. But even centralized firms take financial information much more seriously than other sorts of information; whatever the style of organization, full, reliable, and immediate financial information is considered to be a *sine qua non* of control, [10] and this is usually made very clear to the business units.

Twenty-five per cent return on net assets. That's a key figure. And profit 10 per cent.

All you absolutely have to do is hit the profit mark every month. If you get yourself into trouble, the auditors start visiting. If you keep your nose clean, [the firm] leaves you very much alone.

All large firms institute systems to ensure that the centre receives the desired flow of financial information from the periphery. Inevitably, these are formal systems. It is no part of the current task to explore how well these function, though it is intriguing that the field of accountancy seems much more concerned with how well financial information informs shareholders, government, and the public generally than with what it reveals, and does not reveal, to senior management. [11]

The operations of one large engineering firm provide confirmation of the basic supposition that formal channels do not accommodate all the information needed to ensure sound strategic decisions. In this case, the firm had been expanding its leasing operations in one overseas region, with its customary concentration on the projected financial performance of existing businesses and possible acquisitions. It may be that local managers simply felt inordinate pressure to perform, but it does seem that the means by which they reported their performance to headquarters were as conducive to illegal activity as to legal. Local managers ensured they could deliver quite excellent financial returns by hiring gangsters to coerce payment from customers, a tactic which inexorably led to their own involvement in a range of associated criminal activities. Although this had been going on for years, it became public only through a government inquiry into the industry as a whole. And it was only when the inquiry's revelations made headlines in the regional press that corporate headquarters discovered something was amiss. The inquiry and the press demanded to know what involvement the centre had had in what was being revealed as an exceptionally sordid affair. The inquiry was unconvinced that headquarters had been unaware of what was going on.

Yet, the centre does indeed appear to have been totally ignorant, this despite a visit by the Chairman just eighteen months before the storm broke. [12] Within a week of hearing what was emerging from the inquiry, the responsible London manager rushed to the region and eventually gave evidence. [13] It was not well received. The Commissioner assumed that a cover-up was under way and was extremely critical that headquarters had yet to take disciplinary action against its management: [14] it 'should not "take the position that it is in England and I'm in [the region] and the safest place for them is in England" '. [15] Two weeks later the London manager dismissed local managers *en masse*, and then resigned himself. [16] The board has now decided to minimize the damage to the company's reputation by withdrawing entirely from all its leasing business in the region. Perhaps the ultimate irony is that the same board had actually paid considerable attention to the subsidiary's managerial strengths in its deliberations over acquisitions in the region.

A further important reason for expansion is that [the subsidiary] is very sensitive to the quality of its management, in particular at branch and senior management levels. The company is fortunate in having a crucial competitive advantage in this area, with management strength in depth throughout the organization. To sustain this advantage, [the subsidiary] must be continually providing new challenges and opportunities for career advancement. [17]

This is a case of information critical to the firm's strategy not being acquired by the centre. Headquarters remained satisfied with the information it received through formal channels, financial information which the illegal activities of local managers ensured would be thoroughly satisfactory. Though the inquiry revealed that their practices had long been notorious in the region, there were no informal channels by which this information could have reached headquarters. Indeed, local management had a positive disincentive to create such channels, one encouraged by the company's reliance on its formal information system.

Where the formal communication is so rigid and you demand people go through certain channels and if it's not truly effective, people try and work a way around it, but they are doing it surreptitiously. They are afraid of being caught because they are breaking the rules. That's what causes the problem.

The more devolved the firm, the more strategic decisions are taken at local level. In theory, the smaller the operation and the closer it is to the environment in which it operates, the more it replicates the small firm and consequently the more its information-gathering and information use can imitate those of the small firm. Reality is less tidy than theory. The information systems of business units in even the most devolved of large firms are not totally uninfluenced by the formal systems of the corporation. Consider the case of another large engineering firm, its devolved structure encouraging as many decisions as possible to be taken in its business units. Only financial information is targeted direct at corporate headquarters, dispatched regularly and frequently in uniform format from all points on the periphery. Indeed, a single, on-line computer system has been installed to achieve this. In terms of the centre's access to financial information, the system seems to work well, but this itself has implications for access to other sorts of information. The firm recently brought in consultants to advise on whether the expansion of other IT systems should remain the responsibility of the divisions, or be integrated with the financial information system as a corporate responsibility. As is so often the case, the Finance Director was assumed to be in overall charge of IT strategy and it was he who took charge of the inquiry. The demands of devolution triumphed and financial information retained its singular entitlement to the only corporate-wide IT system. The divisions continued to develop their own IT systems, though there were distinct similarities between these and the central financial system. The model of a financial information system, commanding the regular submission of highly codified and highly objective information from the periphery, was to be less appropriate for other sorts of information.

One division, with hundreds of sales engineers installing the firm's products at thousands of customer sites round the world, provided each engineer with a portable terminal giving instant access to a divisional database of previous installations. The intention was not only to pool the experience of all the division's engineers to create a resource from which all could draw, but also to provide an expert system, giving guidelines on what information should be used.

This was a program which could run on a laptop computer, and could ultimately be carried by sales engineers to their customers. The program used Artificial Intelligence (AI) techniques to embody the expertise of the sales engineers as a whole, as well as the engineering department, and asked the user a response-dependent sequence of questions. After gathering the responses, the program would provide a [product] suitable for the application, according to a standardized selection procedure. [18]

This was not universally popular with the engineers, who often preferred their own solutions, [19] and resented a system supposed to secure 'delivery of all elements of corporate expert knowledge required for [the] critical task of [product] selection to the appropriate point in usable form'. [20] Nevertheless, it was from this unsatisfactory base that the system was further developed. There was little choice in that the resource pool required topping up with new knowledge that could come only from the engineers. The improved system was to be a technical engineering database (TED), continually supplemented with information supplied by the engineers from the installations on which they were engaged. Though this input was absolutely fundamental, the new system was still described as its predecessor had been, in terms of distributing information from the centre, not of receiving information from the periphery.

TED has been confirmed as a key technology transfer tool. . . . the primary vehicle for avoiding duplication and repeating design and applications efforts around the world and locally. [21]

While technical specifications could certainly be codified, the general circumstances surrounding each installation could not. Nor did individual engineers have much incentive to place information from their experiences—information which they tended to see as at least partly their own property—in a system which promised no personal return. They were particularly disinclined to report failures, especially failures occurring—as was typical—some time after installation. Well aware from their own behaviour of the system's deficiencies, engineers in the field came to rely less and less on the IT system and more and more on alternative informal information systems. Basically, they made contact with other engineers to ask if they had experience with particular sorts of installations, or knew of anyone who had. They exploited personal networks—networks encouraged by the division's own international technical conferences—to hear of similar problems and to pick up tips, and inevitably they contributed information of the same sort to these networks. [22]

The concept of the sales guy, every applications engineer on a global basis, being able to walk around with this little laptop on which he was able to bring up all that information, I mean is . . . I can understand why [the responsible Director] would really buy into that, but what you have to do is to now stand back and look at the operation you have got and see whether there is a chance in hell of that actually being employed.

Although managers were aware of the deficiencies of the institutional information system, they were unable to prevent information from it contributing to strategy. The technical information system was used to help formulate strategy in much the same way as the centre used its financial information system. [23]

Indeed, this seemed especially apposite as the centre had declared that the whole corporation would no longer be led by its own technology, but would concentrate on developing the technology required by its customers instead. With no access to the personal networks of the field engineers, it was all too easy for divisional headquarters to believe that the technical information system gave an exact account of customers' technological requirements. In consequence, information from the system came to be relied upon to shape the division's technology strategy.

> That information which is down in the database gets filtered into the engineering department as to what the likely problems are . . . We then formulate some sort of strategy based on that as to what we need in terms of product needs. On the basis of that, we formulate what we need in terms of research needs.

INFORMAL INFORMATION FOR STRATEGY

It would be convenient to assume that the organization avoids market transactions in information wherever possible because senior management is well aware of the characteristics of information and consequently of the difficulties these present in the market. The temptation should be resisted. Management typically concedes that information is a valuable resource, but its instinctive response is simply to hoard that which is precious. This mercantilistic attitude regards information as something to be contained by the organization, not traded in the market. Resistance to market transactions in information is probably much more a product of other functions that information performs within the organization, functions in which the knowledge that information can provide may be only incidental. Information is valued for the power it bestows and the control it allows. [24] In the context of the organization, information systems confirm the existing power structure and its means of control. It is the nature of information which dictates that market mechanisms cannot cope efficiently with information transactions. The market must often fail, but the organization would seem to fail too. [25] Organizational considerations are probably more instrumental in the preservation of existing information systems than any appreciation of the problems posed by market transactions in information.

Several obstacles lie in the way of the large firm which would exploit informal information for strategy, none insurmountable, but all problematic and some less than obvious. The most basic of these is that informal information flow is, by definition, beyond the control of the organization. The irony is that the firm which does not value informal information flow, and which therefore makes little attempt to organize it, may benefit more than the firm which appreciates its value and attempts its control. Thus, gatekeepers—those individuals who gather external information and translate it for selective use inside the organization—can contribute most when they function informally. [26] To control the informal flow of information is to render the flow formal, a temptation to which firms seeking what seems to be an efficient structure for their activities are likely to yield.

[The Chief Executive] and I went to Spain and were met on the night we arrived in Madrid by about five people, all of whom claimed to be [the firm's] representatives in Spain. [He] and I took one look at all these bods and said, 'They have got to go.' We didn't know who in the hell they were.

The firm now has a single branch office in the capital and is isolated from both its customers and its industry.

Beyond the problems inherent in the organization acquiring information informally, there lies the problem of this information reaching levels within the organization at which strategy is determined. The organization's screening mechanisms are fine-tuned to reject information which might make a contribution to strategy but which is simply different from the information that customarily contributes. [27] It is no coincidence that the organization's information systems conform to its hierarchical structure. [28] Screening procedures are installed, designed both to weed out information that will not be valued at higher levels and also to bring together separate streams of information so that only the highest echelons have access to the filtered information from all streams. This singular access provides the apex with both the information required to control the organization and the channels by which it may deliver information to implement this control. [29]

The purpose of screening is not only to reduce the bulk of information acquired by the periphery to manageable proportions, but also to ensure that the information which the centre receives is that which is most valued. In an ideal world, those at the periphery and between the periphery and the centre would know what it is the centre wants to know, and would screen accordingly. In the small firm, where everyone has at least a rough idea of what everyone else is doing, this might happen: in the large firm, it is hardly feasible. Large firms must depend on established structural systems to filter information from the periphery. While these can be tailored precisely by the centre to let through just that information which is demanded, they cope less well with information which would also be useful at the centre, but which is not demanded.

No matter how large the organization, its employees will still communicate with each other informally. Working together means talking together and modern telecommunications and transport have done much, though less than is often claimed, [30] to reduce the need for physical proximity. Much of what information is transferred by these informal means is trivial and ephemeral, of no use to the centre at all. Mixed with this farrago will be some bits that are, and that are not available to the centre through the firm's formal information channels. In particular, information from beyond the organizational perimeter, where the firm's writ does not run, may be able to penetrate the boundary informally. A valid observation is that no large firm can allow adaptation to its strategy to be dependent on the chance acquisition of miscellaneous information from its periphery. However, there is more structure and purpose to the informal transfer of information than management may care to admit. Indeed, it can be argued that informal mechanisms are more appropriate to information flow than formal information systems. While the latter tend to be mechanisms of hierarchy and procedure adapted to the processing and transfer of information, the former are specialized mechanisms dedicated to information transactions. The advantages of such informal exchange are usually appraised by comparison with market transactions in information, but they also have advantages over the formal transfer mechanisms of the organization. All firms contain informal information networks. Few firms seem able to make much use of them to supply information from the periphery and beyond to the centre.

It is easily assumed that the conjunction of modern telecommunications and computer technology melds formal and informal means by which information is handled. The same technologies which permit global corporate communication also allow employees to communicate informally with other individuals. [31] Yet the commonality is more apparent than real. Electronic data interchange on a vast corporate network has little in common with individuals sending each other e-mail messages. The attraction for large firms of telecommunications and computer technologies is the facility these offer to handle information formally. Studies of the means by which individual employees procure the information of most value to their firms tend not to rate advanced telecommunications highly. [32] Even in telecommunications companies, chief executives do not often use electronic means to acquire information, especially what they regard as 'quality' information. [33] The capacity of telecommunications to deal with information transfer does not necessarily extend to dealing with information transactions. It does, though, fit neatly with the structure and control requirements of organization, so neatly that it is easy to overlook that it is these requirements that are being satisfied rather than requirements for information.

INFORMATION AND TELECOMMUNICATIONS

Take the example of a large telecommunications company in which, perhaps predictably, the conviction that telecommunications should satisfy all communications needs—those of its customers and certainly its own—is universal. Travel, for example, will no longer be necessary, nor will libraries with books, nor teachers in classrooms.

The aim of modern telecommunications is to reduce the need for transport to zero.

You will only ever get a paperless office by totally eliminating the paper.

Any information manipulation job can now be located anywhere in the world.

A new commercial ethos pervades telecommunications companies, especially those which have joined the private sector.

Strategic information is now to be closely guarded and awareness of the capability of telecommunications to transfer strategic
information only makes security seem all the more essential.
Linearity suggests that the R&D Department contains some of
the organization's most valuable information. Therefore, R&D
information is to be secured and the traditional means by which
scientists and engineers exchange information with their peers
outside the organization discouraged.

The old club atmosphere is going. There is a new gloss on what [the
R&D Department] does. We used to get warts and all. Now [R&D] has
commercial secrets to guard. Some time ago we stopped [R&D] giving
papers externally.

R&D people are naïve from a business point of view. They will tell you
confidential stuff. I'm just amazed by the leakage that can occur.

At the same time, this is a company which, just like the engineering company, is determined to be market-led, to rely on its customers rather than its own R&D to direct technological innovation.

We must stop the [R&D] approach. There were three projects doing the
same damn thing last year.

If you start giving people too free a hand, then everything gets out of
hand and diluted.

There is no harm in these mind-blowing statements as long as they are
detached from 'And this is what you are going to have next week, guv.'

The transition for any company from being led by its own
technology to being customer-led can be traumatic. In some
companies, the change has occasioned the elimination of the
company's own R&D to allow full concentration on customer
requirements. More significant are the consequences of the
Marketing Department seizing a new opportunity. [34] The
efforts of Marketing to draw closer to customers, especially large
customers, can lead to the distancing of engineers from these
customers. [35] Engineers may come to have little opportunity
even to meet customers, at least not without an escort, much
less to test the complementarity of their own information with
that of customers.

Why should anyone but Marketing have contact with the customers?
The customers are our business. We keep other parts of [the company]
informed on a need-to-know basis.

'Market-led' does imply that Marketing knows what customers need and tells Research. Without that, Research would be directionless.

[Researchers] have direct contact with [the customer], but always with a minder from Marketing or Sales. A lot of us are quite naïve about selling.

The research labs are not in charge of customer linkages. The account managers and marketeers make it clear that there can be difficulties with *ad hoc* approaches.

We couldn't have our customers meeting an engineer with a cup of coffee and a fag hanging out of his mouth.

The problem is exacerbated by the low priority which senior management in many organizations attaches to telecommunications, and to information generally. Few companies have anything like an information strategy, and overall responsibility for information is commonly given to the Finance Director, the individual already in charge of the information reckoned to be of most importance. Responsibility for telecommunications is usually delegated to a middle manager with neither the authority nor the incentive to consider the total information requirements of the organization. For a telecommunications company offering its customers only telecommunications, relating to these telecommunications managers presents few problems; the same language is spoken, the same interests in networks and systems for organizational efficiency are shared. But for the customer organization tackling the problems of acquiring information for strategic change, the chances of finding telecommunications solutions are all the more remote.

Customers complain that it's no fun coming to [the R&D Department] any more; you only get to see the plush, sanitized version.

In this case, strategic change in the telecommunications company has disrupted the flow of the informal information which previously contributed to its strategy formulation. It has also directed information from customers, a major source of information for innovation, [36] along entirely new channels. Perhaps more profoundly, the telecommunications company, providing only a commodity which its customers must exploit as best they can, seems less able than ever to assist in their use of telecommunications to serve the information requirements of their own strategic change.

INFORMATION IN STRATEGIC THEORY

Some would argue that modern information technology now provides the firm with all the information it could possibly want from its environment. [37] So great and growing is the ability of the telecommunications network to handle information that this alone is often thought to determine the shape and direction of economic activity. [38] Those of this persuasion often cite R&D as an activity now unconstrained by borders and distance. [39] Yet, Patel and Pavitt insist that technological knowledge is still concentrated in the home countries of even the largest international firms. [40] Once again, understanding of a sort not normally offered by strategic theory is required to resolve such obvious conflict. Some Swedish thinking suggests that an information perspective is appropriate.

The Uppsala model and its derivatives are unusual in their approach to the study of corporate strategy in that they do address the acquisition and use of information as a central and distinct issue. [41] This centrality has allowed the development of the basic model to include such sophisticated issues as the acquisition and transfer of tacit and embodied information, informal methods of information transfer, and the role of those who give and acquire information. Other models of strategy pay rather less attention to such issues. Compare approaches to the role of the network in strategy. The Uppsala school is able to explore the complexity of network relationships and particularly the sophisticated means by which they facilitate the multilateral exchange of information; other models see the network largely as an alternative structure for the firm, [42] at best a metaphor for the range of relationships firms have with their environment. [43] The Uppsala school provides no prescription, [44] it is too ridden with uncertainty to support any grand design, and refuses to simplify what management must learn. It does, however, offer an intellectual satisfaction in its treatment of information which is denied by much other strategic theory. For example, the Uppsala approach adds a new dimension to the fundamental strategic conflict between central control and devolution of authority. [45] The more information is channelled in the firm, the greater would seem to be the ease of control, but the more difficult is learning. The less information is channelled, the more learning may be assisted, but the more difficult is control. [46] This would seem to suggest that the three strategic imperatives comfortably identified by Doz, Prahalad, and Hamel—control, change, and flexibility [47]—are fundamentally incompatible. Both change and flexibility require learning, which requires information, information that the demands of control may distort or exclude. After two decades, the failure of the Uppsala school to make any significant impression on the main body of strategic theory suggests that interest in information for control is somewhat greater than interest in information for strategy. [48]

Those who study the acquisition of information for strategy purely from an organizational perspective pay little attention to information systems which are not instituted by the organization itself. Nor are senior managers, beset with the primary responsibility of making the best use of the information they already have, well positioned to see their task from anything other than this perspective. They rely upon the organization to provide the information they are expected to handle. In such circumstances, only personal eccentricity accommodates the informal acquisition of information, [49] and in many large organizations, personal eccentricity is tolerated only at the very top.

This isn't a democracy. Firstly, you have got to get used to [the Chairman], because if he wants to know something, he will pick a telephone up and he will ask somebody. If he wants something about a guy who works two levels below me doing something, he will phone him. I might find out three days later, or I might never find out at all. . . . I think that . . . an hierarchical approach gets in the way.

There is often an underlying assumption that informal information is really of most use to small firms, to new firms, to firms in volatile industries, to specialists within the organization with their specialized demands for information. Informal information should not be needed to fulfil the primary information requirements of the organization. In any other than extraordinary circumstances, its use indicates the inadequacy of the organization's own information systems. In an ideal world with ideal organization, it is implied, there would be no need for informal information. The larger the organization, and the more fundamental the use for which it requires information, the more nearly it is expected to approach this ideal situation.

Yet it should not be impossible to expose strategy formulation to informal information without bringing down the whole organizational edifice. The solution is not, of course, an organizational system for informal information flow, for that would render the informal formal and nullify whatever advantages it offers. [50] It may have to be accepted that the organization can do little to encourage informal information flow. The organization can, however, avoid discouraging this flow. [51] Using informal information is particularly demanding of experience and judgement. Yet these are surely managerial qualities, exercised daily and certainly required in the formulation of organizational strategy. No quantum leap in capacity is required to use information acquired informally. What is needed is an acceptance that, though information is used to control the organization, information itself cannot be controlled in quite the same way. [52] To attempt this control may be to deprive strategy formulation of the information it requires, and ultimately to risk losing control of the organization.

REFERENCES

1. Stuart Macdonald, 'Learning to change: an information perspective on learning in the organization', *Organization Science*, 6:2 (1995), 557–68.
2. James Leontiades, *Multinational Corporate Strategy* (Lexington Books, Lexington, Mass., 1985); C. K. Prahalad and Gary Hamel, 'The core competence of the corporation', *Harvard Business Review*, 68:3 (1990), 79–91. See also Richard Whittington, *What is Strategy—and Does it Matter?* (Routledge, London, 1993); L. J. Bourgeois III, 'Strategy and environment: a conceptual integration', *Academy of Management Review*, 5:1 (1980), 25–39.
3. Frederick Gluck, 'A fresh look at strategic management', *Journal of Business Strategy*, 6:1 (1985), 4–21.
4. See Charles O'Reilly III, 'The intentional distortion of information in organizational communication: a laboratory and field investigation', *Human Relations*, 31:2 (1978), 173–93.
5. Liam Fahey, William King, and Vadake Narayanan, 'Environmental scanning and forecasting in strategic planning—the state of the art', *Long Range Planning*, 14 (1981), 32–9.
6. See, for example, Sidney Passman, *Scientific and Technological Communication* (Pergamon, Oxford, 1969), 66–72.

7. Stuart Macdonald, 'Nothing either good or bad: industrial espionage and technology transfer', *International Journal of Technology Management*, 8:1–2 (1993), 95–105.

8. e.g. F. J. Aguilar, *Scanning the Business Environment* (Macmillan, New York, 1967); Warren Keegan, 'Multinational scanning: a study of the information sources utilized by headquarters executives in multinational companies', *Administrative Science Quarterly*, 19 (1974), 411–21.

9. Mary Culnan, 'Environmental scanning: the effects of task complexity and source accessibility on information gathering behavior', *Decision Sciences*, 14 (1983), 194–206.

10. Michael Goold and Andrew Campbell, *Strategies and Styles: The Role of the Centre in Managing Diversified Corporations* (Blackwell, Oxford, 1987).

11. e.g. Alex Dontoh and Joshua Ronen, 'Information content of accounting announcements', *Accounting Review*, 66:4 (1993), 857–69.

12. Malcolm Brown, 'Dismissal deal for guilty denied', newspaper report, 5 Sept. 1991.

13. Pieter Bruce, '[Company] man "avoided dealing with issues"', newspaper report, 5 Sept. 1991.

14. Malcolm Brown, 'Executive returns to UK with a warning', newspaper report, 9 Sept. 1991.

15. 'Gyles warns against stalling', 8 Aug. 1991, 6.

16. Malcolm Brown, '[Company] head resigns amid scrutiny', 21 Sept. 1991.

17. Board papers concerning an acquisition, July 1987.

18. Harvard Business School report, 1991.

19. Ibid.

20. Internal company document, n.d.

21. Company report, 19 Nov. 1992.

22. Stuart Macdonald, 'Information networks and the exchange of information', in Cristiano Antonelli (ed.), *The Economics of Information Networks* (North Holland, Amsterdam, 1992), 51–69.

23. See Lokman Mia, 'The role of MAS information in organizations: an empirical study', *British Accounting Review*, 25 (1993), 269–85.

24. Andrew Pettigrew, 'Information control as a power resource', *Sociology*, 6:2 (1972), 187–204.

25. Don Lamberton, 'The information economy revisited', in Robert Babe (ed.), *Information and Communication in Economics* (Kluwer Academic, Dordrecht, 1993), 1–33.

26. Stuart Macdonald and Christine Williams, 'Beyond the boundary: an information perspective on the role of the gatekeeper in the organization', *Journal of Product Innovation Management*, 10 (1993), 417–27. See also David Jemison, 'The importance of boundary spanning

roles in strategic decision-making', *Journal of Management Studies*, 21:2 (1984), 131–52.

27. William Egelhoff, 'Information-processing theory and the multinational corporation', in Sumantra Ghoshal and Eleanor Westney (eds.), *Organization Theory and the Multinational Corporation* (Macmillan, New York, 1992), 182–210.

28. *cf.* Harlan Cleveland, 'The twilight of hierarchy: speculations on the global information society', *International Journal of Technology Management*, 2:1 (1987), 45–66.

29. S. J. Kobrin, 'Strategic integration in fragmented environments: social and political assessment by subsidiaries of multinational firms', in Neil Hood and Jan-Erik Vahlne (eds.), *Strategies in Global Competition* (Croom Helm, London, 1988), 104–20.

30. Richard Whipp, Robert Rosenfeld, and Andrew Pettigrew, 'Managing strategic change in a mature business', *Long Range Planning*, 22:6 (1989), 92–9.

31. Lee Sproull and Sara Kiesler, *Connections: New Ways of Working in the Networked Organization* (MIT Press, Cambridge, Mass., 1991).

32. Stuart Macdonald and Christine Williams, 'The informal information network in an age of advanced telecommunications', *Human Systems Management*, 11:2 (1992), 77–87.

33. Ethel Auster and Chun Wei Choo, 'Environmental scanning by CEOs in two Canadian industries', *Journal of the American Society for Information Science*, 44:4 (1993), 194–203.

34. Stuart Macdonald, 'Too close for comfort? Implications for strategy and change arising from getting close to the customer', *California Management Review*, 37:4 (1995), 8–27.

35. See Massoud Saghafi, Ashok Gupta, and Jagdish Sheth, 'R&D/ Marketing interfaces in the telecommunications industry', *Industrial Marketing Management*, 19 (1990), 87–94.

36. Eric von Hippel, *The Sources of Innovation* (Oxford University Press, Oxford, 1988).

37. e.g. John Stopford and Louis Turner, *Britain and the Multinationals* (John Wiley, Chichester, 1985), 33–6.

38. e.g. E. Eidenberg, 'Unprecedented force for economic stimulation', *Financier*, 15:3 (1991), 37–9; M. Lyons and M. Gell, 'Companies and communication in the next century', *British Telecommunications Engineering*, 13:2 (1994), 112–16.

39. J. Howells, 'The internationalization of R&D and the development of global research networks', *Regional Studies*, 24:6 (1990), 495–512; Arnoud de Meyer, 'Tech talk: how managers are stimulating global R&D communication', *Sloan Management Review*, 32:3 (1991), 49–58; Mark Casson, Robert Pearce, and Satwinder Singh, 'Global integration through the decentralisation of R&D', in Mark Casson (ed.),

International Business and Global Integration (Macmillan, London, 1992), 163–204.

40. Pari Patel and Keith Pavitt, 'Large firms in the production of the world's technology: an important case of "non-globalisation"', *Journal of International Business Studies*, 22:1 (1991), 1–22.

41. See Jan Johanson and Jan-Erik Vahlne, 'The internationalization process of the firm—a model of knowledge development and increasing foreign market commitments', *Journal of International Business Studies*, 8:1 (1977), 23–32; Jan Johanson and Lars-Gunnar Mattsson, 'Internationalisation in industrial systems—a network approach', in Hood and Vahlne (eds.), *Strategies in Global Competition*, 287–314; Jan Johanson and Finn Wiedersheim-Paul, 'The internationalisation of the firm—four Swedish cases', *Journal of Management Studies*, 12 (1975), 305–22.

42. Sumantra Ghoshal and Christopher Bartlett, 'The multinational corporation as an interorganizational network', *Academy of Management Review*, 15:4 (1990), 603–25.

43. Leif Melin, 'The field-of-force metaphor', in Lars Hallen and Jan Johanson (eds.), *Advances in International Marketing* (JAI Press, Greenwich, Conn., 1989), vol. 3, pp. 161–79.

44. See, for example, Kenichi Ohmae, 'Planting for a global harvest', *Harvard Business Review*, July–Aug. 1989, 136–45.

45. Ulf Holm, Jan Johanson, and Peter Thilenius, 'Network position and strategy orientation in international firms', paper presented to the Strategic Process Research Conference, Oslo, June 1991.

46. Kobrin, 'Strategic integration in fragmented environments'.

47. Yves Doz, C. K. Prahalad, and Gary Hamel, 'Control, change, and flexibility: the dilemma of transnational collaboration', in Christopher Bartlett, Yves Doz, and Gunnar Hedlund (eds.), *Managing the Global Firm* (Routledge, London, 1989), 117–43.

48. See Lars Engwall, 'The Vikings versus the world: an examination of Nordic business research', *Scandinavian Journal of Management*, 12:4 (1996), 425–36.

49. See Donald Hambrick, 'Environmental scanning and organizational strategy', *Strategic Management Journal*, 3 (1982), 159–74.

50. Lawrence Rhyne, 'The relationship of information usage characteristics to planning system sophistication: an empirical examination', *Strategic Management Journal*, 6 (1985), 319–37.

51. Stuart Macdonald, 'Industrial espionage and innovation', *Interdisciplinary Science Reviews*, 21:2 (1996), 209–14.

52. See Mats Forsgren, 'Foreign acquisitions: internalisation or network interdependency?', in Hallen and Johanson (eds.), *Advances in International Marketing*, vol. 3, pp. 141–59.

Concluding Thoughts

Agreement is unanimous—indeed, ubiquitous—that information is important: this is very far from consensus that information should be taken seriously. Sweeping assertions that information is everything do not actually allow information to be anything in particular. Just as on ceremonial occasions chief executives feel obliged to pay tribute to the company's most valued resource, its employees, so it is customary for those in senior positions to make ritual obeisance to information. They are less forthcoming about just why information should be held in such esteem. There are good reasons for this reticence. Just as fulsome praise of the workers helps sanction their being disregarded in matters of moment, so acknowledgement of the importance of information allows exploitation of information without any particular concern for information itself.

There is some further advantage in a simple and unqualified declaration that information is important. If it is openly acknowledged that almost anything can be done with information these days, then it is less surprising, less outrageous, when almost anything is done. Erosion of privacy and civil liberties is masked by the proud accomplishment of what is achieved with massive databases, surveillance cameras, and all manner of technology to monitor the performance of employees. But more fundamentally, what is done with information is what those who have control of information, be they individuals or organizations, want done with it. Above all else, what they want is consolidation of their positions. Information is used to reinforce existing structures. Information is portrayed as virtually synonymous with information systems, and information systems are designed to fit within—to serve—greater institutional systems. There is no room in such a model for information that is errant, disruptive, or even different.

Information systems are well suited to some of the characteristics of information, but not to others. In consequence, the vast capacity of these systems is not only directed towards an institutional purpose, but is also confined to certain sorts of information. Other sorts—basically the tacit, the uncodified, information from irregular sources, information which does not fit neatly, which demands transactions for its acquisition rather than mere transfer—exist in another world. The gulf between the two worlds is growing: with increasing sophistication in the handling of one sort of information, and increasing reliance on the use of the sort of information handled in this way, there is even less interest in using other sorts that must be handled in other ways. In a very real sense, the divide is between formal methods of handling information and informal. The latter, if they are acknowledged at all by those who depend on the formal, are considered primitive and unreliable—the very opposite of the qualities for which formal information systems are valued.

The result is that information is used more and more efficiently for what is already being done, and that information for doing things differently, and for doing altogether new things, is increasingly disregarded. There is, of course, considerable incentive to do better what is already being done, but the capacity to do the same thing better erodes the capacity to do other things altogether, to change. It does this most obviously by reducing the incentive to change: if the existing can always be improved, there is less interest in replacing it. Perpetual incrementalism substitutes for radical innovation. Massive investment in complex information systems confirms trajectories from which deviation becomes ever more impractical. More fundamentally, the greater the reliance on formal information systems, the greater the reliance on the institutional systems of which they are an integral part. To question existing ways is to challenge not just the organization's systems, it is to question the organization itself. But the capacity to change is also reduced by the actual rejection of new and awkward information, the information that is most critical for change. Without this wayward influence, the information available for change comes only from the system. The system is not designed to reveal its own inadequacies.

Yet the pressure for change is unrelenting and mounting, fuelled by the forces of competition, the lessons of experience, and the questions posed by curiosity. Resistance to these pressures is thoroughly understandable: change, even successful change, brings disruption and uncertainty, and change is' not always successful. Why then, if change is so problematic, is there so much praise of its virtues? Is this simply making the best of the inevitable? Not quite. It is notable how often the most voluble advocates of change are the least likely to have to change themselves or to be adversely affected by change. They encourage change as they acknowledge information, as something contained within a system. This is change the product of process, and process is firmly embodied within a system that is immune from change. This is change which is sufficiently ordered to be studied, to be modelled, to be learnt and taught, to fit into existing policy and strategy. This is change which is always constructive, which can be depended upon to make a positive contribution to organizational goals. This is the change of mission statements and vision statements.

It has been argued throughout these pages that change—innovation—above all else betrays the inadequacy of the customary treatment of information. Change requires new information, information which information systems are unlikely to be able to provide. The systems response to the need for new information is an infinity of information, processed to infinity, and transferred to infinity. The systems response to the problem of information transactions is to process and transfer more and more information on the grounds that the more information offered, the greater the chance that some of it will be wanted somewhere. Such systems are not well equipped to handle information transactions. There is nothing so much as the need for new information to highlight the importance of the transactions required to get it. The unaided market does not cope well with information transactions. Aided by policy more appropriate to the nature of politics than to the nature of information, the market seems to cope even less well. But the organization fails too: its own information systems are geared to internal transfer rather than transactions, and their extension beyond the organizational boundary is less to enter the market for information than to capture blocks of external information, to internalize the external. There are, of course, other means by which information transactions may be conducted, such as network exchange among individuals. Appropriate as these may be to the characteristics of information, they are not appropriate to the characteristics of organization. It may be, then, that organizations are typically resistant to change not just because of the threat posed by change itself, but also because of the much greater threat to stability posed by the means by which the information for change is obtained.

To appreciate the importance of information transactions is to recognize that most information exists in scattered bits which have to be found, acquired, and mixed with others before they can be used. Such recognition is rare. Familiarity with the information package is common enough—the politician's soundbite, the school syllabus, the management fad, the media story—but it is familiarity with the pre-packed, prepared for the profusion of information technology and information systems which transfer information so very efficiently. Its assembly takes place elsewhere, accomplished by experts, most obviously public relations specialists and advertising folk, serving and uniting in common purpose the leaders of just about all walks of life. Even academics have their literary agents these days, and academic research, once a bastion of independent thought, now designs and disseminates packages for users. The result is that users—individuals and organizations—while probably more knowledgeable than ever before, are losing the facility to find, acquire, and mix information for themselves. They know what they are told. The fast-food, pre-packed, take-away society has its information equivalent.

There is, of course, no conspiracy of those in power to remain there by denying the nature of information. It is just that, because they are where they are, their experience of information, and of change too, is indirect and remote, removed from the immediate. So instinctive is their attitude to information that any other seems unnatural, to defy intuition. Nowadays information is power as much as it ever was and there is no inclination among those who have power and who wish to retain it to see information in any other way. So, the only information taken seriously is that which bestows power, that which the system produces and controls, that which fits within systems; and the only characteristics of information which are of interest are those which allow information to fit within the system and to be used by the system. Thus are strategy and policy formulated by the system for the system. It is no accident that companies have such trouble coming to terms with information strategy and governments with information policy. From their perspectives, the concepts are meaningless. Information is simply something that bolsters everything else, something that serves strategy and policy, not something sufficiently distinct to have its own.

What we have, then, is a view of the world as an ordered sort of place, and a view of information as that component of the system which keeps everything in its place. They are illusion. The world is a place of some order and of much confusion. And information is not just the oil that lubricates the economic system, not just the glue that holds together existing systems, not just the cotton wool to cushion and pad out inadequate strategy and ill-considered policy. In the real world, there is sickness and unemployment, riot and revolution, traumatic events which have no place in these safe and sanitized models of change. What place frustration, despair, failure, serendipity, envy, and imagination in this sterile view of change? An information perspective breathes life into notions of change, but each breath makes it harder to accept that information has only those characteristics that are suited to information systems. To admit the relevance of its other characteristics is to question the efficacy of information systems and all that they and comfortable views of information uphold. This is why there will continue to be vapid assertions about the importance of information, and this is why an information perspective will soon be buried where it can do no harm. In a very real sense, information is far too important to permit an information perspective.

INDEX